Library of
Davidson College

The Passing Guest

Henry Kingsley, from a photograph in the National Portrait Gallery, originally a carte-de-visite.

The Passing Guest:
A Life of Henry Kingsley

J.S.D. Mellick

St. Martin's Press   New York

© University of Queensland Press, St Lucia, Queensland, 1983

All rights reserved. For information, write:
St. Martin's Press, Inc., 175 Fifth Avenue, New York, NY 10010
Printed in Hong Kong
First published in the United States of America in 1983

ISBN 0-312-59777-0

Library of Congress Card Catalog 83-3285

For
Letty and Jill

> . . . a passing guest,
> Where he became a being — whose desire
> Was to be glorious; 'twas a foolish quest,
> The which to gain and keep he sacrificed all rest.
>
> Byron, *Childe Harold's Pilgrimage*

Contents

    List of Illustrations   *ix*
    Acknowledgements   *xi*
    Abridged Family Tree   *xii*
1. Ancient Tales and Origins   *1*
2. Life at Home   *7*
3. Life at School   *15*
4. Chelsea   *21*
5. Oxford   *29*
6. In Transit   *40*
7. New Beginnings   *45*
8. Sydney Bound   *54*
9. The Monaro and Gippsland   *61*
10. Prelude to Home   *68*
11. Homeward Bound   *77*
12. Eversley   *86*
13. Wargrave   *102*
14. The Editor   *125*
15. The Last Years   *144*
    Notes   *168*
    Bibliography   *185*
    Index   *207*

Illustrations

Black and white
Henry Kingsley, from a carte-de-visite   *frontispiece*
Chelsea Rectory during the tenure of Rev. Gerald Blunt   6
Essex House, Chelsea   22
The *Gauntlet*   42
The "first place of abode" of Kingsley and Venables in Australia   47
Kingsley's traditional campsite at Warrandyte, Victoria   69
The Union Hotel   75
Henry Kingsley in 1861   94
Henry Kingsley in the garden at Eversley   95
Henry and Sarah Kingsley at the time of their marriage, 1864   105
High Street, Edinburgh c. 1870   126
Kingsley in his later years   159

Colour
between pages 101 and 102
Watercolours by Henry Kingsley
"Buninyong. Near Ballarat"
"Mount Cole (Tuckerimbud) and beyond Lanengeryn"
"The Summit of the Mistibithwong"
"The 'King' River"
"Emu Creek in the Portland Bay District"
"The look into Gipps land"
"Ben Nevis, Eastern Pyrenees, Australia"
"The dear old station"
"An undiscovered gold gully"

List of Illustrations

Photographs by the author
Langi Willi
Where Henry Kingsley slept and worked at Langi Willi
Henry Kingsley's cottage at Eversley, 1975
The Kingsleys' house at Wargrave, 1975
The Kingsleys' Edinburgh home at Morningside, 1975
The Kingsley home at 29 Fortress Terrace, Kentish Town, 1975
The Cuckfield home, Sussex, 1975
Henry Kingsley's grave, Cuckfield churchyard, 1975. Photograph by Mrs Joy Carter

Map
South-east Australia, showing Henry Kingsley's travels, 1855–56   58

Acknowledgements

Any work of this nature owes much to earlier researchers, libraries, institutions, and individuals. In this case inquiries were so widespread that all who helped could not possibly be listed here. I have therefore had to content myself with stating that those who contributed in even the slightest way are mentioned in the dissertation on which this work is based. I must, nevertheless, mention particular help received from the following: Professor R.B. Martin; Dr Brian Elliott; Mr C.H. Hadgraft; Dr L.T. Hergenhan; Dr H.F. Garlick; Dr R. Jordan; Miss B.N. Knowles; Miss S.A. Krimmer; Ms J. Huddleston; Mr and Mrs E.D. Mackinnon; Mr and Mrs Robt. Barr-Smith; Mr and Mrs J. Richardson, and Mr S.O.A. Mellick; while Mr Roger Venables and Mr John Crosthwaite deserve a special mention.

Permission to use manuscripts was given by the Trustees of the Henry W. and Albert A. Berg Collection (New York Public Library, Astor, Lenox and Tilden Foundation); the De Coursey Fales Collection, New York; the British Library; the Edinburgh Public Library, National Library of Scotland; Trustees of the Mitchell Library, State Library of New South Wales (including Henry Kingsley's watercolours); the departments of Special Collections, University of California and University of Illinois; the Baillieu Library, University of Melbourne (watercolours of H.P. Venables); Princeton University Library; Brotherton Collection, University of Leeds. Ready co-operation was given by the archivists of King's College, London; Sidney Sussex College, Cambridge; and the Master and Librarian, Trinity Hall, Cambridge. Family papers were made available by Mr R. Chirnside; Mr R. Jamieson; Mr and Mrs B. de B. Persse; Mrs E. Richardson; Mr and Mrs R.J. Scott; Miss A. and Mr J. Hunter. The owners of the Kingsley family Bible and other Kingsley documents wish to remain unnamed, but their assistance is recorded here, as is that of Mrs A.F. Ball, who typed the manuscript. Finally, my thanks are due to my wife, Letty, who helpfully accepted the loneliness this task imposed on her.

J.S.D. Mellick

Abridged Family Tree

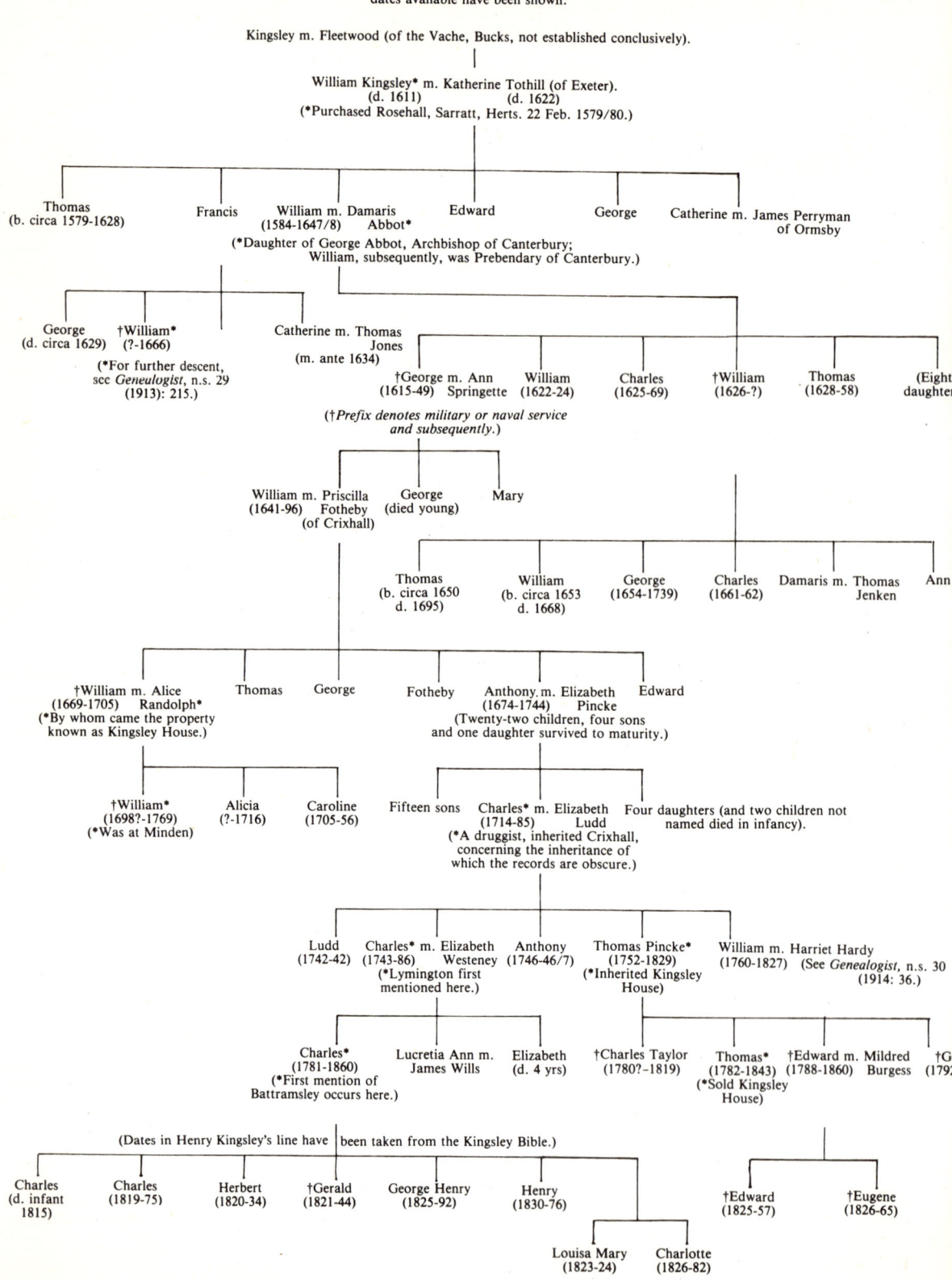

Abridged family tree of Henry Kingsley. From the *Genealogist*, n.s. 29 (1913): 212-24; 30 (1914): 35-38, 86-94; dates available have been shown.

1
Ancient Tales and Origins

According to the Kingsley family Bible,[1] Henry Kingsley, eighth and last child of the Reverend Charles and Mary Kingsley, was born at Barnack, Cambridgeshire, on 2 January 1830. His family believed its origins ancient, its estates forfeited, and many of its forbears soldiers.[2] Such beliefs helped create the Kingsleys' image of themselves in an England undergoing social and industrial change. "We are an ancient house laid low," asserted Henry's brother Charles to his wife, Fanny, in 1843, "with manner and fashions riding roughshod over our heads. Our Kingsley is a ruined grange in Cheshire in the depths of Delamere Forest and we lost it fighting the battles of our Country and our God against Charles, the miscalled Martyr."[3] These, Charles Kingsley claimed in 1857, were the battles of Naseby and Marston Moor, where his forefathers lost "broad acres for their Puritanism" fighting with Cromwell as Independents.[4]

Ancient the family was, but not laid low in the manner Henry's brother and others of his family believed. Indeed, if legend could have been separated from fact, the family's knowledge regarding its forbears and its heritage would have been found illusory in some respects. Nevertheless, these beliefs inspired Henry and his brothers; they also help explain the romantic sallies of Henry's future life, his adventuring, and his irresponsibility. Seemingly unknown to the family, when their direct ancestor, William Kingsley, died in 1611, early connections with Vale Royal in Delamere Forest, Cheshire, and with "Rannulph de Kingsley, grantee of the Forest of Mara and Mondrem from Randall Meschines, anto 1128", had long disappeared.[5] In fact, William acquired his estates, Rosehall and Sarratt, not by inheritance but by purchase, and when Henry was born, the properties, far from being forefeited, were owned by a descendant of William Kingsley on the distaff side, Sophia Charlotte Williams. So far as armed service was concerned, while the Kingsley family at large could claim some of its members as soldiers, the only one on Henry's direct line of descent, George (1615–49), served not the Independents but the King, and then as chaplain.[6] Such wealth as Henry's father, Charles (1781–1860), could claim was also acquired in the not so distant past. Henry's grandfather, another Charles (1743–86), inherited some property and a legacy of ten thousand pounds from a first cousin, Anselm Beaumont, and then seems to have spent much of it during his lifetime, for at his death his only asset was a home in the parish of St George, Canterbury.[7] This was also the case when his wife's will was admitted to probate in 1800. Henry's sister-in-law Fanny claimed that the Kingsley inheritance was squandered during her father-in-law's minority.[8] No doubt this was true, but the evidence shows that Henry's grandfather, and to some extent his father, appear to have been primarily responsible for losing any wealth or property which might have been bequeathed to either Henry or his brothers. What was left were obviously confused tales of property, rank, and achievement, and the family crest — a goat's head couped argent — proclaiming clearly, *Be Strong,* an exhortation much needed by Henry in later life.

Before the Kingsleys' arrival at Barnack, the career of Henry's father was characterized by inactivity and a lack of initiative. He matriculated at Brasenose College, Oxford, on 12 December 1800, aged nineteen, his address being given as Battramsley House, Boldre, near Lymington.[9] This is curious, for it is unlikely that this was part of his parents' estate, and evidence shows that he himself bought Battramsley in 1809, only to sell it in 1811.[10] As it was, Kingsley senior left Brasenose abruptly in February 1801, with only himself to support, and presumably spent six years at the old family home in Canterbury, where he devoted himself to literature, languages, and painting, as well as shooting and riding. By 1807, when he entered Trinity Hall in the Easter term, after matriculating as a fellow-commoner, he had married and spent three terms studying law.[11] What happened to his first wife is unknown, but on 24 August 1813 he married Mary Lucas[12] and in 1814, at her behest, returned to Cambridge. Now too old for the army, he entered Sidney Sussex College[13] to prepare himself for the priesthood, believing that in the Church were reasonable expectations of a good living and a continued presence in the "upper and governing classes".[14] On 12 April 1815 the Kingsleys' first child, Charles, was born but survived for only three days. Four years were to elapse before the next child, also named Charles (1819–75), was born, by which time Kingsley senior was in Holne, Devonshire, having taken his degree in 1816 and been the examining chaplain for the bishop of Peterborough, Dr Herbert Marsh. Subsequently, seven other children were born,[15] while Kingsley held successive appointments at Burton-on-Trent, North Clifton, and finally Barnack, where the old and partly ancient rectory, now known as Kingsley House, was Henry Kingsley's birthplace. The medieval portion originally formed part of a priory and was known in Henry's time as the North Room, where roamed a genial ghost, Button Cap. His existence was later to be denied by Henry's brother Charles in a letter in 1864 to Mrs Francis Pelham.[16] Whether spectre or rumour, Button Cap undoubtedly survives, though in the character of the ghostly Lady Hillyar in Henry's third novel, *The Hillyars and the Burtons* (chap. 5).

She it was who occupied the room with the great dormer window — Reuben's room — in old Essex House, or as Kingsley called it, Church Place, Chelsea.[17] Other information regarding Barnack days is sparse, but Mary, Henry's niece, records that Henry's sister Charlotte (1826–82) and his brother George (1825–92) wheeled the infant Henry "in a garden barrow into a pond and abandoned him there". She wrote further "that no harm was done, owing to the gardener, under Providence, having need of that barrow".[18]

Henry's mother was the daughter of Nathan Lucas, Rushford Lodge, Norfolk, and Farley Hall, Barbados, where he had been a judge and a man of books and science.[19] He knew Gibbon, was an intimate of Captain Phillip later Governor Phillip of New South Wales — and also of John Hunter, the eminent physiologist and surgeon, who is buried in Westminster Abbey.[20] To Mary Lucas were attributed such leanings as her children had towards travel, science, literature, and a sense of humour. Her education was finished in England, and she records that Byron, whom she met at a Norwich county ball, "looked like a butcher boy, his face was so red". In later years she was sufficiently competent for it to be said that "it was only her sex which kept her from being a good parish priest herself".[21] "My father", wrote Charles in 1865, "was a magnificent man in body and mind, and was said to possess every talent except that of using his talents. My mother, on the contrary, had a quite extraordinary practical and administrative power."[22] Despite this letter, Fanny Kingsley in her husband's biography carefully avoids any suggestion of youthful mismanagement by her father-in-law. Her caution is understandable. Henry, at the time the biography was being compiled, had an already established reputation for financial instability and for soliciting money. Any hint, therefore, of mismanagement in the family background risked interpretation as a family trait, a possibility that had to be avoided in the interests of her own children. Her wisdom was confirmed in later years when her son Grenville was financially assisted to Australia by John Martineau after an affair with a married woman.[23]

By 1830, when the Barnack living was required for the bishop of Peterborough's son, the Reverend Charles Kingsley was suffering from what Fanny Kingsley called ague, arising from many visits to the nearby fens, and the family had to move. Furthermore, according to Fanny, her father-in-law "could not root himself at either Clifton or Barnack and the health of the children suffered".[24] Hence it was that the infant Henry was taken in 1830 to Ilfracombe and thence to Clovelly,[25] where in 1831 Sir James Hamlyn Williams gave his father a curacy and in 1832 a rectorship.[26] The move to Devon preceded other Devon links; it was to Devon, years later, that Henry Kingsley returned to prepare for Oxford, and it was to Devon he turned for the backgrounds of *The Recollections of Geoffry Hamlyn* (1859), *Leighton Court* (1866), *Ravenshoe* (1862), and *Oakshott Castle* (1873).

At Clovelly, the Kingsley children had their boat, their ponies, and occasionally the excitement of accompanying their father, who could, in Fanny Kingsley's words, "steer a boat; hoist and lower a sail, 'shoot' a herring net, and haul a seine as one of his fishermen parishioners".[27] In autumn, too, they watched the boats set out at sunset, after a quayside service, to drive for herring and for mackerel.[28] These early memories of wind and wave, of sermon and solemnity, were to make their mark on Kingsley's work.

Lundy Island, with its stories of invasions and a history reaching back to the days of Henry III, lay across the water, a symbol of medieval days, while Clovelly Dikes near by provided a link to even earlier times, with ancient fortifications dating back to both the Iron Age and the days of the Romans. Romance, adventure, and history were all present in the Clovelly years, but sadness was there too, when some, caught in storms at sea, returned not at all or returned on the tide to be buried. It only remained for death to happen at first hand for a lasting impression to be made on the minds of the young Kingsleys. In 1834 Henry's elder brothers, Charles and Herbert (1820–34), both fell ill while boarders at Helston Grammar School, Charles with cholera and Herbert with rheumatic fever. Herbert, initially stricken severely but apparently recovering, suddenly died. The effects of this on Charles can be seen in the references to death and madness in his poem "Hypotheses Hypochondriacae". Whatever the funeral and the mourning did to Henry cannot be known, but he was due to encounter his full measure of family grief, for Charles fell sick again — this time with brain fever.[29] These events, as well as another family death in 1844, left their traces in Kingsley the writer. Two examples will suffice to show how death and its consequences occupied his thinking.

In *Reginald Hetherege* (1874), Kingsley has Charles Hetherege, after asking his father, Reginald, whether death was extinction, comment, "Ay ay; so cold, so calm. She hardly seemed dead. I thought that she smiled when I kissed her forehead. They had done up her hair as she used to wear it . . . the child looked so pretty in death" (chap. 6). But any hint of tranquillity in death is understandable. Kingsley at the time the book was published was beset with ill-health and lack of money, and death meant peace and freedom from worry. In an earlier book, *The Hillyars and the Burtons* (1865), he shows another aspect of his reactions when one of the characters, Samuel Burton, speaks of the "terror of the act of dying — which was undoubtedly a nuisance so great, that at times it made life not worth having" (chap. 68). The probable futility of life contributed to Kingsley's psychic insecurity — he felt life's impermanence keenly.

But if there was sadness, there was also joy when the family explored Clovelly beach, sometimes taking shells to Dr William Turton in Bideford for identification.[30] Additionally the Clovelly fisherfolk provided drama with their constant wresting of a livelihood from the sea — a struggle so much more lucrative when the moon was hidden, the night dark, and the weather thick. Kingsley's opening paragraph of *Oakshott Castle* shows how lasting were his memories:

> The weather had been dim and wild all day, and the sea had begun to tumble in heavily from the south-west; but when the fishermen had gathered round the fire inside the screen, there was one matter of congratulation among them all: there was not one single boat out; the catch had been good, the hucksters had been ready, the fish were gone, the money was paid, the women were seeing to the nets, and each man had in his pocket a sum of money allowed him by his wife for liquor.

If Kingsley's childhood seemed in some respects near idyllic, it is also true that awareness of event and circumstance was accompanied by an insecurity which arose from the action of a father as capable of leading his villagers in devotions and sailing as being of "uncertain temper" in the handling of his children. Fanny Kingsley's handwritten note on her proof copy of her husband's biography makes clear the point of Charles Kingsley's injunction not to let "anger and punishment be the *first* announcement" of a boy's having sinned, for it caused "blind dread" both of the parent and of the punishment "he expects to fall upon him any moment.... Alas! for such a childhood!"[31] Fanny identified "such a childhood" as being that of Charles, "which was not a very happy childhood from the uncertain *tempers* of those around him", and she wrote further that both parents were "of excitable natures and poetic feeling".[32] Parental irascibility, therefore, formed part of the pattern of memories that resulted in Henry's becoming attached to his elder brother Charles, an attachment that in later years he described as "a love which only grows stronger as we both grow older".[33] On the other hand, Kingsley senior apparently won the respect and affection of his children, for Charles, in a letter deleted from the published biography, wrote to his eldest son at school that grandfather "was a *gentleman,* and never did in his life, or even thought, a mean or false thing, and therefore has left behind him many friends, and not an enemy on earth".[34]

In 1836 the easy childhood ways of Clovelly ceased for Henry when his father accepted from Lord Cadogan the living of St Luke's, Chelsea. Leaving the West Country with its seascapes and near-by moors was to mean for the whole family a different kind of parish life. The rectory in Old Church Street, Chelsea, constantly busy with "district visitors and parish committees", meant that Charles and Mary Kingsley were, day by day, fully occupied and the children left more to their own devices.[35] The house, originally built by the Marquess of Winchester in 1560, was acquired as a rectory in 1566 and rebuilt in 1725 after a fire destroyed the earlier Elizabethan structure. The surrounding two acres of ground laid out in gardens had at least one mulberry tree known to have been growing there[36] before the "new" St Luke's replaced the old church, which was thereafter called the Parish Chapel. But the secret places of the garden and its walks were to appear little, if at all, in the later recollections of Henry Kingsley's Chelsea days. Such memories were to be of Chelsea itself, and Henry's response to Chelsea was one of imaginative identification compared with that of his brother Charles, who regarded the Chelsea rectory as a prison.[37]

Chelsea Rectory during the tenure of Rev. Gerald Blunt. From a photograph in Kensington and Chelsea Public Libraries.

Chelsea was to figure prominently in *The Hillyars and the Burtons*, and in its closing paragraphs Kingsley wrote nostalgically of an old Chelsea landmark, Essex House, which had long been pulled down. Kingsley's encounters with death had left their mark. His insecurity and doubt had developed a tendency to see change in terms of the pathos of mortal things, and his awareness of the present was to be ever tinged with a nostalgia for the past.

2
Life at Home

The Kingsleys found Chelsea a very different parish from Clovelly. In one way the living at Clovelly suited Mr Kingsley. In the Church he had little expectation of advancement, having entered the priesthood at an age later than most, while the attractions of Clovelly met his interest in natural history and offered much for the "dreamy days of boyhood", as Henry's brother Charles described them.[1] The father's limited means, nevertheless, determined what had to happen, for extra income in the Kingsley family came only from the bequests given to Mrs Kingsley by her father. These in turn were linked to the Lucases' West Indian plantation interests, and the abolition of slavery meant a lowered income from 1833 onwards. As a result there was little money available to educate or give to the young Kingsleys. They would have to depend on themselves to make their way in the world.[2] Little choice, therefore, was present in the decision to accept the more lucrative living of St Luke's, Chelsea, and there many of Henry's formative years were spent, when he explored the streets or escaped into a world of books in the rectory library.

The subjects that interested Kingsley in later years are indicative of the extent of his reading. According to Mary Kingsley, daughter of Kingsley's brother George, books of travel, illustrated treatises on natural history, and adventure tales were readily available, "dating from that happy age when the artistic imagination wandered free in a paradise that was untainted by the presence of that serpent Scientific accuracy". Present too were records from Barbados and Demerara belonging to Mrs Kingsley, whose forbears had been there for generations. These, along with tales of pirates, and voyagers such as Dampier and Cook, fired Henry's imagination, as they did his brothers before him.[3] The accuracy of Mary Kingsley's description of the library in the introduction to her father's book, *Notes on Sport and Travel* (1900), is confirmed by her reference to journals belonging to General William Kingsley, a cousin of Henry's great-grandfather, who served at Dettingen and Fontenoy. Two of the general's sketches, mounted in an album, were sent years later by Fanny Kingsley to her son Grenville in

Australia, along with photographs of European royalty and many prominent Victorians.[4] If far-away places could excite the young people's minds, then these first-hand sketches, from Tepelini and Apollonia, were evidence enough of the family's first-hand encounter with history.

Present too were Nathan Lucas's documents, including his "Journal of a Voyage to Demerara from Liverpool in 1806–7" of two half-sheepskin quarto volumes totalling 166 pages, letters to Charles, Henry's brother, and "other papers, chiefly concerned with Barbados".[5] There was much for Henry to dream over, and, as Mary Kingsley wrote: "Don Quixote never lingered more lovingly over the fascinating pages of *Feliciano de Sylva* than George Kingsley and his brothers lingered over the pages of these enchanting books: never recalled with more enthusiasm the brave deeds of Bernardo del Carpro and Rinaldo de Montalban than they recalled Anson's capture of the Manilla Galleon, and Morgan's march on Panama." In the library, Mary believed, lay the seeds of Henry's interest in exploration, both in Australia and Africa, apart from his own travels. "It seems to be extremely probable", she wrote, "that this desire in George Kingsley and his brothers was, at least in great measure, an outcome of their early dreamings over their grandfather's books and journals."[6]

Such freedom to read and romanticize had other effects when Henry's studies began at King's College. Some of his attitudes and his reluctance to settle down to routine work are evident in his references to Charles Hawker in *The Recollections of Geoffry Hamlyn*: "When he was thirteen, there was a regular guerilla-war between him and his mother, on the subject of learning. . . . His natural capacities were but small, and, under any circumstances, knowledge would only have been acquired by him with infinite pains. . . . In vain his mother scolded and wept, in vain Tom represented to him the beauties and excellences of learning – learn the boy would not" (chap. 23). In *The Harveys* Henry reveals a dislike, too, for the way Latin was force learned:

> The *cui bono*? of classical drudgery must very often present itself to the minds of those schoolboys who have no chance of being prize-winners; it is a wonder so many of them stick to work through a mere blind sense of duty, for the work is, as a fact, thoroughly disgusting to them; two-thirds of every class grind steadily on the old mill without hope of *kudos,* and without dread of disgrace. In a class of sixty the ten best are actuated by ambition, and the ten worst by fear of birch; the rest, as a general rule, work from a sense of duty, and at work, too, which to them is thoroughly mechanical, not to say disgusting. [Chap. 11]

Life in the rectory was not a happy time for the young ones. A constant stream of clergymen came and went, their conversations revealing their ecclesiastical preoccupations, while other visitors were equally disenchanting. Charles Kingsley wrote: "The girls here have got their heads crammed full of schools, and district visiting, and baby-linen, and penny clubs . . . and going about among the most abominable scenes of filth, wretchedness, and indecency to visit the poor and read the Bible to them. My own mother says the places they go into are fit for no girl to see, and that they should not know such things exist."[7] With his parents absorbed in church work,[8] Charles in studies, his other brother, Gerald, away in the navy,[9] and George closer in age to Charlotte, their sister, than himself,[10] Henry was most of the time left to his own devices in a home where all public amusements were forbidden and where, under the demands of work, Henry's father had all but abandoned his love of painting.[11] The remoteness of the Kingsleys from their parents at this time was such that Charles was constrained to write: "The only persons before whom I am dull are my father and mother. I know not why, but I cannot try to make them smile. They set me down so."[12]

Something of the Kingsley's family values and their need for "respectability" are also to be seen in *The Harveys* (1872), when Charles Harvey muses, after having left college, that he had put nothing but his own talents between himself and the workhouse: "I had deserted all the traditions of respectability as they had been beaten into my head by that poor mill-horse of a father of mine" (chap. 12). This was what, of course, with hindsight, Henry saw himself as having done.

Despite this latter-day judgement, Henry still had time to ponder the difference between life in the rectory and that near King's College. "School traditions are nonsense," he wrote in *Fireside Studies* (1876), "a school exists and flourishes because it is wanted in a particular place."[13] By itself the comment seems innocuous, but in the 1840s the King's College area was notorious for prostitution and was a thieves' kitchen. The then Wych Street, since rebuilt completely, was particularly notorious, the area constituting a danger to young men's morals; it was a subject of much discussion in the *Mechanics Magazine* of 1829 when the college was established. Thieves, prostitutes, and pornography were freely available, and Bookseller's Row opposite the entrance to the college was well known for pornography.[14] What Kingsley writes, then, in *Ravenshoe* is more than relevant both in respect of King's College and the question of what he did in his time away from home or school. In *Ravenshoe* he argued against keeping a school in a crowded, unhealthy neighbourhood because of tradition instead of moving it into the country, and observed that such action visited "the sins of the fathers on the children with a vengeance!" (chap. 42).

While education and environment played their part in Henry's youth, inclination was also a factor. Of George Hillyar in *The Hillyars and the Burtons,* he wrote, "His story sets one thinking — thinking on the old, old subject of how far a man's character is influenced by education; which is *rather* a wide one." Then, reflecting further on education and the saving power of wealth, Kingsley observes:

> There is a certain sort of boy with a nature so low, so sensual, so selfish, so surrounded with a case-hardened shell of impenetrable blockishness, that if you try to pierce this armour of his ... you lose your temper and your time, and get frantic in the attempt. I don't

say that these boys all go to the bad; but in an educational point of view they are very aggravating. If you miss them from the Sunday School and want to see anything more of them you will find them in Feltham Reformatory: though among the upper classes the future of these boys is sometimes very different. "Now this vice's dagger has become a squire. Now he hath land and beeves." [Chap. 61]

In *Reginald Hetherege* he favours an easy discipline at school, "of giving boys liberty, of letting each boy find his place", and goes on to say, almost as a comment on himself — and his class:

It is objected to some of our public schools that they throw boys into *temptation*. We ask which of them throws a boy into half as much temptation as a boy of the labouring class has to endure? We ask the oldest College tutor this question — What class of boys are the *most trouble to him*, the public school boys, who have seen life and know to some extent the value of money, or the poor unhappy babies who come straight from their mothers' apron strings? We think that college tutors will say that the public school men give them the least trouble. [Chap. 5]

In many respects his schooldays resembled those of "the poor unhappy babies" as will be seen when they are examined more fully. He was ill-prepared to conform or to cope. The answer lies in his isolated childhood and the personal traits of his parents in dealing with their children.

A description of Henry's parents survives. J. M. Ludlow, founder of the Christian Socialist movement, with which Charles Kingsley was associated, saw the father as "a tall, courtly mannered old gentleman, not unlike his son Charles, but much better looking... his mother an active clever old dame, from whom her son [Charles] seemed to have inherited a good deal of his quickness. She did virtually all the work of Chelsea parish, her husband virtually nothing beyond the preaching."[15] Other information points to Mrs Kingsley's strength of purpose and firmness of belief, and to her ability to rule "her part of the parish with a just, inflexible hand. Her firm belief that a first offence punished severely would stop any further misdemeanour" was tempered by her readiness to help the wrongdoer after punishment had been meted out.[16] Yet if Mrs Kingsley was strict, her husband moved Charles to anger. In a letter written by Charles to Fanny in 1851 from Europe, where the Kingsley family had been holidaying, he wrote, "I confess it is hard to keep one's temper, when one sees her so bullied — and yet slaving on. It makes my blood boil; but I have not had any unpleasantness as yet. Oh pray for me that I may not quarrel with him." And of his mother he wrote: "What a woman that is! I know not which is the larger, her heart or her head."[17]

In Henry's family circumstances, then, there existed tension and apprehension, aroused to some extent by the mother's standards but equally by an authoritarian, early Victorian father irked by a competent wife. Out of this situation arose some of the factors that helped Henry develop as he did. Born the last child in the family, when his father was forty-nine and his mother forty-four, Henry arrived late and managed to displace George and Charlotte — the youngest members — both of whom were adolescent when they arrived in Chelsea. With isolation came introspection and also the acceptance of Charles, eleven years older than himself, as another authority figure. The age differences left him a watcher of the others, hardly an equal; to use his words in *Geoffry Hamlyn*: "All through my life's dream I have been a spectator and not an actor" (chap. 22).

The religious intensity and other-worldliness of Charles Kingsley and the questionings of the younger Henry are easily discovered in the following exchange between Cuthbert and Charles Ravenshoe:

> "I can tell you but little to interest you, Charles. You are of this world and rejoice in being so. I, day by day, wean myself more and more from it, knowing its worthlessness. Leave me to my books and my religious exercises, and go on your way. The time will come when your pursuits and pleasures will turn to bitter dust in your mouth, as mine never can. When the world is like a howling wilderness to you as it will be soon, then come to me, and I will show you where to find happiness. At present you will not listen to me."
>
> "Not I," said Charles, "Youth, health, talent, like yours — are these gifts to despise?"
>
> "They are clogs to keep me from higher things. Study, meditation, life in the past with those good men who have walked the glorious road before us — in these consist happiness. Ambition! I have one earthly ambition — to purge myself from earthly affections, so that, when I hear the cloister gate close behind me for ever, my heart may leap with joy, and I may feel that I am in the antechamber of heaven."
>
> Charles was deeply affected, and bent down his head. "Youth, love, friends, joy in this beautiful world — all to be buried between four dull white walls, my brother!" [Chap. 11]

In the closing pages of her book, *Charles Kingsley: His Letters and Memories of His Life,* Fanny states that her husband, as early as 1856, looked forward to death with an intense and reverent curiosity.[18] Mary Kingsley's view of Henry was that she believed him to be like his own creation, Charles Ravenshoe.[19] The similarities need little elaboration. As Ravenshoe groped, so too did Henry. There was no present reality to grasp, for life was a paradox: divinely granted, its gifts were worthless.

Contrary to what might be expected, Henry indicates, with the passing of the years, a decided preference for his father rather than his mother. "A father leaves a much more certain mark upon his son than the best of mothers can," he wrote in *Fireside Studies*. "The merest common sense, the most ordinary knowledge of the world, proves that fact so clearly that it is hardly worth ink to write it down." There were affairs, he believed, concerning which, in "every great man's life", he could speak to a father but not to a mother. "The loss of a good mother is bitter enough in all conscience," he went on. "But the loss of the father, the dear friend, the tender, gentle companion, from whom nothing is concealed; the man who understands you beyond all others; the man in whose broad, kindly bosom you bury secrets of disappointed love, of idleness, of carelessness, of a thousand things only known to men, and which, while forgiven by the mother, cannot be sympathised with; that loss — the loss of the father — is more than irremediable."[20]

Henry's view of his father, then, varied from that of Charles. Nothing suggests that the father indulged Henry more than his other children, though a clue might lie in Mr Kingsley's having provided a private tutor for Henry in 1848 before he entered Oxford. On the other hand, Henry's subsequent performance there could hardly be described as that of a grateful son. On the evidence, the father appears to have had less compulsion to be the pastor than his wife and, despite his authoritarianism, was secular enough to understand the way of youth. Certainly there are instances in Kingsley's novels where his characters speak of fathers with understanding and trust. In *Valentin* (1872), for example, Kingsley introduces chapter 30 with the sentence: "I do not like a man who will speak badly of his father." In "Malmaison" the narrator, who is "little more than a schoolboy", is not reluctant to tell his "father the whole truth" after he had written an anonymous article for a newspaper (part 1). Comments of a different order but no less significant occur in *Geoffry Hamlyn* when Dr Mulhaus, thinking of Mary Hawker's father, the vicar, reflects, "What a pity that a man with such a noble intellect should be buried in a country village, a pastor to a lot of ignorant hinds. And yet he is fit for nothing else, with all his intelligence, and all his learning. He has no go in him, — no back to his head" (chap. 8). As already noted, Charles Kingsley wrote of his father that he possessed every talent except that of using his talents; Mary Kingsley was to write, in the years to come, an almost identical comment concerning her uncle Henry: "All his life long he seemed to those who loved him ... to squander alike brilliant talents and brilliant opportunities without attaining happiness."[21] Was there, then, a degree of rapport between father and son that caused Henry to be less critical than Charles? It seems so.

Charles Harvey's comments in *The Harveys* support this view: "Very early in life my father had begun to fail, and, in fact, was a ruined man in the opinion of the most experienced Dons long before he took his degree.... What ruined my father was his persistent culture of modern literature, and painting. The dear man never *could* paint to a marketable extent, but he never did anything else if he could help it" (chap. 2). Underlying the writing is an attitude that contrasts strongly with that of Charles. In 1860, when his father died, Charles's regrets were contained in a letter to his son Maurice: "How every wrong word or deed to ... that good old man, every sorrow I caused him ... rise up in judgment against one."[22] The responses engendered in Charles savour more of duty and argument than love. If, in artistic temperament and sensitivity Henry resembled his father, then Charles was his mother writ large. His own drive to succeed and the high level of religious achievement he set for himself put him, even before his father's death in 1860, in a pre-eminent position in his own family councils as well as those ecclesiastical. Another of Charles's letters, written after his father's death, shows how seriously he viewed himself: "[I have] the awful feeling of having the roots which connect one with the last generation seemingly torn up, and having to say 'now *I* am the root, I stand self-supported, with no older stature to rest on'."[23] While the sentiments may not be disputed, it is pertinent to observe that his mother was still alive and that there were other "roots", namely two brothers, George and Henry, through whom the Kingsley line might conceivably continue. With Charles it was almost as if primogeniture was a factor — only there was no title and no estate. He assumed the role of "head of the family". While Henry was growing up, then, it meant that in matters affecting his career his older brother would not be an uninvolved party. The pattern was to be repeated in Henry's later life.

On the lighter side there were some recreations. In the garden was a great sloping poplar on which George and Henry climbed,[24] and there were holidays. In June 1839 Charles returned from his first year at Cambridge in time to join the family for a holiday at Ipsden in the Chiltern Hills. Gerald was home on leave from the navy, and George and Henry also were present.[25] As it turned out, it was here that Charles met his future wife, Fanny. There had been, too, before Ipsden, a visit for Henry to Cambridge, as Charles records in a letter dated 31 May 1839 to his father: "Henry and Mrs. Knowles were over here yesterday and stayed with me till evening."[26] Mrs Knowles had been Charles's nurse when he was on holidays at Tunbridge Wells in 1828[27] and was an old servant of Mr Kingsley's family.[28]

A few years later, in July 1842, Charles preached his first sermon at Eversley, and Henry's holiday there[29] was the first of many visits to the village where he was later to live and where he formed a friendship with Augustus Granville Stapleton (1832–1921), co-author with Henry in 1860 of "The Navies of France and England". At Eversley, too, Henry spent time when Charles was free, walking in the near-by woodland and visiting farms to see the threshers in the barn and workers in the fields. Some idea of the routine is given in a letter of Charles to Fanny in August 1842: "I have since nine this morning, cut wood for an hour; spent an hour in prayer ... written six or seven pages of a difficult part of my essay; taught in the school; thought over many things while walking; gone round two-thirds of the parish visiting and doctoring."[30] Other attractions were present. R. J. King in 1875 recorded, "The commons and the green roads, some of them of great antiquity, that pass through the firwoods, are the favourite haunts of a great gypsy tribe, and it is rarely that the smoke from one of their encampments is not to be seen curling upwards against the forest background." The gypsies, he wrote, formed part of Charles Kingsley's parish, and Charles helped many of them over the years.[31]

The sea was not completely overlooked, even if, as Maurice Kingsley recollected, his grandfather saved Henry from drowning in 1846.[32] In October 1848 Henry was at the coast again, this time with Charles and Fanny. They were at Bournemouth when he arrived — much to the consternation of Fanny, who thought Charles overworked and anxious and in no way fitted to cope with problems Henry had brought from King's College.[33] She may have been right, for Charles in a letter to J. M. Ludlow had already said "that Henry had been sobbing like a child".[34] Admittedly the sobbing arose from laughter, but excessive emotion was precisely what Fanny did not want for Charles while he was on a recuperative holiday — a view with which Ludlow concurred.[35] In some ways Henry presumed that where Charles was he could be also. Fanny did not necessarily accept this, and she made her point with Charles, for he wrote to his mother on 16 December 1848 saying that Henry seemed to be under a misapprehension about going to Ilfracombe with him. "I heartily wish I were equal to the exertion of taking him in" he explained to her — "but I am equal to no exertions at all."[36] Fanny understandably saw Henry as a hindrance to Charles's recovery but did not confine her blame to Henry alone; she blamed Charles's "kindred" rather than "his pen" for his condition.[37]

3
Life at School

Kingsley makes the point in *Tales of Old Travel* (1869) that "one comes across little points, small in themselves, which force one to believe the whole".[1] That this is the case with Kingsley's own writing was confirmed by the American critic Laurence Hutton, who attended the novelist's funeral in 1876. Hutton, when travelling to Cuckfield, met another mourner, from whom "much was learned concerning the man Henry Kingsley, and his life, and his surroundings; and all that was learned was good and pleasant to hear and record. It seemed that the author had put not a little of himself and his own people in his stories. I learned upon whom the different creations were based, and how far they were real and how far elaborated; and I was told that I should meet the original 'Hetty' which I did."[2]

In *The Harveys* the "little points" that indicate Kingsley's own background are the many reminiscences of school, remembered by him because of his sensitivity, his shyness, and his being "delicate in health".[3] Of Charles Harvey's first schooldays, Kingsley wrote: "I was to go to the North-West London Grammar School, in connection with King's College" (chap. 4). Kingsley himself went to King's College School; his entry in 1844 is recorded in F. Miles's *King's College School Alumni 1831–66*. Like Charles Harvey, Kingsley was tutored for some time at home, and his brother Charles was himself teaching him as late as autumn 1843. Other references in *The Harveys* suggest that it was the King's College School Kingsley was writing about when he referred to the North-West London Grammar School.

F. J. C. Hearnshaw, in his *Centenary History of King's College*, mentions schools "in connection", and the relevant College Calendar states that pupils educated at "Schools in Union" could contend for junior scholarships.[4] This Kingsley saw somewhat differently. "We were entitled to compete for some scholarships at King's College," he wrote in *The Harveys*, which none of us ever went near to getting"; and he observed, "The only community between my school and King's College was that of school books and prayers; to go further, I should say that our communion was confined to the fact that we used Major's

Grammar instead of Valpy's" (chap. 4). The grammar was J.R. Major's, headmaster 1830-66, and the Valpy, either A.J. Valpy's *Gradus ad Parnassum,* or E. Valpy's *Elegantiae Latinae.* Conveniently, too, the headmaster in *The Harveys* is referred to as "Dr. M".

If Kingsley's reference to schooldays in *The Harveys* is accepted as autobiographical, then it seems that he led a fairly free existence while being tutored at home in classics and art, and as a result he found school a burden:

> The Bohemianism of my father's house had taken root in my soul, and I rebelled utterly against school. It was fortunate for me that my Bohemianism took the form of an intense love for art, or I might have been a pirate for aught I know. I had been accustomed to come and go as I chose, and to do exactly what I liked. Now I was to be bound down to set seasons and times. It was, to me, unbearable, and I only bore it for the sake of my father, whom I loved then, and love now in a way greater than that I have ever loved any man in the world.... I was nervous because I am very sensitive, and I hate "chaff." I knew that I should have a great deal of this, and also that I was not physically strong enough to fight it down. [Chap. 4]

Kingsley entered King's College from King's College School in 1847, owing to — as Kingsley says of Charles Harvey — "my being put into work I knew by heart" (chap. 10). No doubt, like Charles, having been taught Latin by his father, he did know it by heart, but he loathed "the drudgery of returning to classical work" (chap. 11) where, for him, the reality was a thousand times worse than the anticipation. He entered the General Literature and Science Department, but he was, he said, "only a pupil, and but a poor one of a pupil".[5] Among his peers, though, there were ways to cope. Of being physically weak, he observed in *Valentin* that "a strong boy, who is a gentleman, can get on by sheer strength of will. A weak boy, who is a gentleman, can get on by submission. A boy, who is neither strong nor a gentleman, has a very hard time of it" (chap. 29). The significance of this becomes clearer when he writes in *Geoffry Hamlyn* about the necessity for a new boy to smooth his way with cakes and pocket-money among his school fellows: "Till these are gone," he says, "he must be a weak boy indeed who cannot (at a small school) find some one to fight his battles and fetch and carry for him" (chap. 16). In *Tales of Old Travel* he notes that having pocket money was being "splendidly provided for", and like "the old tip one used to get when one went to school".[6] But if weaker boys were exploited, masters were also fair targets. In *The Harveys* he records that playground fights were "carried out in the half-hour from one to half-past one" (chap. 6) and the boisterousness carried over into the school room wherever a master was weak. "Boys demand as inexorably as a master a man they can respect and fear," he wrote. "Boys require a Rhadamanthus. To require a boy to *love* the man whose duty it is thwart him on all occasions is requiring too much. Respect and fear is all that ninety-nine out of every hundred schoolmasters have any right to hope for" (chap. 10). What Henry Kingsley saw with hindsight and what he did were two different matters.

Religious instruction consisted primarily of Wednesday afternoon lectures by the principal upon the Thirty-nine Articles of Religion, and further lectures on Saturdays by the chaplain on the Greek New Testament. Examinations on religion were held on alternate weeks. Henry's interest in the subject can best be gauged from a school report which shows him absent from four of the twelve classes held, the tutor's comment being "very little done". The report was almost too courteous concerning his attendance at chapel, merely noting that Henry was "not quite regular". In fact, he was absent thirty-seven times out of a possible fifty-four.[7] But there was more to it than this and good reason to believe that Kingsley had himself in mind when he wrote in *Reginald Hetherege*: "They would have thought that a boy of fifteen is not the person to decide about the mortality of the soul. Charles Hetherege did that at fifteen years old, and was very emphatic on the matter." He also credits Hetherege with trying to "prove logically the mortality of the soul, and the utter extinction of the spiritual part of us after death.... it could have been a good thing if that had been his only eccentricity in that great school of learning" (chap. 5). In short, Kingsley suffered a crisis, if not a loss, of faith during his years at King's College — absences from chapel and indifference to religious studies being the outward signs of his inward doubts. A few years earlier he had again faced the problem of death. His brother Gerald, after a routine voyage on HMS *Royalist* in the Gulf of Carpentaria, died of fever at Port Essington, Australia, on 17 September 1844,[8] only ten years after Herbert's fatal illness. Small wonder, then, that Charles had hurried to Chelsea "to comfort his parents, and try to explain the meaning of life and death to his young brother, Henry".[9] After his arrival, Charles wrote to his wife, Fanny, on 26 February 1845:

> It is sad — very sad — but what is to be said? I saw him twice last night in two different dreams — strong and well — and so much grown — and I kissed him and wept over him — and awoke to the everlasting No! . . . On 17th of September he died too, and so faded away, and we shall never see him more — for ever. God that saved me knows.... O God, Thou alone knowest the long withering baptism of fire, wherewith the poor boy was baptised, day and night alone with his own soul. And yet Thou wert right — as ever — perhaps there was no way but that to bring him to look himself in the face and know that life was a reality, and not a game! And who dare say that in those weary, weary months of hope deferred, the heart eating at itself, did not gnaw through the crust of vanities (not of so very long growth either) and the living water which he did drink in his childhood find vent and bubble up! Why not — seeing that God is love?[10]

This undoubtedly was the substance of what Charles also said to the adolescent Henry, who in his later writings still showed an almost morbid preoccupation with death and the soul's survival. Admittedly the circumstances by which the family learned of Gerald's fate were singularly unfortunate. Henry's father, reading in the Chelsea Public

Library on 24 February 1845, overheard a chance conversation intimating that Gerald had died on service.[11] Not only was the family shocked, but its effect on Henry was overwhelming. He was almost fifteen years of age, precisely that at which Charles Hetherege decided the soul was mortal. Hetherege's "eccentricity" was, in short, autobiographical rather than fictional. Charles's explanations availed little, and Henry made up his own mind. Man was mortal, and so was his soul.

The results in Kingsley's other subjects — English, history, and mathematics — also tell the story. "English" is not shown on the school report as such, but is included in the category "History etc.". In this area Kingsley gained a "satisfactory" rating despite being absent seven out of thirteen required attendances. Either he had a natural competence in the subject or the report was deliberately vague. In fairness it should be stated that Henry tried, during 1848, to establish a magazine for the college and the school in conjunction with Frederick Harrison, Martin Irving, F. J. Fleay, Edward Dicey, D. C. Cathan and C. H. Pearson. The project was short-lived, for the principal of the college, Dr Jelf, discouraged the idea.[12] This was Henry's first known literary effort, an effort frustrated at the time but recommenced later at Oxford. The remaining subject, mathematics, covered a wide range — in the first year, Euclid, arithmetic, algebra, plane trigonometry, and elementary differential calculus; in the second year, elementary mechanics, the theory of equations, differential and integral calculus, and parts of Newton's *Principia*. Varied as they were, Henry's reaction was predictable. The mid-year school report for 1848 was not enthusiastic — in fact, somewhat brief. Kingsley was present for thirty of the thirty-four classes held: "Attentive when present. (Mr. Kingsley is stated to be constantly in the habit of leaving the lecture room shortly after the commencement of lectures.)" The gravity of Kingsley's indifference to the reality of his situation may best be judged in relation to a view of the period: "The society of the 1830's was characterised by a grim atmosphere of just retribution, and sometimes unjust retribution, where nobody got away with anything apart from the occasional relief of an act of deliberate charity. A world where nobody got anywhere without somebody of impeccable background 'to speak for them' and the unashamed soliciting of testimonials."[13] Under the circumstances, it is easy to see why Henry's father acted as he did. On 5 July 1848 he wrote to the principal in somewhat formal terms implicitly transferring the responsibility for Henry's performance and seeking an explanation:

> I am much surprised at the terminal report of Mr. Henry Kingsley's attendance at King's College which I have just received, as he is reported irregular in every department.
>
> As no intimation of his absence from King's College has been sent to me during the last term as he regularly went from home towards College, and as I have full confidence in his honour, I am at a loss to understand this report without further explanation, which I am sure that you will kindly afford me as soon as convenient.[14]

The consequences of the explanation led to a family conference on the problem of his education and required more than a day to solve. In fact, September arrived before the matter was concluded. Truth, then, rather than fiction, lay behind the letter Netherclift wrote to Charles Harvey's father in *The Harveys*: "I had a confidential tete-a-tete with your son to-day, to see if I could find any clue to his recent extraordinary behaviour. After bearing the highest character, he suddenly abandoned himself to a dead, obstinate torpor, from which no punishment seemed able to arouse him. I have very seldom failed to get to a boy's heart, and his was very easily reached" (chap. 11). Netherclift continued that Charles Harvey was devoted to art, a precarious calling, but not "so precarious as his staying here. In conclusion, dear Sir, I must tell you this in all Christian candour — either he must reform, or I shall expel him."

The result of his spiritual upheaval and the pursuit of his own inclinations was really a setback for Kingsley. He had no interest in study, lacked purpose, and, on his performance, was almost, if not already, an apostate.

In 1895 Kingsley's nephew Maurice recollected that only Henry's most intimate friends knew that "he could use the brush and pen equally well but, alas, he rarely took up the former!"[15] To describe his view of himself at this time, Henry used Charles Harvey as a mouthpiece, and painting as a means of explanation: "The other day, after everything was over, I came across a portfolio of my drawings which I had done at this time. I have burnt them. I found that the deep, black selfishness of my heart at this time was so truly mirrored in them, that they were horrible to me as I am now ... I burnt them; but they again are burnt into my heart. I cannot forget what I once was. May be, it is best that I should not" (chap. 11). B.E. Martin, referring in his book *Old Chelsea* to Kingsley's paintings and his career problems, wrote that Kingsley's "parents had intended that he should take holy orders, hoping perhaps that he should succeed his father in the living of St. Luke's; but he felt himself utterly unfitted for this profession, as he also, although with less reason, believed himself unfitted for that of the journalist." Martin went on to say that Kingsley "had true artistic talent in another direction, too, inherited from his grandfather; and he may have been just in judging himself capable of gaining far greater reputation as a painter than as a novelist, even. His skill in drawing was amazing, and the few watercolours left to his family — and unknown outside of its members — are masterpieces."[16]

The year was one of failure for Kingsley, but one memory stood out — he met Thackeray. He was, he recalled, as a "raw boy of eighteen ... asked to dine and meet the great man." His host was John Parker, printer to Cambridge University and later publisher of Charles Kingsley's *Hypatia*. "There before him was the great man himself, at last," Kingsley wrote; "there was the head of hair so familiar afterwards, though not so grey sixteen years ago; there were the spectacles, and the wonderful up-looking face. There was an equal of the great man's at table, but this lad engaged himself entirely in watching Thackeray... the most remarkable face he had ever seen."[17] The identity of the equal he did not reveal.

Kingsley's problems had by now become known further afield. In referring to his schooldays, J. M. Ludlow recollected in a letter that Kingsley's "family were at one time in great trouble about him, he having got into bad courses while at King's College. It was then I first knew him, and I liked the lad notwithstanding his misdoings. There was a good deal of resemblance in character between Charles and Henry but Henry was much weaker, and with lower aims, though a really good fellow at bottom."[18]

Charles Harvey, speaking of what must have been Kingsley's own last days at school, said, "I knocked under, and sat sulky at the bottom of the class, a marked boy with accumulating impositions. I took to coming late, with lessons unlearnt. I must have appeared... what I was, a graceless, sulky young dog.... Other guidance I had none: for what could wild boys of my own age do for me? My friends, the boys among whom I had accidentally been thrust, had but one creed — that of succeeding at school. They were as kind to me as ever; but they had a feeling that I was a disgrace to the old lot" (chap. 11). As well in *The Harveys,* father and son relations were strained as a result of Charles Harvey's failure to apply himself to his studies, and Harvey's father removed him from college. Kingsley's father did similarly. On 18 September 1848 the Reverend Charles Kingsley wrote to King's College stating that Henry would not be returning — "as I have placed him with a private tutor in the country."[19] In an authorial intrusion in *Silcote of Silcotes* (1867), Henry Kingsley asks his reader to "recall, if you are not too old, the last time you were *glad*; and you will half do my work for me. But it was so long ago, you say. Still try to recall it. I suspect that it was the day you left school, or the day you first went to chapel in your cap and gown, or if you are in another rank in life, on the last day of your apprenticeship" (chap. 36). In his own case he had left King's College and was to spend a month with Charles and Fanny at Bournemouth.[20] For the moment the more serious aspects of his encounter with life were being put aside. If not glad, he was at least relieved.

Soon afterwards, Kingsley was placed with Thomas Drosier, the rector of Colebrook, Charles's former tutor at Cambridge,[21] to be prepared for matriculation to Oxford University. A year later, on 12 September 1849, Charles wrote from Colebrook to his father. Henry had spent three days with him and he was "most delighted and satisfied", both with Henry and "with that excellent man's [Drosier's] account of him."[22] The father was specifically enjoined in the letter to "tell her [Mrs Kingsley] also", as Charles's assessment of Henry's progress had been awaited anxiously by both parents. For them the news was a relief. Henry, at last, was on the way — or so it seemed.

4
Chelsea

"The river, the church, the intimacy of Chelsea life and the fellowship of centuries"[1] stayed in Henry Kingsley's imagination long after he had ceased to live at the rectory. Kingsley certainly spent time in Chelsea after his return in 1858 from Australia, but the incidents and descriptions used in his work seem mainly those of his boyhood and pre-Oxford days — Essex House, demolished between 1840 and 1842, being one of the more significant of his recollections. Essex House, or Church Place as Kingsley called it in *The Hillyars and the Burtons*, was occupied as late as 1829 when Thomas Faulkner recorded that it was then "the property of William Sloane Stanley, Esq." and let as tenements despite its very dilapidated condition.[2] Here he encountered the conditions he records in *Geoffry Hamlyn* and which his mother considered "fit for no girl to see":

> They went in.... A squalid, damp, close room, with the earthen floor sunk in many places and holding pools of water. The mother smoking in the chimney corner, the eldest daughter nursing an illegitimate child, and quarrelling with her mother in a coarse, angry tone. The children, ragged and hungry, fighting for the fireside. The father away, at some unlawful occupation probably, or sitting drinking his wages in an alehouse. That was what they saw, and what any man may see to-day for himself in his own village whether in England or Australia, that working man's paradise. Drink, dirt, and sloth, my friends of the working orders, will produce the same effects all over the world. [Chap. 8]

To B. E. Martin, Kingsley's reminiscences were those of his boyhood, and in *Old Chelsea* Martin wrote, "Henry Kingsley especially appeals to us, just here, for that he has given us, in 'The Hillyars and Burtons,' so vivid a picture of modern Chelsea — its streets and by-ways, its old houses and its venerable church, in delightful detail, as he saw them when a boy." Martin, in search of information, interviewed many of Chelsea's older residents, and subsequently wrote that "Henry, the youngest, was a sensitive, shy lad, delicate in health; and the old dames in this neighbourhood tell of his quiet manner and modest bearing. Many of the poor old women about here have a vivid

Essex House, Chelsea. From a painting in Kensington and Chelsea Public Libraries.

remembrance of 'the boys,' and speak of the whole family with respect and affection."[3]

In writing of Essex House, Kingsley recorded that Joe Burton "had, with Mr Faulkner's assistance, made out the history of the house". Thomas Faulkner's book shows Essex House with stone-mullioned windows and doorways and the prominently featured dormer window described by Kingsley in *The Hillyars and the Burtons*.[4] Drawing on Faulkner for more detail, Kingsley went on to claim that "Thomas Cromwell, Earl of Essex, son of the blacksmith at Putney, first opened that hospitable old door", and "there was no doubt we were treading on the very same boards which had been trodden, often enough, by the statesmen and dandies of Queen Elizabeth's Court, and most certainly by the mighty woman herself" (chap. 43). Unfortunately his sentiments were misfounded, as Alfred Beaver Elliott writing in 1892 shows: "Faulkner mentioned the tradition that the Earl of Essex, the Parliamentarian General, once lived there, but like many other Chelsea traditions, this cannot be traced to any satisfactory source, and Dr Martin falls into the curious error of associating with this house Thomas Cromwell, Earl of Essex, the son of the Putney blacksmith, who became Henry VIII's vicar-general, and went to the block in 1540, just one hundred years before the house was built."[5] Kingsley, unaware of the truth, made good use of Faulkner's report in that a blacksmith's son having first opened the door of Essex House, a blacksmith's daughter closed it "up for ever". Kingsley went on: "When mighty America was only a small irregular line on the chart of the world, that pile of brick and stone was built up; and we, poor worms of a day, have seen it stand there, and have weaved a child's fancies about it" (chap. 43). A reverence for antiquity pervades his comments, and regret is in his closing remarks in *The Hillyars and the Burtons*: "The old house at Chelsea is pulled down, this long while past. It stood, when I was a boy, where the south side of Paulton Square stands, I think; but the place is so much changed that I am not certain to a few yards. *Truly, its place knows it no more"* (chap. 80).

That Kingsley was in the house itself is evident from his description of the view from the dormer window:

> When it came to my turn to look out of window, Joe kept watch. I looked right down on the top of the trees in the Rectory garden; beyond the Rectory I could see the new tavern, the Cadogan Arms, and away to the north-east St. Luke's Church. It was a pleasant thing to look, as it were, down the chimneys of the Black Lion, and over them into the Rectory garden. The long walk of pollard limes, the giant acacias, and the little glimpse of the lawn between the boughs, was quite a new sight to me. [Ibid., chap 5]

But it was not to the new and imposing St Luke's Church that Henry Kingsley's boyhood allegiance was given:

> It is so long ago since we began to go to the old church, on Sunday afternoon in winter, and in the evening in summer, that I cannot attempt to fix the date. It had grown to be a habit when I was very, very young, for I remember that "church" with me used at one time to mean the old church, and that I used to consider the attendance on the new St. Luke's, in Robert Street, more as a dissipation than an act of devotion. [Ibid. chap. 23]

He was, he writes, astonished to find that "people who had died, and had their monuments set up here, were, by very long odds, the best people who ever lived" and that the epitaphs were written in Latin not "for the sake of sparing the feelings of the survivors" but to be "quite as complimentary as the English". Behind the banter, of course, stands the adult Kingsley, who necessarily reveals something of himself:

> It appeared that the older language had been used merely because the miserable bastard *patois* which Shakespeare was forced to use, but which Johnson very properly rejected with derision, was utterly unfit to express the various virtues of these wonderful Chelsea

> people, of whom, with few exceptions, no one ever heard. It used to strike me, however, that, among the known or the unknown, Sir Thomas More was the most obstinately determined that posterity should hear his own account of himself.... The Dacres, with their dogs at their feet are grand; but, on the whole, give me the Hillyars, kneeling, humbly, with nothing to say for themselves.... I always loved that monument better than any in Chelsea Old Church. 'Tis a good example of a mural monument of that time, they say; but they have never seen it on a wild autumn afternoon, when the sun streams in on it from the south-west, lights it up for an instant, and then sends one long ray quivering up the wall to the roof, and dies.... I made friends of them, in a way. They were friends of another world. ... I loved two of them. On the female side I loved the little wee child, for whom there was very small room.... And I loved the big lad who knelt directly behind his father. [Ibid.]

Humorous and gentle, while at the same time subtly pointed in his remarks, Kingsley reveals a preference for a lack of pretentiousness in religion, an attitude he held in contradistinction to the priestly pre-eminence of his brother Charles. The detailed description of the Hillyars's "mural monument" identifies it easily as the family monument of Thomas Lawrence sited on the north wall of the Old Church on which are depicted Lawrence himself, Elizabeth his wife, two sons, six daughters all kneeling, and two babies wrapped in clothes to their chin. It is true, as Kingsley noted, that little or nothing is said of the Lawrences themselves in the inscription:

> The yeares wherein I lived were fifty-fower,
> October twenty-eight did end my life.
> Children five of eleven God left in store,
> Sole comfort of theyr mother and my wife.
> The world can say what I have been before,
> What I am now, examples still are rife:
> Thus Thomas Lawrence spekes to tymes ensving,
> That Death is sure, and Tyme is past renewing.

Thomas Lawrence was a goldsmith who at one time owned the old manor house and was the first of five generations of Lawrences buried in the Old Church.[6] The rector's pew in Kingsley's time was directly opposite the Lawrence monument, so it is no surprise that, from his position in the rector's pew, Kingsley was constrained to meditate on life and death. "Death is sure and Tyme is past renewing." faced him, Sunday after Sunday, with its inexorable and inescapable message. His overall impression of Chelsea Old Church appears in the observations of Joe Burton in *The Hillyars and the Burtons:*

> "Four hundred years of memory," continued Joe, "are crowded into that dark, old church, and the great flood of change beats round the walls, and shakes the door in vain, but never enters. The dead stand thick together there, as if to make a brave resistance to the moving world outside, which jars upon their slumber. It is a church of the dead. I cannot fancy any one being married in that church – its air would chill the boldest bride that ever walked to the altar. No; it is a place for old people to creep into, and pray, until their prayer is answered and they sleep with the rest." [Chap. 13]

Small wonder, then, that the youthful Charles Ravenshoe protested to his brother, Cuthbert, that life itself was worth while, rejecting a view which saw life as only a prelude to eternity and secular attractions of little moment. Small wonder also that Kingsley, like his own character, Charles Hetherege, decided that man's lot was finite. His subsequent high-spirited behaviour at Oxford was as much a reaction from the restraints of the vicarage and his earlier meditations on mortality as a release from restraint. The temporal had its place even if the moment was "past renewing".

Chelsea appealed to Kingsley for other reasons as well, its way of life, its people, and its history. His many observations in *The Hillyars and the Burtons* paint a picture rich in colour and activity, of people "among whom", he wrote, "I had been bred up, and whom I had learnt to love" (chap. 27). He wrote sympathetically of a blacksmith in Brown's Row, "a short street which leads into Paulton Square ... now widened" (chap. 33), and presumably the present Paulton's Street, as being "the umpire of buildings – the stopper of fights, and, sometimes, even the healer of matrimonial differences.... [He was] a man possessed of a lively interest in his fellow beings ... [and] ... an ideal of all the blacksmiths" (chap. 2). Kingsley remarked, too, on "the bladders of lard and barrels of size" (chap. 16); on the "fishmonger bawling out, as of old, the audacious falsehood that his soles were alive" (chap. 13); and on costermongers in King's Row, barrows full of whelks, periwinkles, and tripe. Chelsea life had a richness of spectacle which moved him deeply. "Could one ever have been happy in such a squalid unromantic place?" he asks. "Among such sounds, such smells, such absence of fresh air and sunshine, with poverty and vulgarity in its grossest forms on every side of us." He gives his own reply: "Yes, I often feel it now" (chap. 16). Then, too, in a surge of recollection and feeling experienced while in Australia, he wrote of another boyhood memory: "And then and there in the silent forest the Old Chelsea life came back into my soul and pervaded it completely, and the past drove out the present so utterly and entirely that ... the immortal part of me had travelled back into the squalid old street, and *I* was there once again" (chap. 13).

Other sights impressed themselves on Kingsley as well. In Danvers and Lawrence Streets, near the rectory, for instance, he saw "some queer people indeed", especially the owner of a "house in Lawrence Street", a Mrs Quickly, whom Kingsley judged a "foolish and weak woman albeit "singularly civil"; and her successor, Mrs Bardolph, he described as "a great red-faced, coarse Kentish woman, with an upper lip longer than her nose, and a chin as big as both, as strong as a man, and as fierce as a tiger" (chap. 22).

In Reuben, a Cockney lad, Kingsley saw "a sort of small master in the art of cockney chaff: which chaff consisted in putting together a long string of incongruities in a smart jerky tone of voice". Along with this he had a characteristically consummate impudence as well as a rarely violated, peculiar code of honour, combined with a reckless, persistent courage, and fine physique. Kingsley's analysis went further. "The 'Cockney' as those call him who don't care for two black eyes, *et cetera*", distrusted both clergy and aristocracy. He was, said Kingsley, sceptical "of high motives in others" and even if "chivalrous and religious at times", would not admit to being so (chap. 5).

Although some observations clearly belong to a period later than his boyhood, the particulars in *The Hillyars and the Burtons* reveal much of Kingsley's sensitivity and attitudes. Sometime before *The Colleen Bawn* was performed in 1859, wrote Kingsley, Jim Burton, when going to the theatre, noticed a young man of his own rank and age riding a carthorse in front of him. The night was frosty, the road slippery, and the horse, having stumbled, threw its merry, good-humoured rider under the wheels of a passing wagon, where he lay shattered beyond recognition, dead. Man's lot, and the fellowship of disaster, pervade the passage so strongly that one senses Kingsley's own perception of what constituted reality in the streets, as opposed to its presence in the theatre:

> The image of what I had carried up and set on the door-step, an hour before, would not leave me. That a merry, harmless lad like that should be struck down in an instant, seemed to me so lamentable and cruel.... The details would come before me so persistently — the head that *would* hang; the two low, fallen women, who kept saying, "Poor dear! poor dear lad!" and all the rest of it.... The squalor and noise of the street suited my mood better than the gaudy brightness of the play-house; and the bustling reality of the crowd soothed me for a time... this crowd of noisy, swarming, ill-fed, ill-taught, ill-housed poor folks... I was at home among them. [Chap. 27]

On his way home, Burton went into a public-house, where he ordered some porter and heard, as he recollected later, "a waltz which I now know to be one of Strauss's.... It sounded to me like the lapping of the tide upon the mudbanks, and the moaning of the wind from the river among the grave-stones in the old church-yard." Near Chelsea Hospital, the clock struck ten and Burton "came on the broad desolate river, at the east end of Cheyne Walk. The frosty wind was moaning among the trees, and the desolate wild river was lapping and swirling against the heads of the barges and among the guard piles, which stood like sentries far out, stemming the ebbing tide" (chap. 27).

But the Thames was used not only as a desolate image of inward dejection in Kingsley's quasi-autobiography of Chelsea but also for a "fairy voyage" up river to Kew in a barge full of gravel. "Oh!, glorious and memorable May-day!" he writes, "The river swept on smoothly without a ripple, past the trim villa lawns all ablaze with flowers; and sometimes under tall dark trees, which bent down into the water... in one long reach, I remember, we heard... a tiny out-rigger, which creaked beneath the pressure of each mighty stroke, skimming over the river like a swallow, with easy undulations." The return journey on foot by way of Kew Green, Barnes Common, and then Putney Common had its own magic: "In a field, between Penge Wood, where the Crystal

Palace now stands ... and Norwood," he recorded "we found mushrooms" (chap. 6).

Ramblings similar to those of his characters, as well as visits to Charles at Eversley, showed Kingsley that townsfolk could not tell the difference between a summer day in September and a summer day in June: "The town-bred eye does not recognise the happy doze before the winter's sleep. The country is the country to them, and September is as June", and the escaping town traveller finds in late season the "same deep shadows on the grass, the same tossing plumage on the elms, the same dull silver on the windows" (chap. 8). The difference between Henry Kingsley and other members of his family was that Kingsley found what there was to be loved in Chelsea. His mother found it a place of good works; his brother Charles, the antithesis of Clovelly and freedom. Mary Kingsley, his niece, believed he wrote in *The Hillyars and the Burtons* of Chelsea rectory as a refuge from it all: "Henry Kingsley has told us also in that book of the misery, the squalor, and the vice which existed in the many dirty lanes and poverty-stricken courts and alleys by which that peaceful old walled garden was encompassed."[7] Henry saw beyond the wall, saw Chelsea's humanity, and what had been there before, and loved it for itself.

Adding to this view of Chelsea, but with Kingsley's now familiar note of regret for the passing away of former things, is the mention in *Austin Elliot* (1863) of the old red-brick suburban houses:

> Did any reasonable man ever go to walk through the western part of Chelsea on to Walham Green and Fulham, if he could manage to walk anywhere else? Most likely not. And yet there are some houses standing about there which will make a man think, if he chooses to think.... Take a long, low, back-lying house in the King's Road, Chelsea, in front of which they have built shops. That was once a quiet gentleman's house, with elm-trees round it, where several generations of children tumbled downstairs ... and laughed and cried ... until they grew to handsome young men and women ... before Mr. Mullins took it and made a madhouse of it, and the woman who thought she was queen, took possession of the summer-house, and hunted us boys out of it when we dared to go in; and before they put Miss H-, a strong, red-faced woman, with a big throat and thick lips into the old nursery, where she screamed and yelled and tore night and day for above a year, till it pleased God to put an end to her misery.
>
> And when the madhouse was removed to Putney, Waterer ... exhibited his rhododendrons and azaleas there. And all society came to look at them and the line of carriages extended far up and down the King's Road.... And on the very same ground where the author, a frightened boy, looking over the palings, has seen poor Miss H-, in her strait-waistcoat, cast herself screaming down among the cabbage plants and bite the earth with her teeth; on that very same ground all the dandies and beauties of London were walking and talking ... *Sic transit, &c.* That is the story of one suburban house, carefully told, and there are very many with far stranger histories than that. [Chap. 10]

Sic transit, indeed, but one memory on which comment is unnecessary he recalled in "Some Account of the Village of Inverquoich":

"I have been troubled, from boyhood, with a cyclical dream; to wit, that I have awaked, and found myself in broad day, in the King's Road, Chelsea, opposite the Asylum wall, without any trousers on."[8]

Kingsley captured Chelsea life as he knew it, with its river, its church, and its intimacy, as well as the fellowship of centuries enshrined in the Old Church. His childhood was rich and varied, and Chelsea he left, finally, only to prepare for Oxford. The vividness of his writing and the immediacy of his experiences reveal him not just as a keen observer but also as a sensitive, almost introspective, youth, made too soon aware of the pathos of mortal things.

5
Oxford

When Kingsley matriculated at Worcester College on 6 March 1850,[1] he had not only spent eighteen months under Drosier's tutelage but had also increased his knowledge of the West Country, a knowledge later put to good use in his novels. His private tutor in the country lived at Colebrook, situated only five kilometres west of Crediton, and Thomas Drosier's attitude harboured little of a conventional master. He was rector of the village but, according to Charles Kingsley, regarded Henry and his two fellow students as "playfellows" rather than pupils.[2] Crediton is mentioned by Kingsley in *Ravenshoe* (chap. 23) and "An Episode in the Life of Charles Mordaunt", and Devon provided the setting for the opening chapters of *Leighton Court*. *Geoffry Hamlyn* not only perpetuates the Hamlyns of Clovelly but sites Drumston, in the early chapters, within riding distance of Exeter and uses Yes Tor, on Dartmoor, as the setting for murder. The troublesome days of King's College had been replaced by the freedom that characterized Kingsley's early schooling. Academically he benefited by being with Drosier, and his matriculation was taken by his family as an earnest of his ability to apply himself. But the truth was Kingsley, unsettled, wanted to be free.

During 1848 a cousin, J. E. Fitzgerald, visited Chelsea rectory and spoke of a new colony at Vancouver Island. At the time Henry gave little thought to what was said, but in 1850, while at Colebrook, he wrote to Fitzgerald about the venture because, in his own words, "circumstances have occurred which have made me take a deep interest in what you said". He went on:

> First, what is the *smallest* amount of capital that a young man quite unembarassed [sic] can venture to go with —
> Secondly. Is not the colony to be a mining settlement. If so is there any possibility of a farmer's succeeding?
> This last question is prompted by my utter ignorance of the country. I can find it on the map, and see that it must be about the same climate as Canada, but I can find no account of it in any ordinary book, any information will be most gladly received —
> I am getting utterly tired of staying in England doing nothing and what is worse no prospect of having anything to do. It is true I am very, very young only 19 — [sic]

> My Father wishes me to go into the Church, which I *cannot* do, besides who knows where the Church may be this time 3 years. Suppose a revolution were to come, where would the Church of England be? Not a word of this to any one as yet.³

Kingsley's calling was not to the Church, that much was certain; his study with Drosier and his time at Oxford were both marked by a silent rejection of the career chosen for him. He was twenty years of age, lacking in responsibility towards those who bestowed time and privilege on him, and, indeed, a partial victim of the efforts made to educate him. In *Stretton* (1869) is a passage that is revealing in its implications:

> When he won the University sculls he thought himself as fine a fellow as any who fought at Waterloo.... Don't dedicate your son to any particular career, if there is any go in him at all. I once saw a boy of twelve come into a room full of ladies, and I heard his mother say, "There comes another young clergyman." Whereupon the ladies rejoiced and fal-lalled; but from that moment the boy's fate was sealed: he would die sooner than be a parson. I am only speaking of a fact which I think typical. English and American lads of *mettle* and use will not allow themselves to be disposed of without their own will. Lads without mettle will allow this liberty to be taken with them — which accounts for a particular kind of curate. [Chap. 25]

Mrs Kingsley clearly believed Henry's future prospects best assured by the Church. With this he disagreed and promptly went his own way at Oxford. In *Ravenshoe*, which he began writing at Worcester,⁴ he wrote:

> A majority of young fellows at the University deceive their parents, especially if they come of serious houses. It is almost forced upon them sometimes, and in all cases the temptation is strong. It is very unwise to ask too many questions. Home questions are, in some cases, unpardonable. A son can't tell a father, as one man can tell another, to mind his own business. No. The father asks the question suddenly, and the son lies, perhaps, for the first time in his life. If he told the truth, his father would knock him down. [Chap. 8]

Despite the concern Mr Kingsley had for Henry's future, he still had an uncertain temper, and Henry kept from him the fact that he was neglecting his studies.⁵ His activities may have been a preparation for life but hardly for priesthood.

A few days after his arrival in Oxford, Kingsley attended one of Maxwell Miller's "feasts of wine and roses". Miller had a reputation. He "was said to have spent in a single Trinity Term more money on cut flowers than any previous Oxford man had ever squandered on things of beauty and sweetness during an entire year." Through Maxwell Miller, Kingsley met John Cordy Jeaffreson and also Edwin Arnold, who became his lifelong friend. According to Jeaffreson, Kingsley had a "weedy frame and curious visage":

> Resembling Charles Kingsley (who was far from well looking) in the straight mouth, and deep line, descending on either side of the face from the unshapely nose to the corner of the graceless lips, which distinguished the clergyman's visage, Harry Kingsley was far plainer

than his brother. That he was painfully sensitive of his extreme plainness appeared from the frequency with which he called attention to it. When he asked me at the outset of our acquaintance whether I did not think him the ugliest man in Oxford, I could not reply in the negative, although in my desire to soothe his troubled vanity I encouraged him to hope that next term a plainer undergraduate would come into residence.[6]

Even allowing for jest, Kingsley must have had some views about his looks to have written in *The Harveys,* "One of the things which has vexed me very much all my life is that I am anything but handsome" (chap. 2). He was, however, still not beyond trying to make capital of it. Jeaffreson records that a young woman's reply to Kingsley's comment on his appearance was short: "There was no need for you to say so." Nevertheless, concluded Jeaffreson, despite "its obtrusive ugliness, his countenance was not repulsive. On the contrary, the comical unsightliness of his grotesque visage disposed people to like him. The proverbial five minutes were all the time he needed for putting himself on equality with any personable youngster in a woman's regard."[7] The introspection of Chelsea was now being replaced to some extent by a measure of social assurance.

The "delicate" aspect of Kingsley's constitution was attended to without delay. On arrival at Oxford he was slight and lacked physical vigour to such an extent that his aspirations to emulate Charles in rowing were discounted. Nevertheless, by persistent exercise and training, Henry began to excel at sculling and became one of the best of Oxford's rowers. One trophy, on which his name appeared, passed to the descendants of Henry Pares Venables, his companion for a period during the Australian gold rushes, and according to Venables's grandson, Roger, it remained in the family until mislaid during the 1939–45 war. Jeaffreson causes no surprise, therefore, when he records that Henry, a few terms later, "had not only rendered himself one of the best scullers on the river, but so changed the habit of his body that he had the appearance of, as well as the physical capability of an athlete".[8] In *Ravenshoe,* Kingsley drew on his Oxford days and indicates that "the short description of the University boat-race which begins this chapter was written two years ago [1859] from the author's recollections of the race in 1852":

> Putney Bridge at half an hour before high tide; thirteen or fourteen steamers; five or six thousand boats, and fifteen or twenty thousand spectators. This is the morning of the great University race, about which every member of the two great Universities, and a very large section of the general public, have been fidgeting and talking for a month or so.
> The bridge is black, the lawns are black, every balcony and window in the town is black; the steamers are black with a swarming, eager multitude, come to see the picked youths of the upper class try their strength against one another....
> Now the crowd surges to and fro, and there is a cheer. The men are getting into their boats. Now there is a cheer of admiration. Cambridge dashes out, swings round, and takes her place at the bridge.

Another shout. Oxford sweeps majestically out and takes her place by Cambridge. Away go the police-galleys, away go all the London club-boats, at ten miles an hour down the course. Now the course is clear, and there is almost a silence. [Chap. 23]

The Times of 1 April 1852 listed the crews for the event, but Kingsley's name was absent. Four days later the race itself was run, and a comparison of the reports shows the striking degree of animation Kingsley infused into his description compared with that of *The Times*. His interest in rowing was maintained in later years when he lived at Wargrave; the "Shrewsbury Regatta" described in *Stretton* (chap. 15) was based on a Henley event he saw in 1868. "[For Kingsley] to perish of violent delight," wrote Jeaffreson, "as his boat shot past the goal, three clear lengths ahead of the universal champion's outrigger, and the acclamations for the conqueror rent the air and rose to the blue sky, would be a blissful exit from a troublesome life". To die at that moment, "to fall back in his outrigger and expire suddenly at the close of a triumphant match with the champion sculler of the whole universe", was, according to Jeaffreson, Henry's idea "in his merry boyhood [of how] to close a brief and brilliant career".[9] Romantic, undoubtedly, but, in some respects a cry for meaning and a declaration that any achievement before death was at least something. Henry was reacting against Charles's strictures, even if equalling him in prowess.

Jeaffreson graduated in 1852 and endorsed a bill for eighty pounds for a then impecunious Henry. Pestered by creditors, Henry was "incapable of preparing himself for 'smalls' " and Jeaffreson's help gave him sufficient peace of mind to pursue his studies. How Henry met the bill is not known, but Jeaffreson credits it to a legacy left to him, and S. M. Ellis states that the legacy came from an aunt who died in March 1853, a "Mrs. Kingsley of Dulwich, widow of a stockbroker cousin of Charles' father".[10] Henry received five hundred pounds.[11] There is more to Henry's apparent impecuniosity, however, than his Oxford exploits indicate. In June 1852, when Henry sought help from Jeaffreson, Charles Kingsley wrote to his wife from Wales, where he was staying with his brother-in-law, the historian J. A. Froude: "If we want more [money] we must take some of Henry's. He will not want all his till the autumn and it is hard if we cannot do that after all our trouble. The cheque that I sent to Henry on Dampier Grew, Oxford, was for twenty pound. The other I have not sent yet."[12] What these moneys were is also unknown, but undoubtedly Henry was embarrassed to a point where he had to seek outside help. He could neither approach nor reproach Charles because of what he "owed" to Charles and Fanny. On the other hand Charles's arbitrary decision shows to what extent he stood *in loco parentis* to Henry, who is described by Jeaffreson as a "poor boy (yes, boy – though he was something older than myself)".[13] If, as has been suggested, Kingsley saved enough money to pay his passage to Australia, either he did so deliberately to escape from Oxford or the decision was taken suddenly and Henry for once had managed his funds well enough from March to August 1853 to enable him to act.

Jeaffreson liked Kingsley's merry nature and writes of meeting him before leaving Oxford in 1852:

> My university career was in its last week, when Harry Kingsley and his particular friend Willie Langworthy (both of Worcester College) pressed me to tell them by what means I hoped to maintain myself in London.
> "I know just nothing," I replied lightly, "and my design is to make a sufficient income by teaching it to other people."
> On coming out of the long fit of screaming laughter into which they were thrown by this airy speech, my friends begged for a full statement of my plans for getting pupils, who would be willing to pay me for teaching them "just nothing"; but I declined to gratify their curiosity.[14]

The same undergraduate humour caused Kingsley to join Edwin Arnold in a "droll and innocent affair", the formation of a misogynist society called the Fez Club. With fifty or more members, it owed its existence to a belief that "the influence of the gentler sex had increased, was increasing, and ought to be diminished". Jeaffreson, as door-keeper, had to deny entry to non-members and thus protect the secrets of the brotherhood, particularly its proceedings and rules. But the meetings were not all formal. Secret signs of recognition and special articles of costume, including the wearing of a fez, marked the society's meeting for "social enjoyment and fraternal edification" at Dickenson's Hotel and Coffee-House in Turle Street. Breakfast over, the "brethren" smoked oriental tobacco from Eastern pipes, and members who were moved to do so rose and spoke in favour of the subjection of womankind as befitted "light, weakminded and incorrigibly frivolous creatures". Jeaffreson believed the pastime harmless enough. Those present were "fifty young gownsmen who thought it pleasant to play the fool for a season, and who in later time showed themselves healthily eager to associate in lawful wedlock with young gentlewomen of fit quality".[15] But not all were equally fortunate in this respect, as Kingsley carefully but firmly pointed out in *Ravenshoe*:

> No English story about young men could be complete without bringing in subjects which some may think best left alone. Let us comfort ourselves with one great, undeniable fact — the immense improvement in morals which has taken place in the last ten years. The very outcry which is now raised against such relations shows plainly one thing at least — that undeniable facts are being winked at no longer, and that some reform is coming. Every younger son who can command £200 a year ought to be allowed to marry in his own rank in life, whatever that may be. They will be uncomfortable, and have to save and push; and a very good thing for them. They won't lose caste. There are some things worse than mere discomfort. Let us look at bare facts, which no one dare deny. There is in the great world, and the upper middle-class world too, a crowd of cadets; younger sons, clerks, officers in the army, and so on; non-marrying men, as the slang goes, who are asked out to dine and dance with girls who are their equals in rank, and who have every opportunity of falling in love with them. And yet if one of this numerous crowd were to dare to fall in love with, and to propose to, one of

these girls, he would be denied the house. It is the fathers and mothers who are to blame, to a great extent, for the very connexions they denounce so loudly. But yet the very outcry they are raising against these connexions is a hopeful sign. [Chap. 37]

Such comment makes the Fez Club a pastime of nonsense, hardly homosexual, and a way of treating pressures which were not allowed to surface.

Being one, also, of a small group of nondescript dressers may have invited comment and the appellation "The Intellectual Bargees", but this Kingsley shrugged off. He was more involved with finding out some of the mysteries of hunting — an occupation he later condemned for undergraduates on the basis of cost. His familiarity with the world of hunting is clearly first hand:

> The lads were bedding down, and all the great building was alive with the clattering of busy feet and the neighing of horses. . . . The physical appearance of Mr. Dickson was as though you had taken an aged Newmarket jockey, and put a barrel of oysters, barrel and all, inside his waistcoat. His face was thin; his thighs were hollow; calves to his legs he had none. He was all stomach. Many years had elapsed since he had been brought to the verge of dissolution by severe training; and since then all that he had eaten, or drunk, or done, had flown to his stomach, producing a tympanitic action in that organ, astounding to behold. In speech he was, towards his superiors, courteous and polite; towards his equals, dictatorial; towards his subordinates, abusive, not to say blasphemous. [*Ravenshoe*, chap. 12]

Despite his reservations, he had a genuine interest in horse-racing and warned against indifference to its less desirable elements: "Look to your grooms, gentlemen, and don't allow such a blot . . . as some racing stables much longer, or there will be a heavy reckoning against you when the books are balanced" (*Ravenshoe*, chap. 58).

Some of Kingsley's contemporaries had other recollections of his successes. Edwin Arnold recorded that, for a wager, Kingsley ran a mile, rowed a mile, and trotted a mile within fifteen minutes, and won. The Diamond Sculls at Henley he won, too. At the same time he did not neglect sports of another kind. W. G. Wilkinson was happy to recall being with Kingsley in a smoking contest, when, after consuming numerous pipes of Cavendish and strong Latakia tobacco, Kingsley won.[16] The "shy, sensitive lad, delicate in health" was becoming less delicate, less shy, and less quiet. Away from home and the influence of family, he was beginning to stand alone, even if from a practical viewpoint his successes were of little direct use to him. They at least were helping him define his identity.

Another contemporary, C. Kegan Paul, remembered Kingsley for different reasons. Through Kingsley, Paul met Walter Short, Martin Irving, and Herbert Ormerod. Kingsley, Short, and Ormerod, as well as Paul, were all interested in mesmerism, and Kingsley was "remarkably susceptible", so Paul recollected. His being at Worcester was also remarked on by Paul, as he and others considered Kingsley superior to his surroundings,[17] an observation which might perhaps say more about Oxford life than about Kingsley.

Kingsley's writings on Oxford's architecture appear in *Ravenshoe*, where he shows a marked preference for St Mary's in almost rhapsodical description:

> Oxford. The front of Magdalen Hall, about which the least said the soonest mended. On the left, further on, All Souls, which seems to have been built by the same happy hand which built the new courts of St. John's, Cambridge (for they are about equally bad). On the right, the Clarendon and the Schools, blocking out the western sky. Still more to the right, a bit of Exeter, and all Brazenose. In front, the Radcliff, the third dome in England, and, beyond, the straight facade of St. Mary's, gathering its lines upward ever, till tired of window and buttress, of crocket, finial, gargoyle, and all the rest of it, it leaps up aloft in one glorious crystal, and carries up one's heart with it into the heaven above. [Chap. 22]

In 1851 Kingsley and his parents went to the Continent. Charles, much exhausted by work and controversy, left Fanny in England and joined them. From Charles's letters, with his references to "H and I,"[18] and the recollections of Anne Thackeray Ritchie, who was travelling with her father and sister on the boat on which the Kingsleys crossed to Antwerp, come some details of the holiday.

The trip started on a "sleety summer morning" from London Bridge, when the passengers embarked on a packet boat, the decks wet and slippery. When Thackeray and his daughters, aged thirteen and eleven years of age, came on board they were greeted by the Kingsleys. Henry's father, recollected Mrs Ritchie, was sitting "in clerical dress and a lady sitting with an umbrella in the drizzle of rain and falling smuts from the funnel. . . . Mr. Kingsley and his brother were wearing brown felt hats with very high and pointed crowns, and with very broad brims." As the packet pitched and tossed towards Antwerp, Anne Thackeray, unable to sketch, sat miserably beside Mrs Kingsley watching the rim of Charles Kingsley's wideawake rising and falling "against the horrible horizon".[19] Charles stood holding the rigging. Thackeray "wisely retired under a table in the saloon to rest".[20]

On arrival at Antwerp the Kingsleys went to Cologne and thence to Ems. Charles wrote on 1 August 1851 to Fanny from Ems about his visit to Kaulbach's glass at Cologne, "the great triptych of Koloffs, the Adoration", and his trip up the Rhine. Charles and Henry then left their parents and tramped over the hills to Braubach and Marksburg, capturing butterflies and finding, on the way, twenty-five species of plants hitherto unknown to Charles. At Braubach the brothers took the steamer to Bingen, crossed to Assmanshausen, "and walked down the right (the Lurlei) bank to Goar, and back again". The Rhine and its castles, particularly the Sonneck Schloss, delighted them beyond measure. On 4 August, Henry and Charles, complete with knapsacks, left for the Eifel for a fortnight. Three days later they were in Menderscheid after having lost their way the previous night when, about eight o'clock, they had found themselves at the top of a cliff 150 metres high, "with a roaring river at the bottom, and no path".[21] The scenery, characterized by lake-filled craters, roads mended with lava, reapers in rye-fields, and "ravishingly beautiful glens", had been matched by glorious weather as they travelled. By 10 August they had reached Gerolstein, the most wonderful place, Charles claimed, he had visited in his life. He wrote Fanny about the magnificence of the scenery and commented as well on the delights of travelling cheaply: "I am exceedingly well and strong, though I did dine yesterday off raw ham and hock at 9d. a bottle. – Oh! and had no Katzenjammer after it!! My knapsack and plaid weigh about 2 stone, which is very heavy.... Henry's kit is lighter, but I am getting old and luxurious and cannot move without little comforts."[22]

On 13 August they reached Birreborn after having walked from Hillesheim past the Dreiser Weiher, "a mountain fallen into a crater", where they found glassy felspar, olivine, and augite. From there their route took them to Daun and up to the Schalcken Maaren, "three crater lakes in one mountain". But excitement of a different kind was at hand. On 17 August they were at Treves, having been brought from Biltsburg under arrest, and at Treves there was neither comfort nor fun – they spent the night in prison, "among felons and fleas", on the bare floor. The explanation lay in their having been mistaken for political activists associated with Mazzini. Inevitably the affair ended amicably, and they were released. Mr and Mrs Kingsley arrived in Treves to find their two sons being lionized by the town. From here the Kingsleys travelled on to Bonn, Brussels, Waterloo, Ghent, and Bruges before sailing home from Ostend.[23]

Somewhere on the trip it seems that Henry could have been in some position of danger. J. M. Ludlow, writing to Charles in August 1852, asked, "How is the prodigal brother getting on? I heard of your heroism concerning him."[24] Possibly, too, this was the accident to which Maurice Kingsley referred in 1895 when he stated that Henry had injured the sight of his right eye after being blown up by gunpowder.[25] On the other hand, it may have been Ludlow's method of referring to Charles's efforts to keep Henry in ways more productive than those he was following at Oxford, where he was having greater success in sport than in study. *The Times* reported Kingsley's victory on the first day of the 1852 Henley Royal Regatta:

> Yesterday was the opening day of this annual meeting.... The sports commenced with the match for a Silver Cup, between Mr. Burchett, a gentleman well known in London aquatic circles, and member of the Argonauts Club, with Mr. H. Kingsley, of the University Boat Club, Oxford.
>
> The match had been originally made in April, and it was arranged, by permission of the stewards, that it should form a portion of the Henley sport.... Mr. Burchett had the Bucks Shore. The start was very even, and both went off well, and at a good pace. They were almost scull and scull for about a quarter of a mile, and then Kingsley began to show in front, but, taking the bay on the Berks Side, and hugging the shore pretty closely to escape the wind,

his opponent made play in the straight course, and appeared to menace his position. Although Mr. Burchett's efforts were very determined, his opponent was too good, and retaining the lead, won by four lengths.[26]

When Kingsley left Worcester without taking his degree, no reference to him appeared in the college minutes.[27] His departure was predictable, as his studies had been minimal. Before going to Oxford he had sought information about going to Canada, and while there had spent time writing *Ravenshoe*. His writing, sporting, and social activities were more than enough evidence that he was not interested in studying for the Church. His views at this time about academic success were clearly the same as those of Charles Ravenshoe:

> "I don't care for you," bawled Charles; "you're a greater fool than I am, and be hanged to you. You're going to spend the best years of your life, and ruin your health, to get a first.... And when you have got your precious first, you will find yourself utterly unfit for any trade or profession whatever (except the Church, which you don't mean to enter). What do you know about modern languages or modern history? If you go into the law, you have got to begin all over again. They won't take you in the army; they are not such *muffs*. And this is what you get for your fifteen hundred pounds!" [Chap. 8]

In *Stretton*, too, Kingsley questioned the worth of a university education and mentioned the sum of fifteen hundred pounds again. His character, Roland, could "do a better piece of Greek prose" than most, could silence a moderator on the "other side of that dreadful table in those divinity schools... under the most beautifully decorated roof in England", and "could reel off the limits of human knowledge" in science. "I acknowledge that he [Roland] had learnt how to learn," wrote Kingsley, "and that when the world had shown him what it was necessary to know, that he would have learned it. But let me tell you what he did not know." He then cited Roland's ignorance of history, physical science, Darwin, Huxley, and modern languages. "Roland, after [£] 1500 of expenditure, was little fit to cope with the world, as far as education had helped him." Kingsley's attitude was scornful — in the world one had to cope, but undergraduates were "fit for nothing but ushers in schools or curates. Clive or Hastings were not more ignorant, or more helpless before they underwent that great competitive sink-or-swim examination, which is called The World." In some ways he was being honest with himself when he wrote that the ideal Cambridge man was "plodding, thrifty, quiet, diligent, solemn, wise", while the ideal Oxford man was "fantastic, noisy, extravagant, and given to practical jokes" (*Stretton*, chap. 19); only he, of the three brothers, had gone to Oxford — the yardstick was his own.

"I wanted to be a soldier," exclaimed the narrator in "Malmaison", "but my father could not afford it and wanted me to be a clergyman. To this I objected; and the end of it all is that I am a journalist" (part 1). This seems too near the truth, for a journalist and not a clergyman Kingsley became. The struggle to find himself against the pressures of family expectations and a knowledge of his own lack of preparedness for life, allied with his now usual solution — escape — is seen in Charles Ravenshoe's reflection:

> "Thinking, thinking.... He saw that action was necessary, and he came to a great and noble resolution, worthy of himself. All the world was on one side, and he alone on the other. He would meet the world humbly and bravely and conquer it. He would begin at the beginning, and find his own value in the world, and then, if he found himself worthy, would claim once more the love and respect of those who had been his friends hitherto." [*Ravenshoe*, chap. 27]

Later, speaking to Grip, his dog, Ravenshoe says, "I am going to see what the world is like, I shan't come back before you are dead, Grip, I expect.... Very likely I shall go abroad, to the land where the stuff comes from they make sovereigns of, and try my luck at getting some of the yellow rubbish" (chap. 28). Later still, Kingsley wrote that Ravenshoe committed suicide, "deliberate suicide", and that obstinacy carried him through to the end of the decision: "What is suicide nine cases out of ten? Anyone can tell you. It is the act of a mad, proud coward, who flies, by his own deed, not from humiliation or disgrace, but as he fancies, from feeling the consequences of them — who flies to unknown, doubtful evils, sooner than bear positive, present, undoubted ones" (chap. 30). Which was a fair summation of himself, his romanticism and his actions. He would not present himself for the examinations.

But why Australia in preference to Canada? His later comments on Australia were not flattering:

> The discovery of that vast continent which we call Australia is an important era in the history of the world. For it opened, in the first place, a career for young gentlemen possessed of every virtue, save those of continence, sobriety, and industry, who didn't choose to walk, and couldn't afford to ride; and, viewed from this point, its discovery ranks next in importance after the invention of soda-water — a sort of way of escaping cheaply from the consequences of debauchery for a time. But not only did the new country turn out to be the most wonderfully scentless cesspool for a vast quantity of nameless rubbish, convicted and unconvicted; but it gave an opening also for really honest, upright fellows like Charles Morton, with no more faults than most of us, except the very great one of being educated in such a way that no possible career is open to them. What is a fellow to do if his father chooses to play his game of whist with fourteen cards, and if he happens to be the fourteenth? [*The Hillyars and the Burtons*, chap. 44]

Simply, gold provided the motive and Australia the place. With his decision to go, another chapter could begin. The past did not have to be a handicap. Kingsley's apologia comes in his judgment of Charles Ravenshoe:

> I think I have been very careful to impress on you that Charles was not wise. At all events, if I have softened matters so far hitherto as to leave you in doubt, his actions... will leave not the slightest doubt of it. I love the man. I love his very faults in a way. He is a reality to me, though I may not have the art to make him so to you.

His mad, impulsive way of forming a resolution, and his honourable obstinacy in sticking to that resolution afterwards, even to the death, are very great faults; but they are, more or less, the faults of men who have made a very great figure in the world, or I have read history wrong. [*Ravenshoe,* chap. 28]

Now, only "that great competitive sink-or-swim examination which is called The World" remained, and in that he was on his own.

6

In Transit

Kingsley had little hesitation in deciding to go to Australia and so withdraw from his problems. It was a route to be followed by many others in the years ahead, either as escapees to anonymity or as more fortunate remittance men. At Oxford he had become friendly with Henry Pares Venables, a nephew of the Australian explorer Charles Sturt, and with Venables, Kingsley chose to make the journey. Sturt's status and connections in Australia assured them to some extent that they would not be friendless.[1] Fanny Kingsley refers to their hopes in a letter dated September 1853: "Poor dr. Henry started with good prospects and capital introductions from Captn. Sturt — he and Captn. Sturt's nephew went together. His father and mother are just arriving here."[2] Kingsley returned to Chelsea to collect his belongings, a visit which brought second thoughts in later years:

> One more look round the old room! The last for ever! The present overmastered the past, and he looked round almost without recognition. I doubt whether at great crises men have much time for recollecting old associations. I looked once into a room, which had been my home, ever since I was six years old, for five-and-twenty years, knowing I should never see it again. But it was to see that I had left nothing behind me. The coach was at the door, and they were calling for me. Now I could draw you a correct map of all the blotches and cracks in the ceiling, as I used to see them when I lay in bed of a morning. But then, I only shut the door and ran down the passage, without even saying "good-bye, old bedroom". [*Ravenshoe*, chap. 28]

He left for Australia despite the earlier hopes of his parents that he would enter the Church. The eighteen months at Colebrook had been spent to that end. But gold fever ran riot, and its lure, as a short cut to riches, drew more adventurers than Kingsley and Venables to Australia. "No one who has not done a little of the '*exfodiuntur opes*' can understand what the gold fever was like," he wrote in *Tales of Old Travel*. "Mammon's own bait ... for which parliaments legislate first ... [this] indescribable golden gleam out of dirty gravel is a thing which maddens men. See the wondrous sight for yourself before you utterly condemn the men who are driven mad by the lust of it."[3]

Kingsley's plea for understanding by others is enhanced by his own self-judgement in *Geoffry Hamlyn* when he wrote that, for a boyish fancy, he "had cut himself off . . . from all the ties of domestic life" to go his own way (chap. 47). "Who has not seen the misery and despair often caused in a family by the senseless selfishness of one of its members? Who has not felt enraged at such times, to think that a man or woman should presume on the affection and kindheartedness of their relatives, and yet act as if they were wholly without those affections themselves? And, lastly who of us all is guiltless of doing this? Let him that is without sin among us cast the first stone" (chap. 11).

Kingsley and Venables had a self-confidence hardly justified by the adverse information regarding employment in the colony. As one journal explained:

> "Young men accustomed only to the desk, and unfitted for any mechanical occupation, will find it next to impossible to procure employment in Australia." Almost every letter that is sent home from Melbourne, and nearly every newspaper published in the colony, repeats this warning. But in spite of warnings of every kind, young men from shops and counting-houses appear to be the very persons who, for the last twelve months, have filled the greater part of the berths in emigrant ships bound for the land of gold.[4]

Apart from this, they had no idea of the reversal in situation which occurred for educated gentlemen without skills in Australia. The aristocrats of labour were the tradesmen, and land the sign of the squatter aristocrats. The gold seeker was a nomad, and Fortune favoured few with abundance. Of this, though, they knew little. The *Gauntlet*, on which Kingsley and Venables sailed, was one of the new iron-hull ships just then coming into service. Built that year in Dumbarton, it left Liverpool on 20 August 1853 for London on its maiden voyage to Port Phillip Bay.[5] Not a large ship, its tonnage was registered as 784/693; its crew totalled twenty-nine apart from its master, William Inglis; and its passenger list, twenty-three. The ship's records give much detail, but that more directly relevant shows that the ship's surgeon, W. G. N. Manby, had not previously been to sea, and despite the claim made for the increased safety of the new hull, one crew member had second thoughts about the voyage and deserted before the ship sailed. The ship's passenger list shows that Kingsley and Venables advanced their ages by four years before sailing[6] but fails to show the name of another friend, Irvine, hitherto believed to have gone with them.[7] On board, Kingsley's thoughts probably had much in common with Charles Harvey in *The Harveys*:

> Health, freedom, and, in prospect, honour and a grand position! After all these weary years what a prospect for me! As I sat on the deck of the old *Soho* . . . I said to myself that only one thing was left for me to desire in this world, and that one thing was personal beauty. . . . when I was starting on my first holiday journey to new lands, with every chance of relieving the man I loved best in the world — my father — from all future difficulty, I remember, I was jealous of the personal beauty of a lad of my own age, who was on board. [Chap. 18]

The *Gauntlet*. From a watercolour by H.P. Venables.

No record of the outward course taken by the *Gauntlet* appears in its log, but doubtless it followed the Cape of Good Hope route to Australia. A glimpse of this is given in *Ravenshoe,* with its mention of the silence "of the Southern Indian Ocean in a calm at midnight". A sketch made by H. P. Venables shows the *Gauntlet* to have been a three-masted barque, square rigged on all three masts. As drawn, the vessel is scudding in heavy weather and heeling somewhat, with all sails but two close-reefed.[8] These were the days remembered by Kingsley. As he wrote in *Ravenshoe*: "A north-east wind and a mountain of rustling white canvas overhead. Blue water that seethed and creamed, and roared past to leeward. A calm, and the Lizard to the north, a dim grey cape. A south-west wind, and above a mighty cobweb of sailless rigging. Top-gallant masts sent down and yards close hauled.... A dim wild sunset, and scudding prophet clouds that hurried from the west across the crimson zenith, like witches towards a sabbath. A wind that rose and grew as the sun went down, and hummed loud in the rigging as the bows of the ship dipped into the trough of the waves, and failed almost into silence as she raised them" (chap. 51). At such moments Kingsley became intensely aware of what was happening to him. "Few know the feeling which comes upon all men after it is done," he wrote, " — the feeling of isolation, almost of terror, at having gone so far out of the bounds of ordinary life; the feeling of self-distrust and cowardice at being alone and friendless in the world, like a child in the dark"

(*Geoffry Hamlyn,* chap. 17). At long last Henry Kingsley was being educated, and the electrical storms that struck the *Gauntlet* were like the turbulence of his own fears.

Other passages show how deeply his sailing affected him. For example, in *Austin Elliot* he marvelled at the contrast between a ship at sea and a ship in port when he visited either the *Gauntlet* or the clipper on which he returned to England, the *Swiftsure*: "It is hard, when on board a ship in the docks, standing so unmovably still, to realise that one has seen those steady tapering masts sweeping wildly across blotched stars: or those sharp bows leaping madly up towards heaven in the agony of the storm: to recall the reeling, and rolling, and plunging, of the vast inert mass under one's feet, now resting so quietly from her labour" (chap. 18). But his consciousness of event is just as evident in *The Hillyars and the Burtons*.

> One day of one long voyage comes before me particularly clear ... in the trades ... for all space was filled with a divine grey-blue effulgence, which has to my wandering fancy, always seemed to be the trade-wind itself. ... It was not too hot nor too cold ... and the ship was going fast, and heeling over ... going with a gentle heaving motion. There were clouds, slow sailing clouds, but they were of frosted silver. ... there was open sky, but of the very faintest blue. ... where the delicate needle of a top-gallant mast swept ... there were sounds ... of the wind itself, filling space ... the low gentle lapping of the waves upon the ship's side, and the sleepy gurgling and hissing of many eddies around her. [Chap. 44]

Finally, the terror of a typhoon in *Austin Elliott* he captures in prose that leaves no question of its being beyond the bounds of ordinary life: "All was black as ink, but the sea around them was a wild mist of white foam ... [when] wreaths of clouds were not going *with* the wind, but from right to left, nearly dead against it" (chap. 18).

Kingsley and Venables between times made their plans. When they left England, the areas of Mount Alexander, Ballarat, Bendigo, and Forest Creek were regarded as "the most auriferous region in Australia". Of these, the one to be selected was crucial in view of the possible rewards. In 1852, 3.6 million ounces (112 million g.) of gold were dispatched from Australia to England, worth fifteen million pounds[9] — a fortune then, and more so now. The cost of participating in the rush, though, was minimal, and emigrants could reach the "land of gold" at a comparatively trifling expense, whether they embarked at Liverpool or London.[10] To help them, guide books were available. For example, *The Gold-Finder of Australia* in July 1853 offered a first-hand account of living conditions and essential mining information, and *Phillips' Emigrant Guide to Australia,* a slim volume priced at one shilling, sold in thousands of copies to those wanting to sail. From all accounts, Mount Alexander was the obvious choice and without precedent in its yield of gold.[11] Reason, though, was not the only guide. "In the Australian madness of 1852," wrote Kingsley, "how many men do I know who, sick of things here, gave up safe positions in England out of the pure old English spirit of adventure? How many? As many as were Mrs.

Nickleby's lovers" (*Stretton,* chap. 25). Chance and impulse were equally as potent as reason.

On Saturday, 3 December 1853, the *Gauntlet* made landfall near Melbourne after three months at sea, and Kingsley saw the country that was to be his home for the next four years. Ahead lay Port Phillip Bay. "A new morn arises," he wrote, "and flashes a crimson and purple light, in long streamers, aloft to the zenith; and we are sailing slowly along under the high-piled forest capes; more strange, more majestic, and more infinitely melancholy than anything we have seen in our strangest dreams. What is this awful, dim mysterious land, so solemn and so desolate? This is Australia" (*The Hillyars and the Burtons,* chap. 44). His sense of wonder about the melancholy appeal of Australia never left him. Long afterwards, in "The Foundation of an Empire", he remembered the Australian loneliness and wrote: "There lies among the pleasant Southern Seas an island as large as Europe — an island lone, melancholy, until lately desolate. The traveller approaching that island even now is struck with the awful melancholy of its high-piled forest capes."[12]

The *Gauntlet* drew near the entrance to Port Phillip as though almost too eager to end its voyage. Kingsley, on deck watching the headlands approach, heard the pilot who had come aboard exclaim anxiously to the captain, "*I* can't get your ship about; if you can't do it yourself, she will be ashore in ten minutes."[13] The moment was critical, the bay and the heads treacherous — as three wrecks that year testified: the schooner *Colina* failed to answer her helm after being struck by a sudden squall and was lost; the cutter *Mary,* 45 tons, had become a total wreck near Sorrento just inside the bay; and the schooner *Will O' The Wisp,* 150 tons, inward bound from Auckland, had been totally wrecked.[14] With "as ugly a surf bursting half a mile to leeward as anyone would wish to see", the captain barely succeeded where the pilot had failed, and the ship entered the bay.

The voyage was all but over, and for Kingsley the Australian adventure was about to begin. With his own experiences in mind, he recollected in *Ravenshoe*: "He felt like a boy at midsummer, exploring some wood, or distant valley, watched from a distance long, and at last attained; or as one feels when, a stranger in a new land, one rides forth alone into the forest on some distant expedition, and sees the new world, dreamt of and longed for all one's life, realised in all its beauty and wonder at last" (chap. 51).

7
New Beginnings

Kingsley was in Australia from December 1853 to February 1858, a period of his life very different from his earlier years. The fullest account — though of necessity incomplete — of where he went is therefore given because of its importance in suggesting the effects of his colonial experience on him, what was got from it for his novels, and what he left out (as, for example, his hard times). Available information about his stay is limited; nevertheless, a time frame can be suggested from the evidence of his paintings, his writings, police records, and data from other sources, some of which are contemporaneous with Kingsley's visit. This evidence shows, beyond reasonable doubt, that he was in Victoria during 1854 before leaving for New South Wales, returned via Gippsland in 1855, and was in Victoria again from 1856 until he left for England in February 1858.

Like Jim Burton, in *The Hillyars and the Burtons,* Kingsley arrived in Melbourne to encounter a century on the thermometer and a hot northerly wind. He felt, he recalled, "exactly as though I had been doing a hard day's work on a hot day in August, whereas I had only stepped out of a boat, and given a hand, among ten more, to moving our things into a pile on the wharf" (chap. 48). While some of the party proceeded elsewhere, Burton waited in the dust. His experience was typical of other new arrivals'. Cuthbert Fetherstonhaugh arrived in Port Phillip Bay in 1853, landed at Liardet's Beach, and "went up to Melbourne on a jingle [a covered, two-wheel cart], past Canvas Town".[1] Céleste de Chabrillan found Melbourne in 1853 "not yet a town; it was a warehouse. There were shops and depots everywhere, but nothing was restful, nothing intimate; there is something strained and brutal about the first efforts of a new society."[2] John Sadlier wrote, "There is no need to repeat the oft-told tale of how Melbourne and its people appeared to a newly-arrived stranger in the very early 'Fifties.' The dust and general discomfort rather shocked us. The dust is with us still."[3] J. Alex. Allan explained that the tents on Liardet's Beach (Port Melbourne) were the immigrant's answer to scarce — and dear — accommodation, and he described scenes of a kind that awaited Kingsley and

Venables on shore: "The ship *Duke of Bedford* was moored and turned into a lodging-house, where the cheapest rate for bed and board was £2 a week. Four hundred persons from one ship (the *Lady Head*) were thrust on to the Flinders Street wharves without food or shelter, in continuous heavy rain. In one wharf shed a young Scotswoman gave birth to a child.... the streets swarmed with unshaven chins and negligent dress. Everywhere there were men who, with full pockets where empty empty ones had been, had no rational idea regarding the disposal of their riches. Hundreds of mushroom taverns arose, filled with uproarious crowds. Robbery, murder, and outrage prevailed day and night."[4]

The careful detail in many of Kingsley's Australian scenes can in many instances be confirmed both topographically and historically. A brief extract from *The Hillyars and the Burtons* shows how carefully he rendered what he saw:

> There was a row of fine warehouses, built solidly with freestone, along the wharf; but, after one got back from the wharf, up the gentle rise on which the town stands, Palmerston might at that time be pronounced a patchy metropolis.... As an instance, on the half-acre lot next to the branch Bank of New South Wales, a handsome Doric building, the proprietor had erected a slab hut, bark roofed, lying at an angle of say 35° to the street. At the farther end of this, and connected with it, was a dirty old tent, standing at an angle of 35° to the slab hut.... All the place was strewed with sheep skins; and in front of all, close to the road, was an umbrella-tent, lined with green baize, in which sat the proprietor's wife, with her shoes off, casting up accounts in an old vellum book.... I don't know that this was the queerest establishment I noticed that day. I think not; but I give it as a specimen, because the Bank of New South Wales stands near the top of the hill; and, when you top that hill, you are among the noble group of Government buildings, and from among them you look down over the police paddock on to the Sturt river. [Chap. 48]

Palmerston was Melbourne, and Richmond Police Camp, within walking distance of Melbourne town, was "situated at the north-east corner of Richmond Paddock".[5]

As well as the sketch of the *Gauntlet*, Venables made two others. The first was dated 1855 of a vessel arriving with news of the Crimean War; the second, of a tent and its surrounds where the two friends lived after disembarkation. Venables endorsed this sketch: "Our first place of abode".[6] The tent was a standard bush tent with a similar tent attached as an annexe. Here they shared the chores of tent life — one squatting at a smoking camp-fire, one sitting on a log, while both prepare a meal. Both men are wearing shallow-crowned, broad-brimmed hats — the cabbage-tree hat of the goldfields. With no tents near by, Kingsley and Venables pitched tent beyond the dust of Melbourne in undulating country, with only distant mountains for neighbours. In the bay, the rigging of ships showed the settlement's presence only by the density of their masts and yards.

Kingsley and Venables, well out of Melbourne Town, escaped not

New Beginnings

The "first place of abode" of Kingsley and Venables in Australia. From a watercolour by H.P. Venables.

only the dust but also the perils that awaited new emigrants in its streets. Initially, what lay ahead after striking camp at Melbourne would test their gold fever and their finances. Picks, shovels, axes, tin dishes, tent, clothing, blankets, provisions, pots and pans, gold cradle, rope, and bucket — all had to be transported to the diggings and, if not taken, bought there — and prices were exorbitant. Cartage to Bendigo Creek rose from £32 per ton before June 1852 to £150 by mid-winter and early spring. But there were other factors to consider. The route to the Mount Alexander diggings wound its way via Essendon, where the landmark for the first day's trek was "Tulip" Wright's inn, north-west along unmade roads which were deep dust in summer and trampled mud in winter. To escape the threat of thieves and marauders, diggers travelled and bivouacked together for protection.[7] With trudging and digging before them, it only needed the advice of old-timers to be up and away before the sleet and rain of winter came to trouble the travellers more than cursorily. If there was no quick strike, then — short of digging daily in mud and enduring it — winter quarters, and work, would have to be found.[8] Kingsley and Venables were now, however, committed. There could be no question of turning back.

The strikes at Mount Alexander included, among others, that of Sandhurst, later known as Bendigo. John Neill Macartney, sharebroker and correspondent for the *Bendigo Advertiser*, well remembered Kingsley when writing of his early days on the diggings:

> If nomadic, why it was a jolly Bohemian existence. We were free from envy, jealousy, and cankering care. Many a scholarly and polished gentleman's heart beat under the blue shirt of many a digger. Then it was no rare thing to hear a rough, unkempt fellow, speak from the well of English undefiled, in the purest Attic Salt. Henry Kingsley, the author of "Ravenshoe" and "Geoffry Hamlyn," two splendid Australian novels, worked on Epsom, and got the material for his work at Mount Moliagul, near Dunolly.[9]

In the area of Moliagul was much that would have interested Kingsley. The Reverend William Hall, an early arrival in Port Phillip, took over Kingower run in February 1853[10] and in 1856 built Glenalbyn Grange, one of the fine colonial homesteads of the period.[11] He was typical of people with a way of life similar to Kingsley's characters, the Buckleys and the Brentwoods of *Geoffry Hamlyn,* and an entry in Hall's diary of 4 February 1849, when at Ballan, gives some indication of their manners and customs: "Had Service in the morning at Capt. A's station; 20 were present, — many from a distance.... Went in the afternoon and had Service at Capt. A. von Steiglitz's Station (Durdewarra), 14 were present.... two shepherds were present at the family devotions in the evening." From such a milieu came those of Kingsley's characters whom Furphy was to call, fifty years later, "virgin souled schoolboys".[12] Whether they were or not, the presence of such people in the Bendigo area supports rather than discredits Kingsley's depictions of this class.

In fact, while the settings in *Geoffry Hamlyn* are those of the Monaro district of New South Wales and Gippsland, the characters are those of the Western District of Victoria. The area was settled by pioneers from Tasmania and New South Wales after 1830, following its discovery by Hume and Hovell. Among them were the forbears of Malcolm Fraser, one of the two Australian prime ministers to come from the region, the other being R. G. Menzies. Marcus Clarke, who wrote *For the Term of His Natural Life* (1874), also went there for colonial experience, while Adam Lindsay Gordon's presence in the Western District, both as poet and horseman, is well known.

South of Kingower was another settler of some interest, an overlander of 1839:[13] "a thorough-going type of the half-pay military captain, also hailing from the highlands, Captain Dugald McLachlan of Glengower station. He was a little austere as became his rank, was an ardent sportsman, and was usually followed by four or five strong and lithe kangaroo hounds, all ready for the first sight or scent of a lurking dingo, which if encountered was very soon run down and killed, and his brush secured as a trophy."[14] The resemblances to Kingsley's Lionel Horton of "The Two Cadets" are unmistakeable. At The Springs, a homestead near Moliagul, Mrs Hugh Fraser established her school for "young ladies" in 1859, the station itself being mentioned in writings as early as 1853.[15] In short, there was much offering in the way of "charming homes and social customs", and Ada Cambridge did Kingsley a disservice when she wrote: "*Geoffry Hamlyn* was my sheet anchor but did not seem to be supported by the scraps of prosaic history obtainable. We could not verify those charming homes and social customs. On the other hand, cannibal blacks and convict bushrangers appeared to be grim facts."[16] Rather, the Moliagul area supported what Cuthbert Fetherstonhaugh claimed — that *Geoffry Hamlyn* "very truthfully portrayed life in Australia, although bearing the impress of the Britisher who wrote it".[17]

More, though, was to be gleaned at Mount Alexander than gold, sheep stations, and social graces. A magnificent ride from Mount Moliagul to Mount Korong, twenty miles away, was already famous, the horse equalling if not surpassing Widderin's famous run in *Geoffry Hamlyn*.[18] Melville the bushranger made frequent use of caves close to Kingower, where, hidden among towering granite boulders and outcrops, he surveyed the whole terrain. Melville, active in the 1850s, gained some sympathy for being the most daring of the Victorian bushrangers[19] and excited Kingsley's interest by his behaviour, being "the son of a Scotch clergyman ... in utter rebellion against order, law, society ... against God Himself". Kingsley went on to say, "This last man is a puzzle to me still. I would give much to have a talk with him. I had a chance once; I might have got near the man" ("The Two Cadets", chap. 1).

At Mount Alexander some found their fortunes, but not Kingsley. Even the local children whom he saw fossicking on Sundays were still finding gold near Expedition Pass,[20] although their pickings were less than the previous year. James Hodgson, another digger, viewed them doing it with utter disbelief and, still incredulous, wrote from Melbourne on 15 April 1852: "We took a walk in the afternoon (Sunday) and actually saw several boys picking up gold off the grass. The sight nearly turned my brain but that was nothing to what we were to see and hear soon daily."[21] Paintings endorsed by Kingsley show that, as well as being on Mount Alexander, he was on the diggings at Ben Nevis near Avoca, Mount Cole, Beechworth, Buninyong, and the Ovens — all in Victoria. His handwritten notes on the paintings are first-hand evidence of the interest he had in geological and botanical detail,[22] while the paintings themselves are competent watercolours of identifiable scenes. As his friend Henry Campbell recalled, Kingsley explored the adjacent countryside when on the goldfields, an activity that led to another discovery: "It is just worthy of notice how, when one once begins a vagabond life, one gets attached to a place where one may chance to rest even for a week. When one gets accustomed to a change of locality every day for a long while, a week's pause gives one more familiarity with a place than a month's residence in a strange house would give if one were habitually stationary" (*Ravenshoe*, chap. 51). This familiarity Kingsley welcomed in the "strange house" of Mrs Brackenbury, who arrived, alone, in Port Phillip on board the *Croesus* on 9 April 1854.[23] According to his brother George, who met Mrs

Brackenbury in Auckland, New Zealand, Henry encountered her at some stage "on the Gold Fields. She was paralysed at the scientific manner in which he, a most ruffianly looking scoundrel of a miner, described the fish which he had caught." Nevertheless, George recorded, she "took him in and was good to him, the old dear, when he was ill. Her brother was the Consul at Lisbon when I was there in the *St. George.*"[24] Henry's dress, like that of other miners, consisted of a brightly coloured shirt, white dungaree or moleskin trousers, high shiny knee boots, a cabbage-tree hat, and a beard.[25] His clothes, certainly, would have belied his origins as well as his earlier genteel appearances in a drawing-room full of ladies back in Chelsea.

Kingsley had some interesting observations to make arising from his time on the goldfields. Referring to social attitudes, he wrote in *Ravenshoe*:

> I am a great admirer of the old feudal feeling, when it is not abused by either party.... even on the diggings, with all the leaven of Americanism and European Radicalism one finds there, it is much easier for a warden to get on with the diggers if he comes of a known family, than if he is an unknown man. The old colonial diggers, the people of the greatest real weight, talk of them, and the others listen and mark. All people, prate as they may, like a guarantee for respectability. In the colonies, such a guarantee is given by a man's being tolerably well off, and "come of decent people." In England, it is given, in cases, by a man and a man's forefathers having been good landlords and honest men. [Chap. 42]

Drunkenness and disorder on the goldfields he believed equal to, but not worse than, what occurred at an English fair, but of friendship between men he wrote: "At home it would have taken three years to have made these three men such hearty friends as they had become in a fortnight. Friendships are made in the camp, in the bush, or on board ship, at a wonderful rate. And, moreover, they last for an indefinite time. For ever, I fancy: for these reasons. Time does not destroy friendship. Time has nothing whatever to do with it" (*Ravenshoe,* chap. 41). Here Kingsley noted (but could not foresee the full significance of what he saw) mateship, a phenomenon Henry Lawson wrote about years later more fully and with more particularity. Mateship, as such, was to become a recognizable theme in Australian writing by the late nineteenth century, but in *The Mystery of the Island* (1877) Kingsley instances mateship as he recollected it — friendship in action:

> A very sad thing occurred up the Murchison that year. At the very furthest station on that river, a very poor old cockney was hut-keeper to a Scotch shepherd. The Londoner, not a physically good specimen of his class, probably the most plucky in the world, had got the Scotch shepherd's tea ready, and his Bible on the table, when the shepherd came in. The shepherd did not eat his tea or read his Bible. He talked to the Londoner about many things, but he was most certainly ill; he had caught cold in the drenching rains, and he took to his bed with ague.
>
> The Londoner nursed him tenderly. When two men are alone together, far from help or hope, it is a fearful thing for one to fall

sick. No one knows what it is save those who have experienced it. The Londoner read his Bible to him as long as he could hear it; and when the cold stark look of death came into his face, he went for help. [Chap. 12]

The relationship existing here provides a convenient point at which to consider S. M. Ellis's suggestion that Kingsley had a "strain of homosexuality".[26] The Londoner's actions would undoubtedly have been regarded by Kingsley as "noble" conduct — good works arising essentially from concern, or love, for one's fellow man. The passage from "Jackson of Paul's" quoted by Ellis as an instance of Kingsley's "strain of homosexuality" hardly qualifies if incitement to good deeds is examined somewhat more closely: "The two boys had that boy-love for one another which I hope none of our readers have forgotten in the turmoils of life; there is no love except the love of a good woman which surpasses it in the purity and in the incitement to noble deeds." Present in the passage is a latent idealism which treats "love" in terms of "purity", where the sense for Kingsley was related not only to classical concepts of excellence but also to biblical: "Whatsoever things are true, whatsoever things are honest, whatsoever things are just, whatsoever things are pure, whatsoever things are lovely, whatsoever things are of good report: if there be any virtue, and if there be any praise, think on these things" (*Phil.* 4:8). Furthermore, David's lament for Jonathan would not have been unknown to Kingsley: "Thy love to me was wonderful, passing the love of women" (2 *Sam.* 1:26). Kingsley, though, asserts the opposite to David — "the love of a good woman" surpasses that of a "boy-love". The friendship of mining days, the mateship of Henry Lawson, the care of the Londoner for the shepherd, a boy-love which incited to noble deeds, and the love of a good woman shared two things in common — altruism and a pragmatic idealism which could be regarded as being more in the nature of *agape* than *eros*. One final extract makes the point:

> What strange tales one reads of the devotion of men towards one another.... Read the history of Burke and Wills's expedition. When you read of Wills (last and not least of Devon's worthies) dismissing Burke and King, lest they should lose their lives in seeing him die — when you find that Wills sent these two men from him, and chose a hideous, lonely death, sooner than keep them by him till their last hope of safety was cut off — then you get into a clear high atmosphere of tragedy. [*The Hillyars and the Burtons,* chap. 72]

Kingsley writes of his feelings about the lust for gold and human tragedy in *Tales of Old Travel*:

> The compiler, speaking in his own person from considerable experience, has seen strange things from this gold fever.... I have stood, wishing to plead between two angry brothers but have desisted in fear of the "redding straik" (this is the most absolute truth). I have seen wives deserted with promises of return; I have seen wives dragged many hundred miles on mere newspaper reports, and have seen them come back — broken people. I have helped to take out beautiful young men dead, who have gone, in spite of remonstrance,

> into dangerously undermined ground after this same gold. I have sat myself eight hours together by candlelight, at the end of a long dark drive, singing Lycidas and the Christmas hymn, contented and perfectly happy at seeing the metal gleam now and then among the gravel. And more, I have sat on Christmas eve waiting for those who never came, and who will come no more for ever. Dim, fever-stricken ghosts came in from the Buckland, and brought with them still dimmer ghosts from the Omeo; but some who were waited for came not. They had thrown all at the feet of Mammon, and he had devoured them.[27]

With his reference to the ill-fated Omeo rush, Kingsley places himself in Beechworth on Christmas Eve 1854, when the hoax occurred. Two Beechworth papers, *The Ovens and Murray Advertiser* and *The Constitution*, refer to its tragedy.[28] On the loss of life involved, Kingsley wrote: "How great it was we shall never know, but it must have been very great. A man who came into Beechworth on Christmas Eve informed me that he himself had found eight young men dead by the Mitta Mitta" (*The Hillyars and the Burtons*, chap. 72). It was on the diggings, then, that Kingsley was once again confronted with death, an encounter that awakened all his old questionings and his difficulty in accepting its unpredictability:

> Once, in lands far away, there was a sailor lad, a good-humoured, good-looking, thoughtless fellow, who lived alongside of me, and with whom I was always joking. We had a great liking for one another. I left him at the shaft's mouth at two o'clock one summer's day, roaring with laughter at a story I had told him; and at half-past five I was helping to wind up the shattered corpse, which when alive had borne his name. A flake of gravel had come down from the roof of the drive and killed him, and his laughing and story-telling were over for ever. How terrible these true stories are! Why do I tell this one? Because, whenever I think of this poor lad's death, I find myself not thinking of the ghastly thing that came swinging up out of the darkness into the summer air, but of the poor fellow as he was the morning before. I try to think how he looked, as leaning against the windlass with the forest behind and the mountains beyond, and if, in word or look, he gave any sign of his coming fate before he went gaily down into his tomb. [*Ravenshoe*, chap. 26]

Personal feeling lies beneath the subtle wistfulness of the writing and its questionings.

With winter on them, and no strike of any significance, Kingsley and Venables went their own ways, at the latest by June 1854. In 1855 Venables seems to have stayed in Victoria. He was in Melbourne, and the electoral rolls of 1856–57 place him back on the Moliagul diggings, which he left no later than March 1858 to join the Victorian teaching service, as Kingsley has Joe Burton do in *The Hillyars and the Burtons* (chap. 51). Kingsley was on four other fields – Avoca, Daisy Hill, Ararat, and Caledonia. He moved from the Mount Alexander-Bendigo area to Avoca sometime before or early in June 1854. The Avoca field had grown from 2,200 in December 1853 to 14,000 diggers by the time he arrived there. Apart from hearing the story of the child lost in the Pyrenees (*Geoffry Hamlyn*, chap. 30), Kingsley later made use of other local detail. The leading character in "My Landladies: Chapters of a Digger's Life", Mrs MacKinnon, is strong enough to work a windlass. As it happened, the rush started at Donkeywoman's Flat.[29] Of deserted shafts, which themselves point to a late arrival on the field, he recorded: "A man was safer in the Light Cavalry Charge at Balaklava, which occurred at that time." Local knowledge allowed him also to have the narrator ride over "to Mitchell's" (Langi Willi station), and refer to the "cold bitter June of the southern hemisphere", when, as in the tale, the Avoca River floods. But only an intimate knowledge of the diggings allowed him to refer to the lead's being lost and found again, as well as to pink gravel, instead of the more usual white, at the bottom of the Avoca shaft, a hundred and ten feet down.[30]

The floods and cold forced Kingsley in June 1854 to leave the field for a near-by property, where he went "with a party of 'sundowners' ... evidently very much down on his luck".[31] On 21 June 1854 Mrs Philip Russell of Carngham station wrote that her brother was overseeing a near-by sheep station, Langi Willi: "Mr. Mitchell is a very gentlemanly and accomplished man who seems to have spent most of his life in travelling, and is therefore quite unfit for the management of a sheepstation; he spends almost all his time away from home, and Philip is left to manage the station as well as a young man called Kingsley, who is fresh from college and who is expected to benefit by Philip's greater sheep experience."[32] Earlier reports, for reasons that appear later, erroneously placed Kingsley at Langi Willi as a "guest" of Philip Russell, who, however, did not acquire it until 1859.[33] On this occasion, 1854, he helped Philip Lewis (Mrs Russell's brother), not as visitor but as employee, and soon found what being a station hand meant. Erne Hillyar's words suggest his feelings: "I've cut the Bush. I'm sick of it. The place is unbearable since your cousin Samuel has given up coming there; he was the only person worth speaking to. I've read all the books. I'm sick of the smell of sheep; I'm sick of the sight of a saddle; I am, oh! so utterly sick of those long, grey plains.... I want adventure, excitement, movement of some kind" (chap. 58).

Samuel Burton says after Erne left, "[He] may have got to some station on the Ovens, or Mitta, or King, hard up and be staying there" (chap. 69). It is not hard to see Kingsley's own memories here. He was to go to the Ovens, the King, and the Mitta Mitta rivers and was unlikely to be other than what he was in June 1854, down on his luck and consequently hard up.

8
Sydney Bound

It was almost inevitable that Kingsley, with his sense of history, should go to Sydney. At Expedition Pass, Mount Alexander, he camped on Hume and Hovell's 1824 route from Hume's station at Lake George, New South Wales, to Corio Bay, Port Phillip, and where, until a few years before, the expedition's wheel ruts had guided settlers to the Port Phillip district. Through Sturt, Venables's uncle, there was a link with Hume, for Sturt accompanied Hume on his next expedition of 28 November 1828. Gundaroo, not too far from Lake George, had associations with the explorer Edward John Eyre, who became protector of Aborigines on the Murray River and, later, governor of Jamaica. With a chance to experience history almost at first hand, Kingsley decided to leave Langi Willi and work his way northwards along the Melbourne-Sydney road, which largely followed Hume and Hovell's route. His two articles "Charles Sturt: A Chapter from the History of Australian Exploration" and "Eyre, the South Australian Explorer" resulted later from this developing interest in Australian history.

Describing the route (in the reverse way to which he himself travelled it), Kingsley wrote that Hume and Hovell "passed through the towns of Yass, Goulburn, Albury (with the wonderful bridge), Wangaratta, Benalla, Seymour, and Kilmore, until they came to the city of Melbourne"[1] and recollected that he had seen a fifty-pound Murray Cod at "the crossing place of this river [Goulburn River] on the Sydney road (Seymour they call it)"[2] In *The Hillyars and The Burtons* he makes, humorously, a shrewd observation on border tariffs — an issue dealt with fifty years later in the Australian Constitution: "In the good time coming, when the Australian Federation set up on their own account, and, sickened with prosperity, feel the necessity of a little fighting, they need not despair of finding a *casus belli* among themselves. The difference of intercolonial tariffs will make as handsome a cause for a very pretty squabble as the devil himself could desire" (chap. 62). But he had a long way to go before he reached the border and the customs town of Albury. What follows is a circumstantial account of his journey.

From Beechworth, which he left by February 1855, Kingsley travelled along a track that connected Faithful's station, the King River, the Yackandandah Creek, and the lower Mitta Mitta.[3] He learned on the way of the massacre near Benalla of early settlers named Faithful, and of Bogong Jack's exploits, tales that provided material for chapters 36 and 39 of *Geoffry Hamlyn*. While proceeding towards the area of the lower Mitta Mitta, to which he was drawn by Hume and Hovell's route and the Omeo disaster, he added two watercolours to his portfolio, one of the headwaters of the King River and one of the "Mistibithwong". The latter is unknown by that name in Victoria, but tallying both with the height of the "Mistibithwong" and the botanical detail of the feature noted by Kingsley on the painting is Mount Murramurrangbong, approximately twelve hundred metres. Although Kingsley allowed himself much latitude in his paintings, other aspects of the feature help to fix the locality.

The foothills of Murramurrangbong he used as a setting for his sketch "The New Church at the Mistibithiwong *[sic]*", and the discovery of a miner's body, "withered long since by rain and sun, with the cheek pressed in the sand", in *The Boy in Grey* (1871). The mountains form the watershed for streams flowing eastward to the Mitta Mitta and westward to the Kiewa River. Both rivers appear in his sketch thinly disguised as the Neila Neila and the Kauna, which flow where the secret places of the forest were disturbed by "the appearance for the first time since creation, of a lean-faced, bold-eyed young Englishman, who splashed wearily through the river on a tired, highbred horse".[4] The description here of himself on horseback resembles somewhat the painting of himself on his "beloved thoroughbred Mazzaroni", made later in his stay in the Portland Bay district. In *The Boy in Grey* Kingsley subtly structures the conclusion of his Mistibithwong scene, "The Creek of the Last Footsteps", on the Pauline promise, "the trumpet shall sound, and the dead shall be raised incorruptible" (1 Cor. 15:52). It is not that, though, which gives his writing interest, but rather his evocation of the profusion of bird life in the Australian bush: "At this moment there burst on his astonished ear such a ravishing flood of melody that his breath came thick and short with pleasure. Beginning with a few short sharp notes of perfect quality, it rolled up into a trumpet-like peal, and then died off in a few bars like the booming of minster-bells on a still evening in a deep wooded valley, in the land which had become a dim memory" (*The Boy in Grey*, chap. 14).

Kingsley was at this time close to Albury. With winter coming, there would have been only one safe way for a newcomer to travel — on the highway. To the north the next settlement of any importance was Yass, a vital link with distant Sydney and for people moving inland along the tracks made by Hume and Sturt.[5] The Southstone Pitt story in *Geoffry Hamlyn* (chap. 36) and Sam Buckley's separation from his father and the successful battle of Sam's dog, Rover, with a bulldog in the same novel (chap. 22) are all associated with Yass and leave little doubt of Kingsley's visit there.

By now Kingsley — and, no doubt, Venables — had discovered what the Reverend David Mackenzie had already found in 1852: "I must caution you against letters of introduction," he wrote. "If you are without money in either pocket, letters of introduction ... will not even procure you a dinner. When you deliver them to the Sydney great man, you will receive a gracious nod, followed by a few canting common-place phrases.... Place no dependence on the promises or patronage of colonial gentlemen. They came here to benefit themselves."[6] In short, Kingsley was alone on a road where, "as you recede from Sydney, the grass for your horse improves, in the same ratio that the accommodation for yourself becomes worse".[7] Passing through Queanbeyan, Kingsley arrived at Lake George, the location used in *Geoffry Hamlyn* for Tom Troubridge, unknowingly, to meet George Hawker in a public house (chap. 31). The route from here to Sydney was difficult, and it also skirted the former haunts of bushrangers in both the Queanbeyan and Bungonia districts.[8] In *Reginald Hetherege*, it is to that former "Arcadia of bushrangers" (chap. 38) — the mountains south of Sydney — that George Hetherege unwittingly rides, "where all the traps in Sydney would never find him" (chap. 37).

Kingsley arrived in Sydney in 1855 to find a city — not just of churches and commerce but of theatre as well, a city of busy bar-rooms and billiard-rooms. When a man-of-war arrived, he recorded that that "most hospitable of cities in the Pacific surpassed herself", with balls and picnics being given by both army and civilians to the visiting blue-jackets (*Reginald Hetherege,* chap. 36). The architecture of Pitt Street he admired, but he disliked the bullies he found parading there with "long streaming ribands" trailing down their backs (*Geoffry Hamlyn,* chap. 27). He was interested enough to uncover sufficient of the early history of Sydney town to site the gaol correctly in *Geoffry Hamlyn* (chap. 44) — near the harbour.[9] And when, in the same book, he emphasized the emptiness of the Domain by its bough-strewn appearance, he was referring implicitly to the activities of the 99th Regiment's band, which played there in the 1840s to the "fashionables and unfashionables".[10] But these details also point to his using material which was familiar to contemporaneous Australian, but not English, readers — a difficulty he encountered in "My Landladies: Chapters of a Digger's Life". Of more significance was his continued interest in the early days of Sydney, not just the tales of convicts and cells, but also the movement, with their stock, of settlers to the Monaro district further south of Sydney.

Before passing to Kingsley's travels in the Monaro, and from there to Gippsland, a report that he served in the Mounted Police needs to be examined, because it appears to be a colourful myth handed down by one Henry Kingsley commentator to another. Owing to its widespread acceptance, the relevant information is important. Kingsley makes specific mention in *The Harveys* of the "Sydney mounted police", and with that reference differentiates the Sydney unit from those of the northern, southern, and western road patrols and, as well, from those police serving with crown land commissioners. Police forces in the colony were not unified but existed as separate entities. His service is supported neither by the relevant records of the Sydney unit nor by evidence affecting the timing of his travels in Australia. In respect of the latter, suffice to say that Kingsley's movements were governed by weather, the passability of routes, and firm reports of his stay in Victoria.

Doubt about his police service really begins with Kingsley's nephew, Maurice, who wrote: "Shoot well 'tis true he could not; which may be explained by his having been blown up with gunpowder when a boy, and the sight of the right eye injured. But stranger still, he was a poor rider, although for a time in the Australian mounted police. This is the more curious when we see from his writings how thoroughly he loved and understood horses."[11] How curious is this "time in the Australian mounted police" may best be judged from what follows.

Apart from Maurice Kingsley, there are three other references to police service. S. M. Ellis seems precise when he writes that Kingsley served with the "Sydney Mounted Police",[12] and Clement Shorter wrote that "for some little time he was in the mounted police" but resigned in disgust because he had to witness an execution.[13] Edwin Arnold accepted that Kingsley was a "capital and fearless policeman" serving with the Sydney government,[14] but Leslie Stephen's entry in the *Dictionary of National Biography,* based upon information given by Mrs Henry Kingsley, mentions no police service. It suffers the handicap, too, that Stephen could have edited the material supplied, "reducing some copy to a third of its original mass".[15] On the other hand, a need to maintain "respectability" could well have caused Mrs Kingsley to suppress information about Henry's colonial period and, for the same reason, to know nothing of it.[16] To Clement Shorter she said, "He never talked of his Australian experiences although they can of necessity be picked up here and there throughout his novels."[17] In 1894, Edwin Arnold, apparently satisfied with Clement Shorter's memoir, wrote to him saying he rejoiced that the fame of his dear old friend had fallen into such excellent hands. "I could have said a hundred honourable things about H. K. = his was a heart of gold."[18] But this really was pleasure that Henry's memory had been served well, not a confirmation of content.

A brief review of the available data shows that Kingsley was in Victoria until December 1854. He travelled during 1855 to Sydney, remained there until the routes south to Omeo were open in late spring or early summer, and was back in Victoria during 1856. No executions took place in New South Wales in 1856, a particular fact that Kingsley himself noted: "That year [1860] there were twelve people executed in England, while in New South Wales, in the year 1856, *there was not one* — a rather startling fact concerning a penal colony."[19] There is no record in the *Government Gazette* of Kingsley's attendance as a witness of any execution, in any capacity, during the years 1855–57. This was a statutory requirement.[20] Certainly the

The Passing Guest

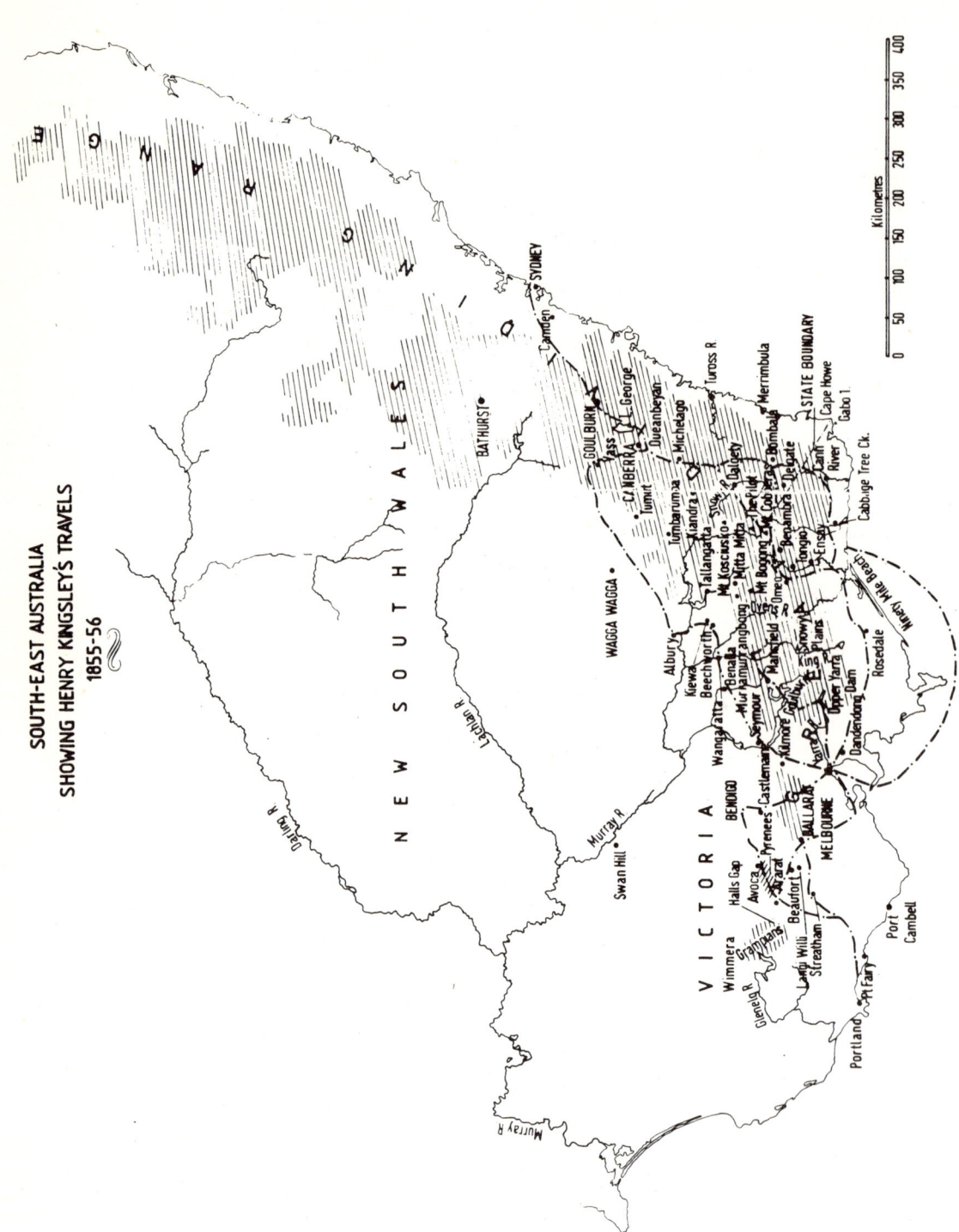

period he was in New South Wales was 1855, with late 1855 being the time of choice for his likely enlistment — *if* it happened. But the matter does not end there.

Mounted police regulations of the time required special application to resign or three months previous notice of intention. Any other course of action resulting in absence from service, sickness excepted, invited a penalty of ten pounds, in default three months imprisonment with hard labour.[21] No mention of special application, previous notice of intention, or penalty exists in the records. Almost, though, as if to dismiss finally the possibility of police service, mounted personnel books — long regarded as irretrievably lost — were discovered during 1973 in an old box of records at a New South Wales Police Force depot. These books, *The Register of Enlistments 1851–62* and the *Financial Pay Records (1854–55–56)* — and, indeed, the *Mounted Patrol and Gold Escort Police Register 1853–66,* also recently found[22] — do not record Henry Kingsley's service in any capacity. In short, the evidence shows that he did not serve.

Kingsley possibly *considered* joining the mounted police, learned of the liability to attend executions, and refrained from doing so. His remarking the fact that no executions occurred in 1856 relates, significantly, to the year he could have been a trooper. He may have realized, with hindsight, that he could have had his mounted service after all, and this, without risk, would have lent some dignity and grace to his colonial period. In recounting the story, family assumptions, the demands of Victorian respectability, and faulty memories did the rest. Certainly the reference in "My Landladies" to the narrator's having been in the police at Richmond, Victoria, only added substance to the belief that his time abroad was not misspent.

That he *was* in New South Wales is confirmed by his review of R. Therry's *Reminiscences* where he rejects Therry's comparison of Killarney and Sydney and with pointed jest wrote: "There are mountains at Killarney, there are none at Sydney. The south side of Sydney harbour is occupied by a city of 80,000 inhabitants; we have heard of no such city at Killarney.... The colony may have changed for the worse since we knew it."[23]

In 1859 Frank Fowler, among other recollections, recalled one in particular:

"Will you buy this Bible?" asked a young man as I stood on the steps of the Herald office [located in 1855 in George Street, in 1856 on the corner of Pitt and O'Connell Streets]. "It is nearly two hundred and fifty years old, and washed ashore in a barrel, on the Cornwall coast, about a century ago. We have had it in our family ever since. My mother gave it to me when I came out, and I would not part with it under any than the most pressing circumstances." "How much do you ask for it?" "You shall have it for a pound." I bought the book; but afterwards found it was too heavy for me to carry home (a hot wind was blowing), so I allowed him to keep it. Five minutes afterwards I passed a public house and saw the owner of the Bible standing at the bar with a decanter of spirits before him, and heard him offer to let the landlord have the book for half a sovereign. That young man I subsequently discovered was brother to a distinguished member of the two great guilds of politics and literature.[24]

The coincidence of some features is evident. Charles Kingsley was a writer and was political in the sense of being an active Christian Socialist; the ancient Bible was washed ashore in a barrel on the Cornish coast — near enough to the areas Kingsley knew and used as settings in *Geoffry Hamlyn* and *Ravenshoe*; and Kingsley refers to "my Bible of 1582" in "The New Church at the Mistibithiwong". Unconfirmed as yet, the tale is, like the reports of police service, curious, though not improbable, and somewhat in character.

9

The Monaro and Gippsland

The Monaro, as known nowadays, is the region enclosed approximately by the New South Wales towns located on its limits — Michelago in the north, Bombala and Delegate in the south-east, and Kiandra in the north-west, an area in general terms of 2,600 square kilometres. The Great Dividing Range abuts the area in the west from Kiandra and runs southwards to the Victorian border. When Kingsley wrote of the "Maneroo", its earlier spelling, the term included what is now north Gippsland in Victoria.[1] Hence, when, in *Geoffry Hamlyn,* Major Buckley in the Maneroo received a letter addressed to "Baroona, Combermere County, Gippsland" (chap. 44), Kingsley was being factual. There was, in his time, a Combermere County located just south of the present New South Wales–Victorian border.[2] To the west lie the Snowy River and the Australian Alps, which form part of the Great Dividing Range.

Kingsley well knew the difficulties of winter travel in the Australian Alps. He wrote in *Geoffry Hamlyn*: "Across the mountain, north of Lake Omeo, not far from the mighty cleft in which the infant Murray spends his youth, were two huts, erected years before by some settler and abandoned ... they had since been inhabited by the men we know ... from Van Diemen's Land, in consequence of Hawker himself having found a pass through the ranges, open for nine months of the year" (chap. 43). But approach routes to Omeo, for a newcomer, were nearly all difficult, whether across the Snowy River and via Benambra, or through Tubbutt and via Bonang, or to Merimbula and the Cann River valley and thence south. Kingsley's arrival in the Omeo area, then — early in the summer of 1855, in good time not to be isolated by winter snows — was determined more by weather than by choice.

He left Sydney, after a "wild dreary day in the spring; a day of furious wind and cutting rain ... when ships creaked and groaned at the wharfs...and the harbour was a sheet of wind-driven foam" (*Geoffry Hamlyn,* chap. 44), and headed southwards. "The Blue Mountains on their right, they rode pleasantly on through forest and over plain, through a beautiful English-like country all the morning, and stayed at a settler's house at midday. It was as good a house as many which he had passed or had entered, but there was a *je ne sais quoi* about the people in it which puzzled him extremely. They were utterly different to the squatters he had met in Sydney; they were not ladies and gentlemen, and were extremely constrained in their manners before him" (*Reginald Hetherege,* chap. 37). Such an encounter with well-to-do "non-gentry" brought home to Kingsley how different the social structure was in Australia, where "every old prejudice was torn up by the roots", and "all old formulas of life scattered to the winds!" (*Geoffry Hamlyn,* chap. 18).

Like his characters Hamlyn, Buckley, and Stockbridge, Kingsley came to the south-east corner of Australia, with the "Snowy pouring eternally from his great curtain of dolomite" (*Ravenshoe,* chap. 21). But he was not only "on the great watershed, which divides the Belloury from the Maryburnong, since better known as the Snowy-river of Gippsland" (*Geoffry Hamlyn,* chap. 18), he was also on a watershed of human experience — seeing life anew in Australia compared with England and its settled class structures. This he treated later, to some extent, in *The Hillyars and the Burtons,* but what he thought of the country then he recorded through the eyes of Geoffry Hamlyn:

> All creation is new and strange. The trees, surpassing in size the largest English oaks, are of a species we have never seen before. The graceful shrubs, the bright coloured flowers, ay, the very grass itself, are of species unknown in Europe; while flaming lories and brilliant parroquets fly whistling, not unmusically, through the gloomy forest, and over head in the higher fields of air, still lit up by the last rays of the sun, countless cockatoos wheel and scream in noisy joy, as we may see the gulls do about an English headland.
>
> To the northward a great glen, sinking suddenly from the saddle on which we stand, stretches away in long vista, until it joins a broader valley, through which we can dimly see a full-fed river winding along in gleaming reaches, through level meadow land, interspersed with clumps of timber. [Ibid.]

The area of which Kingsley writes when he referred to the watershed of the Belloury and Maryburnong Rivers can be identified with some degree of accuracy. The Belloury River, shown on the 1852 Philips *New Map of the Goldfields of Australia,* is the present-day Tuross River, while the name Belloury persists in the form of Belowra Hill, 805 metres, and the town of Belowra, both located in the Tuross River district. As well, John Arrowsmith's *Map of Victoria* shows Kingsley's river as the "Belloury or Tuross River", hence the great watershed of which he wrote in *Geoffry Hamlyn* is the Great Dividing Range to the east of the Monaro. The area, then, where Hamlyn and Stockbridge reined up their horses on the ridge, was the Kybeyan area of the Great Dividing Range, approximately ten miles east of Nimmitabel in the south-eastern portion of the Monaro. This site also meets another requirement for its location — a need to be within a reasonable distance of Hamlyn's station, Durnongs, and the other properties mentioned in the narrative.

The Monaro and Gippsland

To place the stations becomes a question of topography. The Buckleys, on Baroona, lived in Combermere county, Gippsland, while ten miles from them, near a creek, was Mary Hawker's Toonarbin. The Brentwoods, formerly some thirty to fifty miles away, later purchased Garoopna, ten miles distant from Baroona and twenty miles away from the Mayfords. The coast, as stated in the narrative, is thirty miles away; the Murrumbidgee River within riding distance; and, at least, sixty thousand acres of grassed plains land available for Baroona.[3] From these details, the general area of the Cann River valley, then near Combermere County and now near the present interstate border, affords the most likely site for Baroona.[4] No further directions are given for siting the stations, but the locality has sufficient area to include them, to provide the landscape Kingsley describes, and to give an access route to the north.

Kingsley's descriptions were easily recognized by old residents of the Monaro and Gippsland areas. Harry C. Perry, writing in 1928, described Marranumbla, a property acquired by David Parry-Okeden in about 1838, as being situated on Buckley's Crossing on the Snowy River and in "the heart of the wild and beautiful country of which Henry Kingsley was to write many years later in his story of 'Geoffry Hamlyn.' It was a land of mountains and torrents, of rich scrubs and delightful scenery, with the majestic peaks of Kosciusko towering over all. It was a nine days ride on horseback from Sydney to Marranumbla".[5] Mary Howitt Walker in *Come Wind, Come Weather* records how her father, A. W. Howitt, observed on a journey from Gelantipy to the Snowy River: "The scenery is wonderfully wild. . . . six miles down a winding razorbacked spur with a grand view for miles up and down the river, the brown hills changed to indigo blue on the horizon . . . where is the Tinga Ringa Mountain such as is described in Geoffry Hamlyn."[6]

With the passing of winter, a choice of routes was available to Kingsley to go south. Going via Merimbula on the coast would have afforded him an opportunity of seeing the area around Cape Howe and the Cann River:

> A likely and beautiful country when they sighted it one evening with the setting sun blazing behind the forest-crowned peak of Cape Howe, and the ship was becalmed within five miles of land. The men got into the rigging to look at the land, of which so many of them had heard, and where so many of them were to lay their bones, when the weary tossing and tumbling at sea was over for ever. The approach to all the east coast of Australia is dull and solemn, though the first navigators were terrified at it, and said that it was possessed by devils. But it is a kindly-looking coast for all that, and is tenderly loved by those who know the peace, silence, and beauty of the creek and river side beyond the mountain forests, which look a little forbidding to the mariner approaching from the south-east. [*Reginald Hetherege*, chap. 35]

He could then have travelled along the route recommended by Dick, Geoffry Hamlyn's groom, to the police officer, Captain Desborough, in *Geoffry Hamlyn* — a bullock track of ninety miles from Tubbut, via

Bonang, and thence to Omeo.[7] Dick further advised Desborough, when nearing Omeo, to "go round the low side of Tambo, and sight the lake, and you'll be there before him" (chap. 42). The "him" is Hawker, the bushranger, who was fleeing to the almost inaccessible Murray Gates. Desborough, on his way, would have followed the course of the Tambo River, past Bindi and Tongio Mungie stations to Hinnomungie station, all of which are within twenty miles of Omeo.

Kingsley could have proceeded instead — as did the Parry-Okedens — on horseback to Dalgety and made some exploratory tours from there. This does not deny the possibility of his having worked on stations *en route*. Again, coincidence is interesting, for one of the *Geoffry Hamlyn* characters, Major Buckley, bears the name of a crossing over the Snowy River, Buckley's Crossing, which later became the town of Dalgety. Equally interesting too is Kingsley's reference to Buckley's "parliamentary and didactic way of speaking" (chap. 44). Patrick Cody Buckley, who occupied Tongio and Bindi stations for some time, is described as "an uneducated man, but a shrewd judge of stock, and with a natural gift for business. He had a remarkable appearance, and looked more like the Prime Minister of England than an outback squatter." He owned historical Ensay from 1839 to 1849, Woologoramerang from 1851 to 1859, as well as other runs in Gippsland.[8]

From the evidence available, Kingsley's presence on the Monaro can only be inferred. That he was there, though, seems abundantly clear. How he entered Gippsland cannot be determined precisely. That he was there can easily be seen from an endorsement on one of his paintings: "The look into Gipps land from the South. The highest Alp to the right is I believe Kosciusko." Kingsley's "look into Gippsland from the South" depicts what he thought was Kosciusko in the distance with, in the foreground, cabbage-tree palms (*Livistonia australis*). This detail is valuable, since the palms grow in Victoria only in the general vicinity of Cabbage Tree Creek, and when identified by the botanist Baron Von Mueller, in 1854, covered an area only slightly more extensive than at present,[9] — not too far distant from Ninety Mile Beach, which Kingsley refers to in *The Hillyars and the Burtons* (chap. 7). What betrays his presence in the area as well is his mention of the flora — hakeas, acacias, grevilleas, Epacris, and correas — sighted during the *Geoffry Hamlyn* characters' ride to Cape Chatham. All these species grow in the Cape Conran area, near Cabbage Tree Creek.[10] In fact, Cape Conran is really the Cape Chatham of *Geoffry Hamlyn*, although its physical description matches almost precisely London Bridge on the Southern Ocean coast west of Melbourne.

When writing on the back of his watercolour, Kingsley erred because Mount Kosciusko is too far inland to be visible from the coast where the painting was done. The peaks in the foreground, though, correspond almost exactly with Mount Jack and to the west Ruark, and Bald Mountain with beyond it Pike's Hill. Further west again lies the Errinundra Plateau, and beyond that again the high peaks of the Great

Dividing Range with its lofty peaks of Tingaringy, Bulla Bulla, and Black Mountain.

What makes the painting especially interesting, though, is its suggestion that he approached Cabbage Tree Creek from the Cann River area. To have travelled that route points to his having gone from there to Buchan and Woologoramerang, one result of which was his being able, in *Geoffry Hamlyn*, to describe the Murray Gates towards which George Hawker fled:

> [Morning] Long shadows of horse and man are thrown before him now, as the slope dips away to the westward, and he knows that his journey is well-nigh over. It was late in the afternoon before, having left the snow some hours, he began to lead his horse down a wooded precipice, through vegetation which grew more luxuriant every yard he descended. The glen, whose bottom he was trying to reach, was a black profound gulf, with perpendicular, or rather, overhanging walls, on every side, save where he was scrambling down. Here indeed it was possible for a horse to keep his footing among the belts of trees that, alternating with precipitous granite cliff, formed the upper end of one of the most tremendous glens in the world — the Gates of the Murray. [Chap. 43]

Kingsley's description shows that he ventured into what is known as the High Country and then along the Indi River. W. B. Clarke, an early government geologist, preceded him there by some years and noted: "the Indi River [Murray River] ... running with a broad, deep, and rapid current, having all the characteristics of an important mountain stream.... from Mt. Kosciusko the deep and precipitous defile through which its waters flow, is seen far below, and is very distinctly marked for several miles." He mentions, additionally, the slate and granite character of the Indi headwaters, and the defile's steep ascents and descents.[11]

If Kingsley, on the other hand, approached Omeo from the Dalgety area, going to Cabbage Tree Creek later, his route is equally interesting. S. J. Treasure, a mountain-experienced resident of Dargo, Victoria, after examining Kingsley's writings, concluded that "he probably crossed the Snowy River in the vicinity of Jacob and Pinch Rivers and took the old — now almost lost — track to Omeo via the Ingeegoodby River, Mt. Violet and Mt. Cobberas (6000 ft.) and on to Benambra via the Limestone Creek (headwaters of the Indi). He mentions Mt. Tambo which is real and lies S.E. of Benambra. The earliest settlers came this way in 1834."[12] All of which suggests Kingsley, in character, could well have been doing in Australia what he had earlier done in Chelsea, looking at what had preceded him in time, the "former things". Apart from this, his writing has the certain knowledge of observation, for from Mount Feathertop, near Omeo, the "great snow-hills" indeed fold, as he says, "in vast ridges":

> As they crossed the great wooded ridge which divided them from the watershed of the Mitta Mitta, they turned and had a last look at the place where they had suffered so much, and which they were never to see again. The lake lay sleeping in the inexorable heat, sometimes

dreaming into a fantastic mirage like a nightmare, in which the trees and mountains were horribly inverted. All round, the great snow-hills folded in vast ridges.... That was the last of Lake Omeo. That scene photographed itself upon their brains indelibly.... the ridges were steep to climb,... and when they got into the magnesian limestone country, which lies on the left bank of the Mitta Mitta, the water, drawn away underground into infinite crannies and clefts of the rock, began to fail them; and they were forced, will they nill they, to struggle down over the cliffs to the river itself, and fight with the tangled jungle on its brink for very life's sake, sooner than keep the high open leading ranges where walking was so much easier. [*The Hillyars and the Burtons*, chap. 41]

Kingsley's return route to Melbourne cannot be ascertained, and brief passages from his writings must suffice for a guide to areas with which he was familiar. To travel overland to Melbourne from Omeo was no more arduous than any travelling hitherto encountered — especially as he wrote knowledgeably of being able to ride on a "colonial-made saddle" (ibid., chap. 50). Before he left Gippsland, however, Port Albert, the cattle shipment port, was to be seen; this was later to become the "Port Romilly" of *The Hillyars and the Burtons*.[13] In Port Albert, the new steamer service to Melbourne started on 1 February 1856,[14] an event of which Kingsley took note:

The steamers between Melbourne and Palmerston would call regularly at Port Romilly now.... She had sat on the deck all day and all night, watching the coast. There had been long stretches of low sand-beach in some places, and then a majestic cape. Sometimes the land piled itself up into awful tiers of dark forest, one rising behind the other; and sometimes these would break away, and show low rolling plains stretching into the interior, with faint blue mountains beyond. There were islands, too, which one sailed through, on which the foot of man had never rested since the world began; some low, some high and fantastically shaped; but all covered with clouds of clanging sea-birds, and ringed with the leaping silver surf, which never slept. [*The Hillyars and the Burtons,* chap. 54]

He certainly saw, or travelled with, stock for shipment at Port Albert, and the river he mentions is one of the major streams on the coast, the Snowy River being one of them:

But when a hundred miles were gone, the land began to rise and roll into sharp ascents and descents; and one forenoon we came to a steep and dangerous hill. And, while we were going cautiously down through the thick hanging trees, we heard the voice of a great river rushing through the wood below us. As we struggled through it, with the cattle belly-deep in the trubid green water, we had a glimpse right and left of a glorious glen....

"Why," I asked one of the bullock-drivers, who volunteered that evening to show me a place to bathe, "why is the water so ghastly cold? I can scarcely swim."

"Snow, mate, snow. This water was brought down from Mount Hampden by yesterday's sun." [*The Hillyars and the Burtons,* chap. 50]

In summary, then, Kingsley entered Gippsland by one of three routes — along the Cann River valley, along the old bullock track from Tubbutt to Omeo, or by way of the Jacob and Ingeegoodby Rivers to the headwaters of the Indi River. His paintings and his writings, with their reference to flora, confirm his presence in the Cabbage Tree Creek area. Internal evidence in his work indicates he was in the high country above Omeo, and that he wrote from first-hand knowledge of the gorges of the Indi River, of riding along Ninety Mile Beach, and of being in Port Albert.

His choice of routes to Melbourne from Gippsland included going by ship from Port Albert, going by land along established bullock tracks, or going over the mountains from Omeo to Beechworth. In keeping with his spirit of adventure, overland seems the most likely choice, but, whatever the route, Kingsley was back in Melbourne sometime in February 1856. By then he had trekked at least a thousand miles, some of it through country so rugged and remote that, apart from local residents, it is visited even now only by the more adventurous. By any standard, his traversing of plains, rivers, bush, and mountains was a remarkable achievement. Certainly it gave him a continuing interest in Australian exploration as well as the "adventure, excitement, and movement" which his character, Erne Hillyar, also sought.

10

Prelude to Home

Back in Melbourne Kingsley watched with interest "the Queen's ship *Electra*" leave Port Phillip in February 1856, "her yards blackened by two hundred men" ("Travelling in Victoria"). In December 1854 a detachment from the *Electra* had served with the 40th Regiment at Eureka to quell the rebellion by miners against exorbitantly priced miners' licences, an insurrection into which E. P. S. Sturt, another uncle of H. P. Venables, was to conduct an inquiry.[1] Kingsley had now been two years in Australia but showed no signs of returning home.

Leaving Melbourne, Kingsley went back to the bush, this time upstream along the Yarra River valley and across the Plenty Ranges to the Goulburn River valley. In these two areas he spent much of the year; he records how he travelled along the Yarra for "two hundred miles through splendid forests".[2] At Yering he stayed overnight at De Castella's station,[3] before attempting the pass through Insolvent Gap, the route across the watershed of the two rivers. In the early days, squatters used it to escape from creditors who waited on the main Sydney road hoping to catch them on their way home from Melbourne.[4]

In the Goulburn valley at Mangalore station beyond Kitgatanor Creek — the Katgetarnuck of "Wild Sports of the Far South — lived Lieutenant-Colonel Joseph Anderson, who, like the narrator's friend in that sketch, had "electioneered". He was in fact a member of the Victorian Legislative Council. Other coincidences affecting him are too convenient to suggest Kingsley's presence was accidental. Not only was Anderson a friend of David Parry-Okeden, but he was also a former governor of Norfolk Island (1834–39).[5] It is probable he was the principal of Kingsley's recollection in *Tales of Old Travel*: "The Governor of Norfolk Island told me once in private conversation, that he gave 300 convicts 100 lashes a-piece one night. The island was all but gone, but he did not like to shed blood. A gentler or more humane being than this man does not walk this earth. He was a man who got a nickname for his extreme good-nature. He had to do *something*, and he did that — and won."[6] Kingsley was not just intrigued by duty and its consequences but was commenting, as will be seen later, on Governor Eyre and the Jamaica Question.

Kingsley's traditional campsite at Warrandyte, Victoria. Photograph by author.

Kingsley's activities in the Western District of Victoria are better known than those in the Yarra, Goulburn, or Beechworth areas. Certainly he fished, for he records catching the "little correginus?" of the Yarra which was, he noted in "Charles Sturt", "the only one of the Salmonidae which, as far as I am aware, exists to any extent in Australia, seems only to rise to the fly while the waters are clear and green, but go to the bottom in the summer". His observations on the clarity and turbidity of the Yarra, Goulburn, and Ovens rivers are important indicators of the time of year he was in the vicinity of each.[7] He also records that he caught cod, and a strong possibility exists from his reference to Dr Kerr in *The Hillyars and the Burtons* (chap. 11) that he stayed with W. L. Ker of Eglinton station, who studied medicine at Edinburgh University before coming to Australia in 1840. Although a station owner, Ker "acted as a doctor when there was not one available".[8]

In July 1856 Kingsley's old Oxford associate Martin Irving arrived in Australia to take up an appointment as Professor of Classics and English at the University of Melbourne,[9] and in February 1857 Irving directed Henry Campbell, a new arrival, to their mutual friend Kingsley on the Caledonia diggings, not far from Anderson's Creek. L. R. Cranfield, a local historian, records that Kingsley's camp was pitched near the entrance to the present Warrandyte cemetery,[10] and as Campbell remembered it:

[I] walked out to the Camp, and joined his party, and he took me as his mate; I slept in his tent, helped with the rough cooking, and we "toiled and moiled" and met with nothing but disappointment, for it was a very poor "diggings". . . . There was one thing that varied the monotony of digging for gold in hope and finding always Hope Deferred, and that was our Sunday's work, which was what is called Prospecting — poking about the gullies in the Dandenong Ranges. This always tempted Harry Kingsley, for he was always keeping his eyes open for "Colour" in describing Bushrangers' haunts for the book he was even then writing viz., *Geoffry Hamlyn*. When that book came out I recognised some of the places he described. If I remember rightly, Henry Kingsley went on to Daisy Hill.[11]

Kingsley's search for "colour" must have taken him to nearby Ferntree Gully, where the setting is identical in many ways with one of the "bushranger haunts" in *Geoffry Hamlyn*, the scene of the police and bushranger clash. This was undoubtedly the scene Campbell had in mind.

At this time T. A. Browne (Rolf Boldrewood, author of *Robbery under Arms*), having sold some cattle, and on a visit to De Castella's, met Kingsley washing for gold at Anderson's Creek: "He was working away there at a 'Long Tom' with his trousers as yellow as a guinea, and a blue serge 'jumper' on. He's a college-read man, and a brother of the great clergyman at Eversley so he knows both sides. What such a man writes is worth any one's while to read."[12] Before leaving, Browne invited Kingsley to call on him at his station, Squattlesea Mere, an invitation taken up not so very long afterwards.

When Kingsley arrived at Browne's station he was with other "sundowners" and it was night so, having been given the customary rations, he went to the men's hut to sleep.[13] Next day he made himself known. He had been to Daisy Hill and Ararat, after which he had made his way to Browne's. At Ararat, the new eldorado, Kingsley had found enough gold to pay his passage home and provide for his immediate needs. For the first time in many months he had some resources of his own, and was able to visit Squattlesea Mere as an invited guest.[14] Hence at Browne's as well as the adjacent station of Dunmore, owned by Charles Hamilton Macknight and James Irvine, Kingsley had the opportunity to learn what Australian squatter society was like.[15] Not only was there much visiting between properties, but nearby Port Fairy was the centre for an active social life of race meetings, balls, and picnics.[16] Kingsley subsequently went to Port Fairy, where he stopped at Macknight's seaside home, Dunmore Cottage, and while there interviewed Captain John Mason one evening when strolling on the jetty. Mason wrote later that Kingsley was gathering material for a book, as a result of which Mason told him about an old Spanish or Portugese ship which lay buried in the sand near by.[17] Kingsley's reference to the vessel in *Geoffry Hamlyn* (chap. 24) thus becomes one of the earliest to what is now known locally as the Spanish Galleon.

Browne was adamant that class distinctions existed in Australia at that time, the simplest indication of which was the men's hut at each station, where itinerants lodged when receiving "bush hospitality". His own "rank and quality" he made known on his first call to Dunmore by seeking books from Mrs Laidlaw, the Scottish housekeeper referred to in Kingsley's "Eyre's March". He was invited to wait in the library.[18] This, in some measure, explains part of the difficulty involved in finding evidence of Kingsley's presence on stations where he was other than an invited guest. It explains Browne's comment, too, that Kingsley knew "both sides", but there is no record of Browne's reaction to Kingsley's view that squatters were "perhaps a *trifle* fond of hearing of great people" (*Ravenshoe*, chap. 55).

Dunmore enjoyed a reputation for hospitality long before Kingsley's arrival,[19] and its station diary records not only its activities but also his visit there with Browne on 16 May 1857. The Dunmore diary, as well as Browne's records, show that "solid reading [and] intellectual discussions" were commonplace activities at Dunmore and Squattlesea Mere. This may be seen to some extent in Browne's *Babes in the Bush*, which he described as "partly realistic [and] partly imaginary", and listed the characters' identities in his personal papers. Hamilton (Macknight) tells Mrs Effingham (Browne) that Kinghart (Kingsley) believed his obligations "to the (temporarily) lower orders" compelled him not to eat at table unless the servants were present:

> "What nonsense!" said the gentleman referred to, rather hastily; "but I daresay you recognise our friend's vein of humour, Mrs. Effingham."
> "It's all very well, Kinghart," replied Hamilton gravely, "but I feel pained to find a man of your intellect deserting his convictions when they clash with conventionalities. You know the Rector's opinions as to our dependents, and here you stand, ashamed to act up to the family principles."
> "My dear fellow, of course I support Charles's gallant testimony to the creed of his Master, but he had no 'colonial experience,' whereas I have had a great deal, which may have led me to believe that I am the deeper student of human nature. I don't know whether I need assure Mrs. Effingham that she will find me outwardly much like other people."
> "How few beliefs shall I retain henceforth," said Hamilton sorrowfully.
> "Putting socialism out of the question," said Mr. Kinghart, "I shall always regret that Charles did not avail himself of an oppotunity he once had to visit Australia. He would have been charmed beyond description."[20]

After so long as a sundowner and a wanderer, Kingsley could easily believe birth, not reputation, gained such hospitality. He was the brother of the writer and clergyman, "the great, the noble, the world-renowned Charles Kinghart". He could be forgiven for believing such privilege to be evidence that "gentle folk" looked after their own — even in the colonies. Douglas Sladen, twenty years later, was accorded the same treatment in Victoria as a guest of Philip Russell at Carngham, when he spent a year wandering from station to station, and crossed Kingsley's tracks in doing so.[21]

Browne went to some lengths in *Babes in the Bush* to describe Kingsley as he, the squatter, saw him. Kingsley was an "out-and-out-brick", though reserved at first, unreasonably fond of books, and played a good game of whist. He was so "deuced clever" that if there had been any material for fiction "in this confounded country", which there was not, Kingsley could write a book. At Macknight's station he is depicted as quiet and peruses one or two rare volumes until Mrs Laidlaw brings the bedroom candles. His dry humour is unmistakable, as is his knowledge of "classical lore". In short, he is a "first rate fellow". The final judgement, though, is given by Beatrice Effingham (Browne's daughter): "He is a library that can talk, and yet, like a library prefers silence.... He is sarcastic about women, too.... Perhaps he has been illtreated by some thoughtless girl." Browne obviously was unaware of Kingsley's thoughts about younger sons who had little prospect of marriage.

At Dunmore, where Macknight kept bloodstock, Kingsley encountered the three horses Premier, Jezebel, and Romeo — "a chestnut with a blaze and four white feet" which he named in his writings.[22] From these horses he gained his inspiration for the "noble" Widderin of *Geoffry Hamlyn,* naming it after a local feature relatively near the real Baroona station in Western Victoria.

Apart from Langi Willi, where Kingsley went with a letter of introduction from Browne to its owner, Willi Mitchell, the only other station he is known to have visited is Nerrin Nerrin, owned by John Macpherson, father-in-law of Cuthbert Fetherstonhaugh's sister. Nerrin Nerrin is close to Langi Willi, and there too he is reported to have written part of *Geoffry Hamlyn.*[23] As it was in those days, so it is now, for the lakes of Nerrin Nerrin still swarm, as Kingsley noted in "Eyre's March", with a variety of birds "all through the burning summer's day".

Browne, when giving his letter of introduction, prevailed on Kingsley to give up his nomadic life and become like his brother, Charles, a writer.[24] For once Henry listened — because he was already trying to do so before he went home. In Australia he had few worries. He was well received, accommodation was no problem, and he had gold from Ararat to depart when he chose. Apart from which, as later correspondence reveals, he was not really well. Better to rest and recuperate here and write while he did. For him there could be only one decision to take, and Kingsley took it. He went to Langi Willi to see Willi Mitchell — this time as a guest, not as a station hand.

C. Stuart Ross in 1911 wrote his recollections of Mitchell and Kingsley as they were in 1857:

> Wm. Mitchell, who bought Langi Willi from Wright and Montgomery in 1852, was a man of liberal education and refinement, whose large and well selected library attested his broad culture and wide range of scholarship. Mr. Alex Anderson told me that on one occasion when Mr. Mitchell was exchanging solid courtesies with him at Baangal he was sometimes accompanied by a friend, who was his guest for a

considerable period, and he used to say to Mr. Anderson — "I am sure my friend is writing a book, for he usually disappears immediately after breakfast and does not show face again till dinner-time." Mr. Mitchell's friend was Henry Kingsley, and it was quite true that he was writing a book, for there at Langi Willi may still be seen the room in which Henry Kingsley wrote "Geoffry Hamlyn" which easily holds front rank in Australian literature.[25]

The room where the writing was done still stands at Langi Willi, in a small blue basalt building situated close to the original homestead but not part of it. T. A. Browne summed up Kingsley's position as a guest at the station where three years before he had been an employee: "There couldn't be a nicer fellow [than Mitchell], however, and Australia will ever owe him a debt for extending the hand of generous and delicate hospitality to the artist who first worthily illustrated her free forest life, her adventurous sons and daughters fair."[26]

If Mitchell was being "delicately" hospitable he succeeded, for as well as writing, Kingsley painted, rode, and fossicked on Mount Buninyong, where he found sapphires which, not knowing their value, he threw away. Mount Cole, Fiery Creek, Mount Llangeryn, Emu Creek, and the ranges of Ben Nevis all appear in watercolours he executed while he lived and worked at Langi Willi. Mitchell was a friend and frequent visitor of the Richardsons of Gorrinn station near by,[27] and it is here, rather than Langi Willi, that the landscape fits the painting that Kingsley inscribed "The dear old station. I will give no description lest I grow sentimental". As a watercolour of a station property it captures some of Kingsley's happier memories during his last days in the Western District:

> How quaint that old Australian life seems to one! High refinement in many cases, but the devil always at the door. Not, as in India, a sudden, furious, unexpected devil, tearing all to pieces; but a recognised devil, standing always ready. "This is the last of that seal of Lafitte, sir, and the blacks are crowding round and looking awkward." *"The Illustrated London News* is come, sir, but no *Spectator* this mail; and Mike Howe is out again, sir, and has stuck up Dolloy's, and burnt one of the children, sir. Do you think he will take us next, or the Macdonalds?" These are the sort of little marestails you get at the outside edge of that vast cloud of English influence which has now over-shadowed fully one-sixth of the human race. [*The Hillyars and the Burtons,* chap. 62]

On the original manuscript of *The Hillyars and the Burtons* is a deletion which contains his only known reference to Langi Willi. After he had referred to an "abrupt, picturesque little mountain with castellated crags", he went on to write, "Anyone who wishes to see an exactly similar one, may ascend the hill called Mount Emu which is but five miles from the station called Langi-Willi, near the township of Skipton in the district of Portland bay." From the Portland Bay district came his painting of Emu Creek which shows him riding his "beloved thoroughbred Mazzaroni", while from Mount Cole came his painting of "a winter Sunday evening", evidence of his presence there in his last year.

From Langi Willi Kingsley went to Melbourne, late in 1857, to inquire about a passage to England. Some of the details of that visit appear in his article "Travelling in Victoria", in which can be seen how he includes, obliquely, detail that affected him: "I have seen people in 1857 [in Melbourne] with bowie-knives in their belts, and much astonished, instead of meeting bushrangers, at being put into a comfortably padded railway carriage, and whisked up, if it so pleased them, to a first rate hotel."

In the same article, Kingsley showed more than a passing interest in the "great colonial match", between the Victorian horse, Alice Hawthorn, which was to race Veno, from New South Wales. "The long legged chestnut from Sydney" defeated the "plucky little grey" on 3 October 1857, in Melbourne, and Kingsley, having attended the race, went home via Geelong and Buninyong, completing part of the trip on a little railway steamer, the *Comet*. From its deck, he stated in the article, he saw the Blackwall clipper *Swiftsure*, 1,500 tons, which covered the outward voyage to Port Phillip in sixty-seven days from London.[28] In this he was correct, but he omitted to mention that when it left Melbourne for London, on 24 February 1858, he was one of the sixty-one passengers occupying second class cabins on board.[29] He also referred to the *Swiftsure* in *Geoffry Hamlyn* (chap. 48).

"Travelling in Victoria" contains much detail of Australian life as Kingsley encountered it then. Almost jocularly he writes: "That schooner yonder is from ... the Clerance [Clarence River] far away there in the north, while her next-door neighbour is busy disgorging nuts and apples from Launston [*sic*] in Van Diemen's Land (I humbly ask pardon – Tasmania)." His irony is evident. Tasmania, cutting its links with a convict past, changed its name from Van Diemen's Land only in 1854.

One further instance of Kingsley's tendency to make oblique reference to incidents connected with him is worth noting. He mentions in the same article "Mount William, the highest mountain in Portland Bay". But Mount William, as well as being the highest feature, was also the name of a station lying near its foothills, west of but not far distant from Langi Willi. Its owners, the Chirnsides, were not only friends of C. H. Macknight but also owned the horse Alice Hawthorn.[30] It was little wonder that Kingsley was interested, almost personally, in its performance.

Christmas 1857, in Australia, was memorable. Bushfires blazed on the hills near Skipton and on the ranges between Ararat and Pleasant Creek.[31] Christmas at Ararat began with an attendance of four thousand people at the racecourse near Green Hill, all ignoring the realities of an Australian summer.[32] Unemployment was widespread in the colony. The Argus published a letter, signed "Non Mi Recordo", on 8 October 1857 which said in part: "People do not believe in gentlemen-labourers, who, however willing and anxious to perform the work required, are new and inexperienced; they are apt to think that a classical education is hardly calculated to make good navvies or agri-

Prelude to Home

The Union Hotel, mentioned by Henry Kingsley in his writings, is the small building on the right.

cultural laborers." Kingsley, vaguely unwell and somewhat uneasy as a result, could see by now, as did Douglas Sladen after him, that while being a gentleman was sufficient to obtain free, even "delicate" hospitality, one ultimately still had to do something. Sladen decided to study law, Kingsley decided to go "home". His writing reveals the strength of immigrant ties to Britain present, despite translocation, in the nineteenth-century Australian, who was in the main Scotsman, Irishman, Welshman, or Englishman, with little inclination, culture, or capital to want to deny his origins. And even if he had wanted to do so, his accent hardly disappeared with disembarkation.

> If our reader has never been in Australia, he will hardly understand what are the sensations of a man, long banished, when he first realises to himself the fact, "I am going home." Home! No one ever says, "I am going to Europe, sir," or "I am going to England, sir." Men say, "I am thinking of taking a run home, Jim" (or Tom as the case may be). Then you know Jim (or Tom) considers you as a sacrosanct person, and tires not in doing errands for you — will wade the mud of little La Trobe Street for you, and tells you all the time that, when so-and-so happens (when the kye come home, in fact), he means to run home too, and see the old folk. ["Travelling in Victoria"]

From the little known Australian writer Nathaniel Walter Swan (1835–84) came a final glimpse of Henry Kingsley's last days in Australia. Swan "wended his way [from Sandhurst] once more to Melbourne, picking up, on the way, with another blue-shirted and white-moled man apparently equally unfortunate, and also on his way to the sea-board, and thence to England. This was Henry Kingsley (whom we all know so well from his delightful *Recollections of Geoffry Hamlyn,* which he wrote at Langi Willi near Skipton)."[33] From these few days together came Swan's own decision to be a writer.

Kingsley's hotel in Melbourne was the Union in Bourke Street. He mentions it in "Wild Sports of the Far South", where the narrator takes his brother for "iced claret punch, a cool and harmless beverage"; in "Travelling in Victoria", where he says the cuisine there was to be preferred to that of the Wellington in Piccadilly; and finally in a review in the *Reader* of 21 February 1863, where he reveals that his companions of the bar and billiard-room were, like himself, university educated: "Were there no gallant young surgeons, fresh from the hall and the college, in the billiard-room at the Union? Melbourne must be strangely changed if there were not." To the Union, then, Kingsley found his way for the last time. The Australian adventure was all but ended. He was on his way home.

11

Homeward Bound

The clipper *Swiftsure* advertised in the *Argus* on 11 January 1858 and succeeding days that it was sailing for London "positively on 24 February" with or without the wool and gold needed for freight. Dietary scales for the voyage had been lodged with the agents, W. P. White and Co., 10 Elizabeth Street South, Melbourne, where intending passengers were assured of a fast voyage "home" under the command of Captain W. B. Pryce. At Hughes Wharf, Melbourne, the steamer *Sophia* was retained to carry passengers free of charge to the clipper, on whose passenger list Kingsley described himself as a "mechanic" — a term then in general use — and on 24 February passengers boarded the clipper. Next day, the *Swiftsure* sailed for London.[1] "The skipper [said] laughing [that] we have been three weeks in the bay in ballast, trying to get cargo, and have got a little wool and gold. . . . We went into the saloon, and the stewardess, a hard-headed, hard-handed Scotch woman, showed us the vacant berths. There were now, she told us, near 100 passengers, but most of them in the second cabin, between decks. The voyage would pay, she said, entirely through the passengers" ("Our Brown Passenger").[2]

The first entry made in the ship's log on 27 February was the ship's position, and later that afternoon the first death of the voyage was noted: "Departed this life Clara Isabel Hughes 7 years of low fever brought on by seasickness."[3] Another was to occur before the ship reached England. The homeward route lay well to the west and south of Tasmania, thence eastwards around Cape Horn to the Atlantic,[4] a long journey not without perils. By 27 February the *Swiftsure* passed King Island in Bass Strait and caught the Roaring Forties to the south of Tasmania and New Zealand, where the winds were high and the seas mountainous. Kingsley was indeed "under the strange Southern Cross, and Magellan's clouds".[5] Of this he later wrote:

> I remember once being in one of those horrible weltering sixty-foot seas, which one, I believe, only gets in the Southern Ocean, when I saw a tiny cockle-shell of a brig, about 200 tons, faring on her way, at one time as high up over our heads (or so it seemed) as our main-

> yard, in about another minute after sinking slowly, slowly down in the hideous grey valley beneath our feet: yet she was floating comfortably like a cork — making, as the mate said, much better weather of it than we were.... We must have been a splendid spectacle to them, hurling our magnificent length at every conceivable angle, and in at least one-half of all possible positions before and through the following sea; yet I doubt they did not envy us.
> [*Tales of Old Travel*, pp. 123–24]

The last links with Australia were now gone. The pilots in their whaleboats, which met new arrivals at the entrance to Port Phillip Bay, and the pounding surf off King Island were becoming memories. The "quaint little inn [which lay] close to where the shipping lies [and where] thirteen million was annually passing outwards and eleven million inwards"[6] lay far astern and, for Kingsley, gone forever. Ten days after sailing, the *Swiftsure* was far to the east and south of New Zealand.[7] The long haul to the Horn had begun.

Kingsley, in his recollections of the voyage in the high latitudes, described the conditions the crew and passengers encountered:

> I have been in disasters in ships which have got into the trough of the sea while trying to make passages, by scudding before great gales of wind. On the last occasion we ran 1,000 miles in 92 hours, under a close-reefed main topsail and a rag of a foresail. During the full rage and fury of the storm, while the pressure of the wind on the sails was sufficient to keep her before the ever-accumulating and ever-following seas, all went merry as a marriage bell; but when the weather slightly moderated, when the seas began to grow in strength, when it got impossible to get the vast length of the ship round and lay her to — then, I think, that the captain, although noted for his suavity of manner, began to get short, sharp, and peremptory with those passengers who seemed inclined to amuse themselves by staggering about the deck, falling into the lee-scuppers, and getting handed over to the doctor with severe scalp bruises, and a very puzzled expression of countenance. At this time I thought I noticed that the captain looked old; and, moreover, he had to stand behind the two men at the wheel, with his arms in cleats; he had two hundred souls to answer for, this captain, with the pay of a ten-year Home Office clerk, and his wife and children on board, beside.
> [*Tales of Old Travel*, pp. 129–30]

Imperilled by ice and enclosed by night, he also described the prayer for travellers as

> one of the most sublime pieces of uninspired prayer put up by man to his God! — "That it may please Thee to preserve all that travel by land or by water; all women labouring of child; all sick persons and young children; and to show Thy pity upon all prisoners and captives."
>
> Those who do not appreciate fully that passage in the Litany, had better hear it read out by the captain in latitude sixty south, when the sea is thundering and booming, and the ship is reeling and rolling, and the wind is screaming, and the cruel icebergs are gleaming, half-seen, in the snow-fog, and the horrid long night is settling down over the raging ocean. They will find out what "travelling by land or water" means then, I'll warrant them. [*Austin Elliot*, chap. 22]

Nearing Cape Horn, Kingsley encountered at first hand the immensity of the sea, as the *Swiftsure* lunged and pitched its way towards another night of dread. The experience is recounted in *Geoffry Hamlyn*:

> It is March, 1856. The short autumn day is rapidly giving place to night; and darkness, and the horror of a great tempest, is settling down upon the desolate grey sea, which heaves and seethes for ever around Cape Horn.
>
> A great clipper ship, the noblest and swiftest of her class, is hurling along her vast length before the terrible west wind. Hour by hour through the short and gloomy day, sail after sail has gone fluttering in; till now, at night-fall, she reels and rolls before the storm under a single, close reefed, maintopsail.
>
> There is a humming, and a roaring, and a rushing of great waters, so that they who are clinging to the bulwarks, and watching, awe-struck, this great work of the Lord's, cannot hear one another though they shout. Now there is a grey mountain which chases the ship, overtakes her, pours cataracts of water over her rounded stern, and goes hissing and booming past her. And now a roll more frantic than usual, nigh dips her mainyard, and sends the water spouting wildly over her bulwarks. [Chap. 48]

Later, with the vessel well to the south of the cape at latitude 61°30′, there was the fear of ice: "The Horn, storm beaten, desolate, four hundred miles to the North, and barely forty miles to the South, that cruel, gleaming, ice barrier, which we saw to-day when the weather lifted at noon, and which we know is there yet, though we dare not think about it.... The Lord send us safe through the ice" (ibid.). Then, almost incongruous in its haste, came "an enormous American steamship, with roaring steam-pipes, tearing her way furiously and defiantly through a Cape Horn gale and a Cape Horn sea" (*Tales of Old Travel*, p. 124). It was, for Kingsley, an awesome and majestic sight. For Pryce, the master, however, the passage was normal, and he made no reference in the log to the ship's runs, the storms, or the ice. His sole entries for the period were: "4/3. 3 p.m. Jacob Nielsen disrated to ordinary seaman — not able to perform the most simple work of a seaman. 10/3. 1 p.m. Jacob Nielsen's reply not shipped as an able seaman."

Reminiscences of Kingsley's voyages were not always characterized by dangers visible or invisible. He shows himself equally adept at describing the sights and sounds of a clipper ship moving at speed:

> One day of one long voyage comes before me particularly clear.... I can't tell you in what month this day (or these days, it may be) fell; but it was in the trades.... the ship was going fast, and heeling over enough to make everything you leant against more pleasant than a rocking-chair — going with a gentle heaving motion, for which it would be absurd to hunt up a simile, because there is nothing so wonderfully delightful where-with to compare it. There were clouds, slow sailing clouds, but they were of frosted silver; and there was open sky, but of the very faintest blue, save immediately overhead, where the delicate needle of a top gallant mast swept across it in a shortened arc, and where it was a faint purple. There were sounds — one a gentle universal rush, that of the wind itself, filling space; and

others, supplementary voices; the low gentle lapping of the waves upon the ship's side, and the sleepy gurling and hissing of many eddies around her. All things seemed going one way with some settled kindly purpose. The clouds seemed to be leading the wind, and the wind to be steadily following the clouds, while the purple waves, a joyous busy crowd, seemed to be hurrying on after both of them, to some unknown trysting place. [*The Hillyars and the Burtons,* chap. 44]

On such days Kingsley reviewed his Australian adventure, for in such weather there was little else to do but let his thoughts wander. He was on his way home, unlike Venables, who was still seeking gold at Long Gully, near Moliagul in Victoria.[8] Australia was now a gold-mine for the imagination to exploit rather than a place in itself. There were fascinating memories to be recalled, and a need to come to terms, within himself, with the place and its people. Station life, for instance, had its own charm, a romance of development from pioneer shelter to squatter comfort:

See Baroona now. Would you know it? I think not. That hut where we spent the pleasant Christmas-day you know of is degraded into the kitchen, and seems moved backward, although it stands in the same place, for a new house is built nearer the river, quite overwhelming the old slab hut in its grandeur a long low wooden house, with deep cool verandahs all round, already festooned with passion flowers, and young grape-vines, fronted by a flower-garden, all a-blaze with petunias and geraniums.

It was a summer evening, and all the French windows reaching to the ground were open to admit the cool south wind, which had just come up, deliciously icily cold after a scorching day. [*Geoffry Hamlyn,* chap. 22]

But what of the earlier days and the convict system? "Men did not live long in the chain gang, in Van Diemen's Land, in those days, brother," he wrote:

Men would knock out one another's brains in order to get hung, and escape it. Men would cry aloud to the judge to hang them out of the way! It was the most terrible punishment known, for it was hopeless. Penal servitude for life, as it is now, gives the very faintest idea of what it used to be in old times. With a little trouble I could tell you the weight of iron carried by each man. I cannot exactly remember, but it would strike you as being incredible. They were chained two and two together (a horrible association), to lessen the chances of escape; there was no chance of mitigation for good conduct; there was hard mechanical, uninteresting work, out of doors in an inclement climate, in all weathers: what wonder if men died off like rotten sheep? And what wonder, too, if sometimes the slightest accident, — such as a blow from an overseer, returned by a prisoner, produced a sudden rising, un-preconcerted, objectless, the result of which were half a dozen murdered men, as many lunatic women, and five or six stations lighting up the hillside, night after night, while the whole available force of the colony was unable to stop the ruin for months? [Ibid., chap. 21]

But, if out of this was to come a novel, Kingsley knew he would have to consider how to depict the characters. Outward description rather than inner history seemed the better method for him. The aberrant mind intrigued him, but its portrayal was beyond his ability:

> The history of the soul of a thorough-going rascal like Samuel Burton "remains to be written." *We* can't do it; we can only describe the outside of such, and say what we saw them do under such circumstances, as we have done with Samuel Burton. As for what they think, feel, and believe, they lie so horribly and habitually that the chances are ten to one that every other word they speak is false. Samuel Burton's character has been sketched after long and intimate confidences with many convicts. I used at one time to make after a new convict as I would after a new butterfly, and try — hopeless task! — to find out when he was lying and when he was telling the truth. The result has been Samuel Burton. But I have, at all events, found out two things. The first is, that a man who has just told you with infinite glee about the share he had in robbing a church, will invariably deny, with virtuous indignation, that he had any share whatever in the crime for which he was transported. His brother always did *that*; and his wife, in a moment of misplaced confidence, received the stolen property into the house in a basket of greens, which was found standing on the sink when the "traps" came. And the second is that, until we can catch a thoroughbred scoundrel, with high literary ability, and strict regard to truth, we had better not talk too fast about the reformation of criminals. [*The Hillyars and the Burtons,* chap. 69]

Elsewhere in Kingsley's writings are more of his Australian observations. He remembered Australia as a "land with millions of acres of fertile soil ... [calling] aloud for someone to cultivate them" (*Geoffry Hamlyn,* chap. 4). But there were some aspects that he found unacceptable. In *Austin Elliott* he rejected as impossible those who preached morality without alleviating physical adversity:

> Could not he, Austin, do some good, infinitesimal it might be, if he mixed with the other convicts? In the eye of the law he was no better than the worst of them, but he was still higher than the highest of them. Surely he might do *some* good.
> By merely mixing with them and talking to them, we might raise their moral tone, thought he. Speaking to them of higher things would — must — do them some good. One does not like to say that he was wrong; but still it becomes apparent that he had not acquired what we call the Australian instinct — that is to say, did not know a convict or jail-bird when he saw him; did not recognise the class of man as a distinct one; did not perceive the extraordinary difference, in appearance, between an honest man under a cloud, and a rogue. In fact, I am sorry to say, he came to the conclusion that he might raise the moral tone of the convicts around him by talking to them on an empty stomach. [Chap. 35]

The role of visiting parsons who called on any convict was futile, he thought. They understood neither the nature of the men nor the uselessness of their effort:

> Yellow-hair and the hut-keeper are now in loud conversation, and the former is asking, in a loud authoritative tone ... "whether a chap is to be hunted and badgered out of his bed by a parcel of — parsons?" To which Hutkeeper says, "No, by —! A man might as

well be in barracks again." Yellow-hair, morally comforted and sustained by this opinion, is proceeding to say, that, for his part, a parson is a useless sort of animal in general, who gets his living by frightening old women. [*Geoffry Hamlyn*, chap. 26]

Misguided parsons, though, were not the only objects of Kingsley's critical recollections about Australia. Among convicts, those who had served long sentences had a higher status than those who had served a short period.[9] Free settlers, he thought, had too much respect for the old convicts,[10] between whom there was a peculiar form of mateship, arising from sentiment rather than principle.

Reader, if you do not know that a man will act from "sentiment" long, long years after he has thrown "principle" to the winds, you had better pack up your portmanteau, and go and live five years or more among Australian convicts and American rowdies, as a friend of mine did. The one long outlives the other. The incarnate devils who beat out poor Price's brains with their shovels, when they had the gallows before them, consistently perjured themselves in favour of the youngest of the seven, the young friend who had hounded them on. [*Ravenshoe*, chap. 59]

Distrust of religious motives and the presence of a strange code of honour Kingsley had also noted as characteristic of the London Cockney.[11] If, however, he detected a connection between Cockney and convict he made no mention of it. He wrote also about bushrangers:

The first bushrangers were escaped convicts from Sydney. Bushranging began almost as soon as the Blue Mountains were crossed and the great interior opened; making the strict police, possible while the colony was confined to the easward of that mountain chain, now impossible. After this, bushranging spread far and wide: more to the north, towards the Hunter and Clarence at first; but afterwards, as the flocks went south, into the most outlying districts in that direction. The object of these bushrangers was to avenge themselves on the society which they had once defied, by new crimes; and if you will take the newest digest of the criminal laws, and run your eye down the list of crimes, you will find not one which they did not commit. Such were the first generation of bushrangers. The second were hardly so brutal; but, strange to say, young men whose fathers had been convicts, but who were reformed and were doing well – getting rich indeed – joined this second generation of bushrangers from mere love of adventure and of old association. I date the second generation of bushrangers at 1830; what shall we say of 1865 – of the *third* generation – when no road in New South Wales was safe, and when the *grandsons* of the original convicts join the bushrangers and defy the police? On one occasion, in 1865, they actually held a town for two days and gave a ball, at which the policemen were obliged to dance. If it is so in 1865, what must it have been in 1830? ["The Two Cadets", chap. 1]

In the bush Kingsley, of necessity, met many whose diverse histories and characters stayed in his memory long after his return to England: "If you have ever tried the lonely bush for yourself for a few years," he wrote in "The Two Cadets", "and would afterwards honestly confess to us all about the uncommonly queer people whom you have to like in that beautiful but unutterably melancholy solitude, you would tell us a most interesting story" (chap. 2).[12] His observation on the effect of solitude and the bush was echoed many years later by Henry Lawson.

Grooms at the stations he regarded as nearly equivalent to "the dirtiest helper at a University stable".[13] Class distinctions undoubtedly existed and respectability was important, but birth was no indication of behaviour. There were "high spirited men in Australia brought lower than you would fancy".[14] Some, having turned their back on their own class to live with the lower orders, either gave it up as futile and assumed "the position that superior education [gave them]" or else drank themselves "to the devil".[15]

Self-help was clearly needed in Australia to a far greater extent than in England, and any emigration plan based on sending unskilled labourers to the colonies was doomed to failure.[16] On the other hand, the labourer as such was unable to grasp his chance to improve his position in life. Translocation of such people as a social experiment was a failure. Idealism had its place, but opportunity did not ensure independence. Kingsley's attitude, however, as revealed by his writing, is obviously "upper-class" and accordingly made its appeal to those who were "traditional":

> "Oh, but you are over-stating the case, you know, Dean," said the Major. "You must have a class of small farmers! Wherever the land is fit for cultivation it must be sold to agriculturists; or otherwise, in case of a war, we shall be dependent on Europe and America for the bread we eat. I know some excellent and exemplary men who are farmers, I assure you."
> "Of course! of course!" said Frank. "I did not mean quite all I said; but I am angry and disappointed. I pictured to myself the labourer, English, Scotch, or Irish — a man whom I know, and have lived with and worked for some years, emigrating, and, after a few years of honest toil, which, compared to his old hard drudgery, was child's-play, saving money enough to buy a farm. I pictured to myself this man accumulating wealth, happy, honest, godly, bringing up a family of brave boys and good girls, in a country where, theoretically, the temptations to crime are all but removed: this is what I imagined. I come out here, and what do I find? My friend the labourer has got his farm, and is prospering after a sort. He has turned to be a drunken, godless, impudent fellow, and his wife little better than himself." ... "Yes," said the Major," ... there is no social influence in the settled districts; there are too many men without masters. Let us wait and hope." [*Geoffry Hamlyn*,, chap. 26]

Australia, though, was not devoid of charms. As Kingsley wrote in "The Two Cadets": "In that land of untellable melancholy peace called Australia, the setting of the sun — a peaceful event everywhere — is more peaceful, more calm, possibly more beautiful, than in any other country in the world. Once see for yourself those dim, lonely, long-drawn plains of grey grass, and see the sunlight die on the solitary wooded peak which stands out from them twenty miles away, and then you will know what I mean" (chap. 1). There, too, the seasons glided almost imperceptibly into each other marked only by the greenness or otherwise of the grass. The flaming primrose of an Australian morning was a glory to be remembered in the years to come, and even Melbourne's hot tin-kettle of an old post-office in the 1850s, "the sweltering little den", had a charm of its own. It was a link to home: "Old loves, old hopes, old friends, old scenes, old scents, old sounds", he recollected, later, "are threads which, though you draw them the finest silk, are still stronger than iron.... If you have imagination enough to put a voice into these senseless sounds of nature, I should beg to stand with you in the Melbourne post-office on a mail-day, and see what sort of voice would speak to you out of the rustling of a thousand fluttering letters, held by trembling hands, and gazed on by faces which, however coarse and ugly, let the news be good or bad, grow more soft and gentle as the news is read" (*The Hillyars and the Burtons,* chap. 15).

Such memories evoked others less pleasant to recall, as, for example, the boisterous rowdiness and rawness of the scene when a dozen or "fourteen gentlewomen from Mrs. Quickly's old establishment, who having nothing to pay for entrance [to the theatre], and as much drink as they could get the cattle-dealers and diggers to treat them to, made the hall a sort of winter-garden". On this Kingsley commented: "We exhibit our vice and dissipation 'with a loathsome indecency which no other group of nations seem to have rivalled" (*The Hillyars and the Burtons,* chap. 75). Despite such criticism he still envisaged a future for the lonely, melancholy land which lay silent in the Southern Ocean. It would be, he wrote, the place to which "all the unfortunate of the earth" would come, the English factory labourer, the farmer-ridden peasant, the Irish pauper, the starved Scotch Highlander, the German and the Hungarian, for "all the oppressed of the earth" would take refuge there. It would be a land for new beginnings (*Geoffry Hamlyn,* chap. 36).

While Kingsley busied himself on the *Swiftsure* with his writing and his thoughts, Captain Pryce attended to matters of the moment. On 14 April he logged the ship's position as latitude 11° 18' south and longitude 33° 30' west and confined William Morgan in irons on the lower deck for "being drunk, disorderly, insolent, threatening". Two days later the offender was released and the voyage continued without incident until two days out from London, when the second death occurred: "James Brown died — syphilis." For Kingsley, burial in the vast wastes of the sea, almost within sight of home, was a sad reminder of life's uncertainty. Whether or not his parents were still alive was unknown to him, because he had not, while in Australia, written home. Nevertheless, whatever lay ahead had to wait, for the ship was almost in the Channel:

> Two months and a half at sea, and no land seen — nothing but the everlasting ocean.... It is getting colder too, almost as cold as Old England in spring time. It should be spring time there now.... A pleasant month this May used to be in Hampshire, if I remember right.... Ah, there it is — a great purple mountain rising out of a

gleaming morning sea; a hundred happy English valleys wrinkling its broad flanks; a hundred happy English cottages nestling in its misty hollows. They say it is the Start. But I care not what it is, for I know it is England. ["Wild Sports of the Far South"]

He was *home,* and once more a new phase of life was opening up, with all its attendant demands. He had brought back with him his only assets, a great deal of colonial experience and the incomplete manuscript of a novel. The rush to Australia was over — the dross of his finds had now to be discarded, and the real gold retained. With thoughts of what might be in front of him, Kingsley prepared to disembark.

12

Eversley

The *Swiftsure* arrived in London on 16 May 1858.[1] Kingsley went to his old home in Chelsea. It was night when he reached the rectory, and he paced up and down outside the door for more than an hour "fearing to enter lest he might hear that both his parents were dead".[2] Finally he knocked and learned from the curate[3] that his parents now lived at Eversley, not far from Charles's rectory. It was in the country, then, not at Chelsea, that Kingsley was reconciled with his family after what he later described as "so many weary years of separation".[4] Subsequently he took the cottage, Dressors, next to his parents, explaining afterwards that he had not written because he was ashamed of his failure in Australia and dreaded receiving bad news from home.[5]

Towards autumn 1858, the publisher Alexander Macmillan visited Charles Kingsley at Eversley, and Henry was asked to join the group. Macmillan and his brother, Daniel, who started business as a bookseller in Scotland, had opened a bookshop in Cambridge in 1843 and begun publishing the following year. Their first notable success was Charles Kingsley's *Westward Ho!* (1855). Charles was a firm friend of the Macmillans and stood as godfather to Alexander's son in 1850. During 1858 Daniel died and his brother assumed control of the firm.

In the rectory garden Henry and Macmillan were introduced, and thus began an association characterized in years to come as much by friendship as by profit on Macmillan's part.[6] Kingsley read portion of the manuscript he had brought,[7] and, much interested, Macmillan asked for it to be sent to him. Some time later, Henry sent "two or three bricks as a sample of the house". He had taken ill after the meeting at Eversley, in consequence of which he had been writing under difficulties and could not, as requested, visit Macmillan at Cambridge. "I do pray to hear your opinion of these M.S. soon," he wrote, " – Charles thinks highly of them but one's Brother you know would be apt to do that."[8]

Macmillan's opinion, when received, delighted Henry, who replied almost immediately explaining that his pleasure at the verdict arose not only because so experienced a judge approved but because "the ladies" did so as well. "With regard to a purely objective story like mine," he said, "they are the best judges. Their recommendations, and yours shall be carefully attended to." He agreed with Macmillan's view that the story needed to be rounded off, and said, "It is what we painters call *giving it air*, softening the various groups one into another so as to form not a succession of objects, but a picture. I am a young hand but I am confident that I can do it — now that I can see my way as your letter has enabled me to do, I shall give up my whole energies to the work, allowing nothing to interfere. And with God's blessing hope to produce something that will stand as a genuine book." The influence of Macmillan and Charles Kingsley at this stage on the writing of *Geoffry Hamlyn* now becomes evident. Kingsley's original estimate was for a book of thirty chapters averaging twenty-five pages each, based on a calculation that one of the manuscript pages equalled one and a third printed pages. Enough of *Geoffry Hamlyn* had been written for Kingsley to estimate that its length would correspond to that of his brother's book, *Two Years Ago*. He was, he wrote, confident of his future work now that he was well because his first loose efforts had been so satisfactory when he was borne down by ill health. On Charles's recommendation, he was writing different parts of the novel and hoped to send the first chapter "in two or three days".[9]

As it happened, Kingsley's progress was slower than Macmillan wished, and on 19 August he wrote to Kingsley asking after "the gentleman on the moors of North Devon", and added that he had written to the bookseller and publisher George Robertson of Melbourne to stimulate interest in the book. He went on to ask if there was a possibility of its being completed by Christmas and hoped Kingsley's health was better than it had been the week previous.[10] In reply, Henry apologized for not having written earlier because he had been "exceedingly seedy" and had abandoned "any hope of going to Cambridge for the present". Apart from which, his father required a great deal of attention.[11]

Kingsley and Macmillan quickly established a firm friendship, as the humour in their letters to each other reveals. "Pray receive my sincere felicitations on the state of the Thames," Kingsley congratulated Macmillan, "the position of affairs in India, the success of the Telegraph Squadron, and in short the general pickle all public affairs seem to have got into just now." It was a reply, similar in vein to a letter from Macmillan. Shortly afterwards, Kingsley sent Macmillan another chapter which, in Charles's opinion, was the best piece he had so far written. "But," Henry added, "we shall have better before we have done."[12] By late October 1858 Macmillan and his wife had read over a hundred pages of the novel, both of them being "delighted by it". It was, wrote Macmillan to his friend and business associate James MacLehose, "a story of Australian life — chiefly backwoods, partly in England" and went on to describe Kingsley's power of description as akin to that of Charles but dissimilar in style: "It is wonderfully quiet — but yet powerful — a kind of lazy strength which is very charming;

some of the characters too are drawn with a masterly hand. Convicts, emigrant gentlemen from decayed families, farmers emigrant from various reasons — these are characters he draws. Each one stands firm and clear on his feet, like a man in actual life."[13]

A month later Kingsley sent all he had written and said he planned to finish the novel by the end of the month. "I for one shall be most heartily glad," he wrote. Some of what was forwarded had been read at Eversley, and this, with what had been added since, formed the first third of the work. The length, Kingsley indicated, would depend on Macmillan's wishes; however, he had enough matter for a three-volume novel rather than the two that had been discussed. His health was improving, he said, but he had had "a sad bout of it". He concluded humorously, as he and Macmillan were now in the habit of doing, and referred to the Anglican bishop of London's charge before the Court of the Queen's Bench. Details of the case appeared in *The Times* on 25 November, when it was alleged that the Reverend Alfred Poole had been conducting a system of private confession and absolution. "[This] is the hardest hit in the mouth that our two old friends the Pope and the Devil have had this year," wrote Kingsley.[14] At this time he was living at St Leonards,[15] and he proposed going to Cambridge for publication of his book on 31 December.[16] Macmillan agreed and asked that Kingsley stay for a few days before returning to Eversley. Of the work that Macmillan had read, descriptions of scenery, special scenes, and characterization drew his praise, but he disliked "scenes of darkness". According to him they were "powerfully done" but occurred too frequently, and he wanted to talk the matter over with Henry during the visit. His own preference was for "heaps of marriages" and the "merry laughter of happy families in the green forest". He besought Kingsley to read the relevant passages to other members of the Kingsley family to get their opinion, while he, for his part, would do the same with his own family. Understandably the novel had to have appeal to sell, but it is clear that Kingsley's first work was to be formed not just by his own preferences but also by those of his closest friends and critics, the Kingsleys and the Macmillans. Another sixty pages "of laughter", advised Macmillan, were needed to make the first part with the sombre scenes into a volume, and he enjoined Henry to take great pains in "rounding off" the tale, saying that three volumes were needed if this were to be done satisfactorily. "You remember," he told Kingsley, "you have to fight against your noble name."[17] It was not the first time Henry was to find his interests affected by his brother's prominence. In 1863, for instance, he felt compelled to ask Macmillan to delay publication of *The Hillyars and the Burtons* rather than appear in print simultaneously with a work by Charles.[18] It is hard to know precisely what Macmillan meant by "scenes of darkness", but the probability is that he meant, besides those of Hawker and Lee, scenes that embodied other than the romantic attitudes which could be associated with "happy marriages" and "merry laughter . . . in the green forest". Consequently scenes between members of the Hawker family depicting roughness of speech and behaviour, of Ellen and her illegitimate child, and of the undesirable aspects of a nineteenth-century Devon County Fair would have caused Macmillan to hesitate about their inclusion in the novel.

The possibility that the early part of the book might have to be altered worried Kingsley, who was apprehensive of harming, by excisions, what had been written.[19] He agreed that the scenes between Hawker and Lee were somewhat long but preferred, he said, to "throw in three or four chapters of lively 'discourse' ". By way of reassuring Macmillan he added that Charles had read nearly all he had written, hoping, no doubt, that such support would be enough to justify his stand.

In another letter Kingsley makes clear that chapter 30 of *Geoffry Hamlyn* ("How the Child Was Lost") was written in Australia. This chapter, which Charles "particularly swore by", was later published separately by Macmillan in 1871 as a book for children, *The Lost Child*. Its treatment of death in the Australian bush, where feelings of terror are softened by sentimental fancies and thoughts of heaven, would have appealed to Charles. But he was not alone in his admiration. It appealed to others, too, one critic praising it for having "an unaffected and manly pathos".[20]

Kingsley did not get to Cambridge as planned for discussions with Macmillan, owing to a recurrence of his and his father's illnesses, and for the same reason did not finish the book by 31 December. According to Henry's doctor "the coats of the stomach were in a deuce of a state" and would not be better for some time. Hard living in Australia and the strain of writing were affecting him, added to which he had been nursing his father while Mrs Kingsley was in Chelsea attending to the affairs of the parish. The delay worried Henry, even though he told Macmillan that "a man's father you know ought to be paramount to all things".[21] Nevertheless, he had been able to find enough time to plan the novel to allow Mary Hawker to become Mrs Troubridge, "comfortable ... with three children" so that Macmillan's feelings would not be "harassed" unnecessarily.

Early in 1859 Kingsley senior suffered a stroke, in consequence of which Henry could give little time to *Geoffry Hamlyn* despite having the second and third volumes nearly finished.[22] Meanwhile, the Boston publishers Ticknor and Fields offered him, not fifteen pounds as suggested to them by Macmillan, but fifty pounds for the unpublished proofs.[23] This Kingsley accepted[24] after conferring with Charles, who pointed out that he had been offered only thirty pounds for *Westward Ho!*[25] To Henry it seemed that his arrival on the literary scene was marked by monetary rewards quite worthy of the noble name he bore, if not, indeed, a little better. He was by now deeply involved with nursing his father as well as with writing; Charles did what he could by checking the finished work. In the meantime, while he wrote to Ticknor and Fields that "The Reminiscences *[sic]* of Geoffry Hamlyn" comprised "900–1000 pretty closely printed pages", Macmillan, on one of his visits to Eversley, debated with Charles whether one incident in the novel should be omitted to avoid shocking the public. "Strength", wrote Macmillan afterwards to Henry, "is quite compatible with frequent 'propriety' in these respects."[26]

On 4 March 1859 Macmillan received volume 2 of the manuscript with the passage omitted to which he and Charles had objected. "The faults", wrote Henry Kingsley to Macmillan, "I have laboriously mended, against my own judgment in some instances."[27] But this was not the only demand made on Kingsley, for Macmillan's other requests caused the early portion of *Geoffry Hamlyn* to be expanded to almost one third of the finished book, with more of the action being set in Dartmoor and Devon than had originally been planned.[28] Meanwhile, preparations were well in hand for launching the book. During April 1859 Mudie's Circulating Library placed an advance order for five hundred copies of the novel,[29] and Alexander Macmillan sent an incomplete set of the printed sheets to Professor Irving in Melbourne, requesting that George Robertson, the publisher, and a Melbourne newspaper, the *Argus,* be given access to them.[30]

With difficulty, Kingsley continued with his work, though persistent ill health delayed the final proof reading until mid-April 1859.[31] But now there was another problem. In addition to Macmillan's views about the "dark" scenes, and Charles's rejection of the "rough" passages, Kingsley's father wanted him to eliminate "everything in the book which might prevent it lying on a drawing room table". In an attempt to defend his general plan for the novel, Kingsley wrote cautiously to Alexander Macmillan: "A gloomy beginning leading up to a happy and prosperous conclusion is I think within the bounds of true art."[32] As Kingsley was finding out, life experienced was one thing, portraying it in a novel was another. Realism would have to be surrendered if he wanted publication. The realism of "rough" scenes would have to be replaced by romance if he was to meet the constraints of father, brother, and publisher. One can only surmise what was changed or deleted. Certainly he had been in Australia and, in some respects, possessed deeper insights into human nature than Charles, but informed counsels had to prevail. No colonial roughness of scene or expression was to taint his work, or, for that matter, sully the already established mid-Victorian image of the Kingsleys. The fact is that Henry's protests showed he suspected his creativity and narrative mode could be adversely affected, but he succumbed without further struggle for the sake of survival — the need for publication was paramount, and family approval of his work a necessity. In accepting such constraints, Henry lost his newly found colonial independence of outlook. No longer the traveller, he was once again the youngest son of the Reverend Charles Kingsley, Chelsea, conforming to parents, family image, and attitudes. His other brother, George Henry, a doctor, had sought refuge outside the reach of the family and in his repudiation of Christianity, but Henry, needing money, and lacking a profession, could not escape. He could no longer be the free product of that "quaint Australian life".

He was "home" and, henceforth, must write for approval, not to express himself.

On publication, Macmillan, in addition to sending four copies for review to Australia, forwarded *Geoffry Hamlyn* to the editors of thirty-six magazines, papers, and journals. Relatives and friends of Kingsley who received copies totalled twelve, including his mother at Chelsea, his sister-in-law at Eversley, Martin Irving, and Henry Venables.[33] Benefactors in Australia who had hosted him, surprisingly, received none, which seems to indicate a lack of intimacy with them on Kingsley's part even though he had received their hospitality. After all, if Browne is correct, it was he who had persuaded Kingsley to give up the drifter's life for writing; Macknight had been his host at Port Fairy, where some material for *Geoffry Hamlyn* was obtained; and Willi Mitchell had looked after him "delicately" at Langi Willi. Whatever else may be inferred, evidence of widespread personal ties in Australia is not given by the Macmillan distribution list. On the other hand, Tennyson received a copy in October 1859 as "a relief from metaphysico-theological controversy".

After publication in April 1859, Macmillan sent Kingsley a much-needed six hundred pounds, whereupon a grateful Henry wrote: "Allow me to say that I think you have behaved most liberally to me in not adhering to your original proposition."[34] He was referring both to the co-operation he had received in having the book published in America and the payment. In the same letter Kingsley said he was working on *Ravenshoe*, which he revealed had been started in 1853 while at Worcester College, Oxford, and which he hoped to finish by May 1860. He was now trying to turn some of his unproductive university years to good account and mitigate his leaving Oxford without a degree. It was also a way of saying that he was right in rejecting a career in the Church — he was a *writer*.

There were drawbacks, though, in being the younger brother of a clergyman who was also a prominent novelist. The possible comparison of his work with Charles's had caused him to write from St Leonards, before publication, that he saw no "reason for comparison to be made with Charles". Furthermore, he asserted that "this would be like comparing Louis Napoleon to his uncle".[35] Meanwhile, Charles and Fanny were both busy, she with a young family and he with preaching, lecturing, and writing. He proof-read and offered advice to Henry when necessary, but other than that no mention occurs of the Charles Kingsleys being involved to any great degree with the other Kingsleys at this time. The onus of being available to help the parents domestically had fallen on Henry, the unmarried son at home. The prodigal had been forgiven but, either by design or accident, was now making reparations for his waywardness at school and the silent years in Australia.

Whether Henry wished it or not, comparison of *Geoffry Hamlyn* with Charles's work *was* made, both in England and America. In England, although his intimacy with colonial life was acknowledged,

Kingsley's profusion of incident and detail and his lack of control in *Geoffry Hamlyn* were deplored. Henry could learn in this respect from Charles, it was said.[36] In America his originality and vigour were praised, but, wrote the critic, there were "portions of Mr. Charles Kingsley's teaching which drive Mr. Henry Kingsley into a mental corner. He does not care — he drinks his whiskey and water until his big brother is once more in his line" and then goes along with established family doctrine.[37] In short, his independence, as well as the unconscious way he preached Charles's gospel, was noted. From both countries came comment on a roughness of language — in England deplored — in America praised. In Australia, the *Southern Cross* of 19 November 1859 pronounced the book, "in many ways crude, incomplete, and yet while displaying only the merest rudiments of a constructive faculty, the work has everywhere power, a stamp of real life and individuality. It had a vigorous hand and a true one — resembling his brother's, but thoroughly his own."

Fortunately for Kingsley, criticism affected him little. His letters to Macmillan, "his dear friend", contain references to the "inane and silly pomposity of the *Saturday [Review]*", "the honest, true and kindly" review of the *Critic*, and the insolent review of the *Daily News*, which he thought "offset" by "the last notice" in the *New Quarterly*. The fact that Tom Taylor (1817-80), sometime professor of English, London University College, editor of Punch (1874–80), and a well known contemporary playwright, "was raving about his book" was sufficient for him.[38]

As far as Kingsley was concerned, the work was a success. He had written a novel set in Australia some fifty years after the first convict settlement in 1788 at Port Jackson and had introduced the new land's uniqueness in language reminiscent of the Book of Revelation: "A new heaven and a new earth! Tier beyond tier, height above height, the great wooded ranges go rolling away westward, till on the lofty skyline they are crowned with a gleam of everlasting snow.... All creation is new and stirring" (*Geoffry Hamlyn,* chap. 18). Similarly the paradisal quality of the flora and fauna had moved him to write: "Then a green swamp; through the tall reeds the native companion, King of Cranes, waded majestic; the brilliant porphyry water hen, with scarlet bill and legs, flashed like a sapphire among the emerald-green water-sedge" (ibid., chap. 34). He had captured, in his first attempt, an Australia which evolved not from convicts alone but from squatters, of people prepared to risk resettlement in the Antipodes to improve themselves. Apart from which, his bank account prospered. He had, in his own manner, found gold in Australia, and in a way more lasting than most, for he was now able to indulge himself. He complained to Macmillan that it was "too dry for fishing and too hot for riding".[39]

Later in the year a mutual friend of Kingsley and Macmillan, Professor George Wilson, died. Despite being ill for many years, he had been largely instrumental in establishing the Industrial Museum of Scotland and had gained much esteem for doing so. Kingsley, writing to Macmillan about the unexpectedness of the death, thought it providential, as Wilson had "been spared a life of suffering".[40] In the same letter he said that *Ravenshoe* was giving him trouble. He had been writing the first and second parts concurrently and could not effect a satisfactory transition between them. The great difficulty, he said, was doing it "so that the joint may not be seen".[41] But his problem was more a lack of time than artifice. Kingsley, preoccupied with nursing and his father's continued suffering, had not spoken lightly about George Wilson. By February 1860 Charles had to write from Chelsea to the Reverend James Montagu: "Forgive me for my silence, for I and my brothers are now wearily watching my father's death-bed — long and lingering."[42] On 20 February their father died, and their mother went to live with Henry. The family coachman, William Mearing, was discharged,[43] economies obviously being necessary, and Kingsley, for the moment fully involved with his family, had to put *Ravenshoe* aside. On 13 June 1860 he received a further three hundred pounds from Macmillan "for leave to print and publish the Second Edition of *The Recollections of Geoffry Hamlyn*", and in January 1861 serialization of *Ravenshoe* began in *Macmillan's Magazine*. It was to run until July 1862. Now there were no real worries. Despite some economies, he had funds with prospect of more to come, and life at Eversley was relatively comfortable.

William Tinsley, in his *Random Recollections of an Old Publisher*, recollected that Kingsley had a capital sense of fun and true humour;[44] and Charles Kingsley's son Maurice, in an article for the *Book Buyer* written in 1895,[45] recalled that his uncle Henry's "settling in Eversley was a great event". The Kingsley children loved him dearly: "At times he fairly bubbled over with humour; while his knowledge of slang — Burschen, Bargee, Parisian, Irish, Cockney and English provincialism — was awful and wonderful." A photograph taken by George Kingsley in 1861 shows Henry in the garden of his home at Eversley, posed with shotgun for the benefit of his nephews and nieces. "My dears, I likes to be took as a country squire in me preserves," he said in reply to their jeers and derision, "and divvle a soul but yerselves knows I can't hit a barn, and me preserves is in the back kitchen closet." Another photograph, also taken by his brother George, shows him accompanied by Vic, his black and tan rat terrier, and Captain West, who was both neighbour and fishing companion of Charles, George, and Henry. There was no doubt that Henry was the expert when they went fishing. When the others had given up in despair, Henry would cast a fly deftly and lightly into seemingly impossible places and succeed while they watched. He rented a few miles of fishing on the near-by River Blackwater, and also some rough shooting adjoining his fields, more, according to Maurice Kingsley, for his nephew's benefit than his own, "as he did not much care for shooting". Maurice noticed, too, as they had at Squattlesea Mere, that although shy in company, his uncle was really genial and warm-hearted. Henry's paintings, as Maurice recollected them, included oils of scenery near Snowdon, of Yes Tor in Devon,

Henry Kingsley in 1861. Reprinted from the *Book Buyer*, January 1895.

and one of the Auberg which Charles Kingsley kept in his study. Two others were in the album that Fanny gave to her son Grenville when he emigrated to Australia. One watercolour appears to be of a Scottish loch, while the other is of Penmaenmawr, North Wales, with Great Orme's Head in the distance.

On the proof copy of Fanny Kingsley's abridged edition of *Charles Kingsley*, in the margin of Charles Kingsley's poem, "The Delectable Day" (chap. 26), is a gloss "H.K." besides the words "the fool". In context, they imply pity rather than condemnation. Other glosses show that "the great and overwhelming sorrow" hanging over Charles in

Henry Kingsley in the garden at Eversley. Reprinted from the *Book Buyer*, January 1895.

December 1874 was "H.K.'s illness", while earlier "anxieties" of Charles, in the winter of 1872, relate to Henry also. Although it might appear that Fanny omitted references to Henry in her biography of Charles, her glosses show they were there, albeit hidden. Furthermore, a copy of *The Hillyars and the Burtons* and two photographs of Henry, given to Grenville, tend to modify the view that she had little sympathy for her brother-in-law. Maurice Kingsley refers to Fanny's relations with Henry when he says that her volume of *Geoffry Hamlyn* was inscribed: "Fanny E. Kingsley, with the most affectionate love of her brother-in-law, Henry Kingsley."[46] Unfortunately the affinity of the early years was to be changed somewhat after Henry married, mainly because the Charles Kingsleys had little regard for Henry's wife and her mother.

Much freer after his father's death, Henry in 1860 was a frequent visitor to Macmillan's dinners at 23 Henrietta Street, London,[47] using rooms near by, at 19 Henrietta Street, during his visits.[48] Occasionally his brother George was present, but a more frequent visitor was Charles. Some indication of whom Kingsley would have met is afforded by Macmillan's letter of 25 July 1860 to Daniel Wilson, professor of history and English literature at Toronto, when Macmillan said that among those present at his last function were Holman Hunt, Thomas Woolner, Alexander Munro, and Tennyson. It was here that Kingsley, despite his shyness, benefited socially from his friendship with Macmillan, preferring, according to his nephew, "men's talk to women's", although living at that time much to himself.

A glimpse of Kingsley's life at Eversley is given by Professor John Stuart Blackie: "At half past seven I found myself before the dear, rustic, old English Rectory, gracefully shaded by acacias and Scotch firs — the Rector had been out fishing all day, and was glowing in face like a tropical copper sky.... His brother, Henry, came in later, and we all smoked, and drank tea, and talked and went early to bed."[49]

At Kingsley's cottage the routine was uneventful, according to Henry Campbell, who, on his return from Australia, stopped there while Henry was writing *Austin Elliott* and *The Hillyars and the Burtons*:

> After dinner and much smoking, he would retire to his study at the back of the house, overlooking the rose garden, about eleven o'clock, and fortified only by a jug of rum and water would write without intermission until six in the morning. Then he went to bed until luncheon time. In the afternoon he would take long walks, work in the garden, or shoot or fish. Then home to dinner, and the same programme as before, night after night, day after day. It was not a wise arrangement of the twenty four hours doubtless, but one can appreciate how he loved those silent hours of the night, the rose and garden scents, the moon and dawn-light over the fir-woods.[50]

Campbell records also that Joe, a newspaper boy, was the original of Bill Wilkins the shoe-black in *Ravenshoe* and a frequent visitor to Kingsley's Henrietta Street lodgings. Both Joe in real life and Bill in fiction had their pitches by St Peter's Church, Eaton Square. Kingsley, doubtless, met Joe at Field Lane Home for Boys, with whose affairs he was intimate and to which he referred in later years when appealing on behalf of sick children in Edinburgh. As S. M. Ellis points out in his biography, Kingsley mentions this home in "Meerschaum". The original manuscript of *The Hillyars and the Burtons*, of which a portion survives, gives a hint of Kingsley's possible interest in other charitable projects; St George's Workhouse, Hanover Square, is shown thereon as the original of the Nicholas Without Workhouse mentioned in the novel (chap. 49). It was there that the character Dawson once lived.

To some, Kingsley proved a helpful friend. In trying to help the brother-in-law of his friends the Annesleys, who lived in Eversley, he inadvertently revealed a romance prior to his marriage. Seeking Macmillan's help for a "young fellow aged eighteen, a gentleman, innocent, and well disposed ... but horribly deficient in education", he gave as his reason: "I would do almost anything to help him, for some of his sisters are something like sisters to me, and one of them was once something more."[51] The family was in poor circumstances, he noted in his letter, which could well have caused the romance to lapse.

He was probably not financial enough at the time of the affair to bring an impoverished dependant into the Kingsley circle. If this was the case, it is possible that from this romance came the theme of love and duty in *The Hillyars and the Burtons.*

In September 1860 Kingsley moved for a period to Alma Cottage, Wargrave, a few kilometres distant from Eversley, and while there served with the 2nd Battalion, Royal Middlesex Rifle Volunteers.[52] Using the battalion's crested stationery, he notified Macmillan of his change of address and also wrote Edwin Arnold: "The Volunteer Movement is the finest thing that ever happened to the country but it has been hard on particular cases. I am being drilled to death in preparation for Hythe where I shall be ultimately finished."[53] A correspondent in *Macmillan's Magazine* observed that the volunteers comprised "men, and not boys; full grown men with professions and trades to work at, and ... bread to earn for themselves. There is, probably, not one in five of them who has got over the feeling of dismay ... whenever he finds himself walking about the streets in a uniform."[54] As might be expected, Kingsley put service ahead of pleasure. "I must choose the dust and noise and heat of Wimbledon, instead of a delightful afternoon in the garden at Fir Grove [Eversley]," he wrote to Mrs Erskine, who often did proof-reading for him. She was the wife of the Right Honourable Thomas Erskine, a distinguished judge and an intimate friend of Charles Kingsley. In apologizing to Mrs Erskine, Kingsley concluded wryly, "We must thank the Emperor of the French for this and many other things."[55]

Kingsley was not always so dedicated: "Drill is a very good thing, but isn't dinner a better?" he wrote to his friend Bowes of *Macmillan's Magazine,* "Why should you stay to drill next Saturday. Blow drill. Mutiny ... cut it and come to dinner."[56] To Edwin Arnold he apologized for missing him at an army review held in Reading and made the apology good with a humorous recollection of the proceedings:

> I went with my landlord and his son, a very nice intelligent boy [whom I sent to look for you] ... a gentleman in light grey with raw leather accoutrements and yellow gaiters with breeches (meaning you), and tell him that Mr. Kingsley wanted to speak to him. In a quarter of an hour he returned with one of the London Scottish, a Macgregor, or Macpherson or some such name, who wished to know what the devil I wanted with him. ... He was good enough to be satisfied with my explanation, and left us with an air of lofty scorn, and we were humiliated, covered with confusion, as with a garment.
>
> I am sorry to say that the effect produced by the South Middlesex uniform on the population was not such as I could wish. It got into their stupid heads that I was a musician and that I was enjoying a brief respite from my duty of playing on the lute, sackbut Psaltery or dulcimer. On going into a booth to get a glass of soda water and sherry, I was asked for a song, my refusal was taken to be contumacious, and I received personal insults. ... I hope you enjoyed yourself tho' it would have been infinite folly if we had met.[57]

The lighthearted tone of these excerpts shows that Kingsley's "simple, direct, bluff and humorous"[58] personality did not fit easily into the ecclesiastically serious format of the Kingsley family. In *Geoffry Hamlyn* a comment by the narrator betrays Kingsley's own frustration with the restrictions he had to observe: "I suppress the expletives, thereby shortening [conversations] by nearly one half, and depriving the public of much valuable information" (chap. 37). The protest may be humorous, but it is not without point.

Kingsley made steady progress with *Ravenshoe*, keeping his copy two months ahead of publication in *Macmillan's Magazine*. He was now well aware of the need to avoid giving offence if he was to be published, and some years later, in 1866, used *Ravenshoe*'s problems to argue his case: *"Silcote of Silcotes* ain't half so improper as fifty things in *Ravenshoe,* and we made a success there." Victorian expectations and the demands of the drawing-room were for him ever present constraints. In *Ravenshoe,* through what ultimately proves a false report, Charles Ravenshoe ceases to be heir to an estate in Devon and becomes Charles Horton. The former is a gentleman, the latter is not. The situation afforded Kingsley an opportunity to look at society across the class barrier, but through the same eyes — an adventure into the "other-man's-land", as it were, for genteel readers. Towards the end of the book, Ravenshoe says, "When you speak to me, sir, of the distinction between upper and lower classes, I answer you, that . . . I have come to the conclusion that, after all, the gentleman and the cad are one and the same animal. . . . I have been to death's gate to learn it" (chap. 61). Charles Horton, in Victorian fashion, had tried to submerge his personal grief by supporting a noble cause, the Crimean War, where he had been gravely wounded.

At times Kingsley seems to balance the tragic, or near tragic, with passages written in lighter vein. If they are seen in this way they appear less intrusive and more like a deliberate attempt to control the reader's response while maintaining interest and suspense. In some ways, even with its wealth of detail, *Ravenshoe* shows considerably more control of its material than is generally seen in Kingsley's work.

Despite his concern, *Ravenshoe* succeeded admirably, and on 30 October 1861 Macmillan wrote to Kingsley saying that he was looking forward to its success as a book.[59] Publication took place in 1862, when Kingsley allowed it to go "to the world pretty much as it stood". To Macmillan he commented, "It has had a pretty good deal of overlooking. . . . I should like to know when you would be likely to want anything from me for the Magazine . . . the first number will be ready soon."[60] This was a reference to his next work, *Austin Elliott*. In the summer of 1862 Kingsley went to Lanarkshire and Inveraray, a visit which was to help with the Scottish scenes in *Austin Elliott,* and also to Cambridge, where he was Macmillan's guest.[61] In June, he received six hundred pounds for the first edition of *Ravenshoe* (fifteen hundred copies), the same amount he had received for *Geoffry Hamlyn* and a concrete indication of Macmillan's judgement. Kingsley did not escape criticism from the press. This time the *Spectator* looked at his work and, while crediting it with a wealth of life and humour and with a recognizable pathos and humorous incident, considered that its dramatic deficiency lay in the handling of the dénouement, the artistic element of the book suffering accordingly. Kingsley could not cover narrative deficiencies with "large resources of infinite humour", the critic suggested. It was a criticism Kingsley could have well heeded, for it generally marked the way his work would develop in the years ahead. In *Geoffry Hamlyn* he allowed the romantic aspects of a new land and the retrieval of family fortunes to overshadow the exploration of impulse and decision. The web of problems he wove around the Hawkers touched almost on the problem of identity and environment – but not quite. In *Ravenshoe,* Kingsley placed his protagonist on both sides of society through an accident of birth. The idea warranted better treatment than improbability in some of the incidents. Nevertheless, although his conclusion, that upper and lower classes, the gentleman and the cad, were one and the same animal may not have been new, it helped Victorians to continue the debate on the question.

On the continent, Bernhard Tauchnitz of Leipzig, noting the book's success, offered to print *Ravenshoe* in a popular edition. Kingsley accepted without delay, for not only was this Tauchnitz's first approach but his copyright would be safeguarded. On 12 September 1862 he agreed to Tauchnitz's arrangements for translating the work and expressed confidence in what would result.[62]

Any ideas that Kingsley now had of himself as an author must have been confirmed by the way his literary career was going. Published in England and America and on the Continent, it seemed that he had only to write in order to keep himself financially secure. There was, nevertheless, a doubt in his mind whether his future was secure, possibly even whether he could keep up his literary successes. Whatever the reason, he wrote to Charles saying he had decided to read for the Bar. Charles was delighted and considered himself negligent for not having thought of the idea himself.[63] Certainly, it offered Henry a choice of position with the solicitor-general or even a practice itself. With Charles's approval, then, Kingsley applied for admission to the Inner Temple and was accepted on a warrant of admission dated 5 December 1862. He was required to commit himself to a three-year course and provide a bond of sufficient security "to discharge his duties to the House".[64]

The rooms in Henrietta Street, adorned as they were with many portraits of Sims Reeves (the brother of the landlady) in his operatic roles,[65] hardly met the new circumstances, and Henry became resident at 5 Priory Grove.[66] His study for the Bar promised well, but he was still preoccupied with writing. In a letter to Macmillan, he wrote that he would dine at the "United University Club" but thought he "*ought* to dine at the Temple".[67] He then referred to his new novel, *The Hillyars and the Burtons,* and its forthcoming publication in *Macmillan's Magazine.* He could allow himself to be pleased – it was to run as a serial from November 1863 until April 1865.

For Kingsley, 1863 was a good year. He was reading Law; his new story had been accepted; and *Austin Elliot,* a two-volume novel, in addition to being published by Macmillan, had also been accepted by Ticknor and Fields. The narrative revolves around two characters Austin Elliot and the girl he loves, Eleanor Hilton, who strives to return Austin's love while concealing the existence of her ne'er-do-well brother. Locations in North Wales and north-west Scotland give particularity and colour to the work and reveal Kingsley's love of scenery. The story, essentially romantic, seems to emphasize duty and honour as the mainsprings of human action, as, for instance, when a duel kills Elliot's best friend, Lord Charles Barty, while he is trying to protect his own name and Austin Elliot's life. To a modern reader, the actions and behaviour of the characters seem at times unreal, although parliamentary scenes, prison details, and the plight of the inhabitants of Ronaldsay are quite well handled, as is Kingsley's use of a dog in an important part of the action.

Apart from copies for newspapers and magazines sent on 25 May, the only copies of *Austin Elliot* given away were to the Cambridge University Library, the Edinburgh Advocates Library, the Stationers Hall, and to Mrs Charles Kingsley.[68] Henry had persuaded Charles to write novels again, to "increase his fortune". Writing to Macmillan of Charles he said, "I am glad that he has got out of the absurd idea that it was *infra dig* to write novels. . . . A man who has forced his way to the front rank by literature must not throw literature overboard."[69] Certainly times had changed when Henry could take it on himself to advise Charles; the usual state of affairs was being reversed. "I shall be glad enough of some more money if quite convenient," Henry wrote to Macmillan, "for I can get five percent from a safe man. The offer was made to me yesterday by a relative. Of course you can't guess who. This comes of getting appointed a etc. etc. *Don't say a word.* Do drop me a line, I see you have announced a third edition of *Austin Elliot*, but by my calculations you have *four* in hand."[70] To end the year on an even more satisfactory note, Kingsley offered Macmillan a biography of Thackeray, who had died suddenly, to be done lovingly "and gracefully through the characters in the man's books", showing how Thackeray "came to be loved through the people he created".[71] His offer was accepted, although a biography as such never appeared, only an obituary in February 1864.

Kingsley's period of re-establishment on his return from Australia was now over. He was busy. If not wealthy, he was relatively independent and seemed at last to have found his way. He was a successful novelist even if not a great one, and he was preparing to fit himself for a second and more secure career in law. Additionally he had discharged his duty to his parents and had, by his writings, converted his years of non-achievement into recognizable literary profit. He had come a long way, and from what he could see, the auguries for the future were good. However, the criticism of *Austin Elliot* in the *Saturday Review* was admonitory and relevant — the book interested and amused, but unconnected descriptions tended to occur in the story like "purple patches"; and the many descriptions tended to sacrifice plot, overriding it altogether. His treatment of plot and description in *Geoffry Hamlyn* and *Ravenshoe* had previously drawn adverse comments. He would have done well to have heeded the remarks.

The following series of photographs include watercolours made by Henry Kingsley in Australia and held by the Mitchell Library, Sydney. The captions for these are the endorsements taken from the back of the paintings.

"Buninyong. Near Ballarat. You are looking, end on, at the loftiest tip of a great volcanic crater; which on the other side has burst down, and overflowed the alluvial diggings of Ballarat with two distinct bands of lava (?) (blue stone, sometimes taking a crystallized basaltic form, as at the cascades of Lal Lal, not far from here). These bands of basalt are the curse of the miners. Two miles beyond this hill I found sapphires. The height of the peak above the meadows is 1200 feet. And the plan of the hill is this [omitted]."

"Mount Cole (Tuckerimbud) and beyond Lanengeryn. A winter Sunday evening. Between you and the spurs of the nearest mountain almost the richest shallow diggings ever discovered those of the Fiery Creek, which at one time supported a population of 40,000. When this was daubed a solitary desert."

"*The Summit of the Mistibithwong*, granite (auriferous) noticeable for being *nearly* at the Southern level of the pine (araucaria?). The ill indicated forest below you extends for over a hundred miles without a break. Through it lies the track of Hovell and Hume the discoverers of Port Phillip from the Land Side." (A pencilled notation reads: "The lower Mitta Mitta about 4000 feet high.")

"*The King River*. It rises on Mt. Buffalo and is snow fed, never failing in the dryest summer. The ghosts of fern fronds in the foreground I used to believe were those of the *Dicksonia Antartica* at its furthest point East. (The 'King', I should tell you is a river which joins the Ovens, and so the Murray.) But Mueller seems to be certain that even the Dicksonia never crosses the dividing range, and so I am wrong."

"Emu Creek in the Portland Bay District. Self on beloved thoroughbred Mazzaroni. Wedge tailed Eagle following me, and lighting on tree after tree."

"The look into Gipps land from the south. The highest Alp to the right is I believe Kosciusko."

"Ben Nevis, Eastern Pyrenees, Australia."

"The dear old station. I will give no description lest I grow sentimental."

"*An undiscovered gold gully*. The short vista before you with the light through the trees beyond, consists of 1st about 8 to 12 inches of very poor alluvial soil, growing Kennydia prostrata, and many Epacridae. 2d. 2 feet or so of loosish quartz gravel. 3d. of line of *mullock*; or amorphous clay. 4th a band of consolidated gravel, getting coarser, until you come down to the actual boulders, some of them as big as your head, inter mixed with blue clay as fine as soot. 6th and lastly wash dirt, lying on the rock. I cannot describe good and unmistakeable wash dirt, any more than you can describe to me the difference between Beaune and Chateau Margot. But you can tell it as a rule the instant you have it in your hand. A perfectly rounded gravel, with plenty of ironstone, and a *clayey* fracture. You may see the gold or you may not. In some stuff I have seen, going eleven ounces to the load, the gold was so coated with the clay that you could see not a sign of it. I fear that I bore you."

Langi Willi. The structure to the right is of the 1850s; that on the left is an addition.

The doorway to the right is the entrance to the room where Henry Kingsley slept and worked at Langi Willi.

Henry Kingsley's cottage at Eversley.

The Kingsley house at Wargrave, 1975.

The Kingsleys' Edinburgh home at Morningside, 1975.

The Kingsley home at 29 Fortess Terrace, Kentish Town.

The Cuckfield home, Sussex.

Henry Kingsley's grave, Cuckfield Churchyard.

13
Wargrave

Kingsley's views on the novel are given in his 1863 article "A Word of Remonstrance with Some Novelists", and it is relevant to his claim that he wrote an "objective novel", to the place of values in his work,[1] and to the function of the novel as he saw it. It is apparent that for all his contemplation of life and death he had not glimpsed the extent to which he could use the novel to explore what in society, or in an individual, motivated human action. His stance in the article, because of the constraints operating on him, was that of a writer of romances intended to instruct. The frequent lapses into recollection and humour in his work show to what extent he found such writing demanding. His guide was Scott, his ideal Thackeray, and his exemplum Hogarth. Apart from obvious failings, many of the inconsistencies in his work seem to have been caused as much by a limited vision of himself as a writer as by haste in writing:

> We were wont to set store on immortal Will and Sir Walter, and call their art true art, and boast how they had enlightened and bettered the world. How much health and happiness will redound to society through this modern treatment of sin is a very dubious question. For a time our rage after criminal heroines owned certain bounds. It began with a frenzy for supercilious or violent damsels, rampagious young women whose waywardness and perversity, that is their selfishness, folly and slightly-veiled coarseness, came to be harped upon as their chief attractions. We have long passed these respectable bounds. Falseness, dishonesty, murder even, are rapidly claiming our most intense sympathies.... Decidedly the latest, most enticing, engrossing, breathlessly delightful heroine, is she who is in some form connected with the crime of bigamy. I beg to propose, if this style of novel continues in fashion, that the scene be removed to the more appropriate locality of the Mormons' city. By this means a great deal of invention, some improbability, and a few moral and religious scruples may be saved.... I do not protest against the introduction of wickedness into art, living as we do in a wicked world. I believe "terror and pity purge the human heart," but let wickedness be painted as William Hogarth painted it.... Do not let crime or its penalty be the crucible which converts our dross into gold.... I humbly pray our good writers, moralists, satirists,

humourists, by precept and example, ... to exorcise this evil possession of our literature, that we may not have the sorrow and shame of knowing [that] the reign of good Queen Victoria ... will be identified in after generations with the reign of female criminals in English literature.[2]

Kingsley's concern at the changing content of the novel is similar to one made in the August 1860 issue of *Fraser's Magazine,* when the author of the article appealed for some of the "genial *humour* of bygone days" and noted the changes that had been taking place: "Dickens has allowed mannerism to usurp the place of that quality which immortalised Sam Weller; Thackeray's humour is keen and ironical; but the dry humour of Sir Walter Scott, and the graceful, playful *fun* of Miss Austen, Miss Ferrier, or Theodora Hook, have almost disappeared.... when our pity and terror had been qualified, it was not displeasing to find something to excite our mirth.... There is no lack of power, thought, or pathos in the works of Mr. Henry Kingsley, or of the author of *Adam Bede*; but these qualities are relieved by the most genuine and unmistakeable humour."[3]

Both Kingsley and the author of the *Fraser's Magazine* article were commenting on the changing literary scene. But this was not all that was changing. Kingsley recognized to some extent when writing *Geoffry Hamlyn* that he was out of touch with what was happening in Victorian England, as is shown by Geoffry Hamlyn's observations on his return from Australia. In spring 1866 Kingsley commented to Macmillan, "When men have been away for a long time together from civilisation, they make frantic efforts to show that they have kept pace with European thought. The author of *Geoffry Hamlyn* was such a man."[4] Macmillan, too, recognized that circumstances were changing. Competition, he observed in a letter to Kingsley, was not so intense when *Geoffry Hamlyn* and *Ravenshoe* were first published compared with the position in 1866, when libraries and railway stalls could choose from a supply of books that outstripped demand.[5] Hence, while Kingsley's observations on society and the novel were perceptive if viewed from an early Victorian standpoint, his understanding of what was happening and what it would mean to him was inadequate. During his last years he saw this to be so when he referred to his unpopularity with the reading public.

Early in 1864 Henry Campbell stayed with Kingsley and acted as an amanuensis while Kingsley worked on his obituary of Thackeray.[6] Campbell took the finished article to Macmillan personally when it was written, and Kingsley, in the accompanying letter of introduction, told Macmillan that he had started work on a new book of adventure tales, which were ultimately published five years later by Macmillan as *Tales of Old Travel*. As it happened, Kingsley's article on Thackeray was cut by David Masson, the editor of *Macmillan's Magazine,* so that Masson himself could add a tribute.[7] To this Kingsley objected and wrote Macmillan accordingly, at the same time requesting that the matter be not taken further: "I will quietly fight my own battle. Therefore there is no necessity for you to say *one word.*"[8]

On 2 July 1864 Kingsley was nominated for membership of the Garrick Club by E. S. Dallas and George Russell, while C. W. Shirley Brooks and Tom Taylor supported his admission.[9] George Russell later wrote of Kingsley's "insight and sympathy" in *Sketches and Snapshots*,[10] and of his intimate knowledge of Chelsea and its people in *Collection and Recollections*.[11]

Seventeen days later Kingsley married Sarah Maria Kingsley Hazelwood, of 7 Gloucester Terrace. Henry's brother Charles officiated at the ceremony, which took place in St Mary's, West Brompton, the witnesses being E. G. Graham, Ann Hazelwood, and Maria Louisa Gunning.[12] Gerald Blunt, rector of St Luke's Church, Chelsea, recorded the event in his diary: "July 19. Wedding of Mr. Henry Kingsley and Miss Haselwood [sic] (who had been, for a time, our governess) at St. Mary's Brompton. Wedding breakfast at the Rectory. Mr. and Mrs. Charles Kingsley, Dr. Kingsley, and about thirty friends. Croquet in the afternoon."[13] A wedding photograph shows Kingsley in morning dress, clean shaven, carrying a top hat, and standing to the left of his wife who is seated. Sarah, with a somewhat angular face, long, dark, wavy hair parted in the middle, sits with hands folded on a voluminous skirt spread out to her sides and front.[14]

If S. M. Ellis was correct, the description of Miss Lee, the governess in *Silcote of Silcotes,* was a portrait of Sarah, whom Kingsley apparently saw as "beautiful, attractive, and boisterous".[15] Sarah may well have been. She was, in her own way, independent and forthright; in October 1869, when discussing "The Rights of Women", she declared, "I have visited amongst the poor of London and of a country town and village for the last ten years, but I cannot in any way, much as I liked my work, feel that it has done me the smallest good."[16] Being as blunt as this, she may well have been the Miss Lee who "would have marched up coolly to the finest knot of dandies in Europe, and asked one of them to call her a cab; and have driven off in it, with a cold bow of thanks".[17] In S. M. Ellis's opinion, Kingsley's marriage was "unwise".[18] He had in mind the worries that ensued, which he believed contributed to Henry's literary decline. Michael Sadleir noted that a Wargrave contemporary remembered the Henry Kingsleys settling there and attending church on Sundays. " 'Nobody liked them,' she said, 'though why I could not clearly understand. I think the impression was that there was something queer about him. They used to sit in front of me in church. Both were small and insignificant, and the man had unhappy eyes.' "[19]

A brief review of the circumstances of the marriage gives some insight into the event itself and Kingsley's attitude to it. On the surface it seems to have been unexpected. If he were going to live at Wargrave, there seems little advantage in Kingsley's having joined the Garrick Club just before leaving London. On the other hand, having previously lived at Wargrave, he might have thought membership could be a convenience when in London, or even, possibly, for appearance's sake. That he wanted to have matters arranged before he was married is another

Henry and Sarah Maria Kingsley Hazelwood at the time of their marriage, 1864. Reprinted from S.M. Ellis, *Henry Kingsley 1830-1876*.

possibility arising from a letter of Maurice Kingsley's to Laurence Hutton, written from New Rochelle, New York, on 14 November 1894:

> Mrs. Henry Kingsley – *the only one* – was Miss Sarah Hazelwood, daughter of Mrs. Hazelwood of Chelsea, a widow at the time I first knew of her, and a first or second cousin of my grand-father's – I

heard of her as a most peculiar person who was never allowed to darken the door of Chelsea rectory.

On my uncle's rise to fame the old lady threw her very willing daughter at his head, who then assumed the name of Sarah *Kingsley* Hazelwood. Off and on in London, when living at Eversley, he saw a good deal of them, and one day came back to tell my father that he was threatened by the old harridan for breach of promise. My father urged him to fight it, but poor Henry was too weak to face the exposure and married. Whether or not Leslie Stephens *[sic]* is correct about my father's performing the marriage ceremony I am uncertain — her word for it cannot be taken — and my recollection is that my father sadly decided to be present *only* at the Service in spite of my mother's protest. I well remember his sorrow before and after for several reasons, and it seems to me I should have remembered that as well.[20]

Another letter, dated 12 November 1894, refers again to Kingsley's marriage: "What I referred to in my last was poor Uncle Henry's marriage — a most sad one, which drove him to drink, despair and death when a young man, and was a bitter bitter source of grief to my father. The 'fury and fool' spoken of in my father's 'Delectable Day,' were Mrs. H.K. and my poor uncle."[21] Maurice's report corresponds with Fanny Kingsley's glosses in her abridged biography of Charles, the "swindler" in the last line of the poem being "Mrs. Hazelwood". The glosses reveal much of the Charles Kingsleys' view of Sarah and her mother as well as tersely summing up Henry's situation, rather than Henry.

Certainly he had been a visitor to the rectory in Old Church Street, Chelsea and had made friends with his father's successor,[22] but what the "exposure" could have involved is unknown. Charles evidently believed there was nothing about which to worry, and his view must be accorded some weight. He, after all, was a chaplain to the queen and prominent in his own right; consequently any charge or accusation made against Henry was a potentially serious matter to Charles. But even he urged Henry to fight. Equally true was that Henry had a reputation as well and apparently feared both the censure of friends and the effects of any publicity on his literary career. As it was, his law career was to lapse with marriage, as its continuance became an impossibility. But that was not the only change that Henry was to encounter. Sarah Hazelwood changed from a "mass of kindliness, vitality and good-humour", to a poor and sickly woman soon after the marriage. Writing to Macmillan, Kingsley said: "My little wife has been very poorly and so so but is much better now."[23] Much depends, of course, on the meaning of the words "has been poorly and so so" and the length of time the Kingsleys had been married. If Sarah was not pregnant before marriage, then Kingsley's fear of embarassment or exposure seems disproportionate to what could have been said to him other than a reference to the number of visits he might have made to the Hazelwoods, and the appearance of courtship which that implied.

Charles, writing to Thomas Hughes, author of *Tom Brown's Schooldays*, in 1857, showed a tolerant attitude to sexual adventures while still expecting the consequences to be faced: "As for women. I suppose the poor lads will 'get their hands into plackets' while the world lasts: but still there is not the shameless seduction there used to be."[24] And earlier, in 1851, he had written to F. D. Maurice, theologian and leading Christian Socialist: "I do not mind a lad's having been a scapegrace about girls, or even having tried to lie himself out of a scrape, if there is any tolerable substratum of tenderness and chivalry to w. one can appeal. The selfish, silent, sly animal is the only one for w. I see nothing but 'jackass's medicine.'"[25] In view of Charles's attitude, therefore, it is unlikely that he would have advised Henry not to give in to Mrs Hazelwood unless he had satisfied himself about the relationship.

There is still the possibility, of course, that if Henry *were* in love with Sarah he might have feared opposition from Charles because the Hazelwoods were poor. This no doubt had happened with the Annesley girl. Then, too, if Henry married, he alone could not be expected to provide a home for his widowed mother; and Charles, moreover, having just returned from Europe with Froude,[26] was not expecting any such development. Apart from those considerations, Charles obviously disliked both the Hazelwoods, mother and daughter.

In the light of the foregoing, some passages of *Silcote of Silcotes* seem almost self-revelatory:

> In short, it was the old story — Monseigneur amused himself. He was short and sharp with her at times, and at times angry, for the poor girl, though not naturally dull, was dull by habit.... At first she submitted to him, and used her every effort to please, from mingled motives of respect, of fear, and of the wish to attract him ... in short ... the poor girl fell desperately in love with him. He wished he had never seen her a hundred times a week. If he ever in his inexorable plans, "contracted an alliance" (he had no idea of your Darby and Joan marriages) he must have, first of all, "connexion." Such a preposterous action as that of marrying Miss Lee meant ruin, retirement to a college living, and a wasted life. It was not to be thought of for an instant.... A wife whose family was without interest was bad enough too; but a wife who was so utterly without knowledge of some of the ways of the world as was Miss Lee, was quite out of the question. [Chap. 19]

After the marriage, Henry and his bride went to the Needles Hotel on the Isle of Wight for their honeymoon, where Charles Dodgson (Lewis Carroll) called on them. His diary recording the visit reads: "Aug: 9. (Tu). As I know a friend of Henry Kingsley's (Tyrwhitt of Christ Church) I thought I would try the experiment of calling on him at the Needles Hotel. I was received in a most friendly fashion by him and his pretty bride (married three weeks ago). They called at the hotel in the afternoon to see photographs."[27] Kingsley became friendly with Dodgson and in September 1864 attended a party at Dodgson's at the Croft Rectory Common Room, Christ Church, Oxford, where among those present were Tennyson, the Reverend R. H. J. Tyrwhitt, Tom Taylor, Macmillan, and Baron Tauchnitz.[28] Another guest present, the

Reverend R. J. Duckworth, wrote later that while visiting Dean Liddell, Kingsley read the manuscript of *Alice in Wonderland* with the greatest delight and urged Mrs Liddell to persuade the author to publish it.[29] Curiously, in 1900 William Tinsley thought it possible Dodgson and Kingsley worked together: "I had a notion, from something I saw in my office one day when Kingsley was there, that he and the author of 'Alice in Wonderland' and 'Through a Looking-Glass' now and then worked together, for Henry Kingsley had a capital sense of fun and true humour, but I may have been wrong."[30]

After the honeymoon, the Kingsleys bought a home in Wargrave, and Kingsley asked Macmillan for an opportunity to make a collection of English prose for the Golden Treasury series. "The little wife and I could do it together perfectly," he wrote. "I am so much happier than I deserve to be, that I am lost in amazement," At the same time he advised Macmillan not to visit Wargrave on a Sunday — the vicar preached badly.[31] Henry's view of the Church, by now, was a liberal view — the Church comprised not just the clergy, but all the faithful — which also explains Kingsley's reference to the "prophetical balderdash" he was hearing when he wrote to Masson about this time seeking an explanation of some Biblical references.[32]

Meanwhile his income seemed assured. By the end of 1865 Tauchnitz had published *Ravenshoe, Austin Elliot, The Recollections of Geoffry Hamlyn,* and *The Hillyars and the Burtons,*[33] and in America, Henry's popularity was rising while Charles's seemed to decline.[34] From Macmillan, Kingsley was receiving prompt settlement for his efforts; on 6 May 1865 he received three hundred pounds "on account of amount due for the first edition of *The Hillyars and the Burtons*",[35] which Ticknor and Fields of Boston were also publishing. Such widespread distribution of his fourth book might have indicated that Kingsley had overcome some of the problems that had attracted unfavourable comment in his earlier books. His control of the narrative compared with the bewildering turns of *Austin Elliot* was indeed better, but he became lost in another maze. The focus of the novel, ostensibly written about the tension between love and duty, was fractured by two other themes, almost unrelated but of equal importance — the reversal in social status of peer and tradesman in a new land, and the lack of logic in human affairs. Any of these three themes, if developed properly, would have given him a powerful work, but haste, as was always to be the case, denied him the chance of revising what he had written. The surviving manuscript of *The Hillyars and the Burtons* shows few revisions. That Kingsley succeeded at all without revising his work is in a way an indication of his natural ability.

Despite much good writing in *The Hillyars and the Burtons,* it would be hard to argue that it succeeds other than as a novel sensitive to certain Australian conditions of the mid-nineteenth century. Social reversals, gold-mining disasters, inheritances, and colonial politics, as well as the strangeness of the Australian landscape, are treated with reasonable competence. In one respect Kingsley's shortcomings foreshadowed the problem of the Anglo-Australian novel — the unifying of incident and setting in two countries, ten thousand miles apart. Some of his problems lay in the need to interpret the new land and its people to English readers, the most noteworthy examples of this being Gerty's supposedly "Australian" speech after her arrival in England, and the inclusion of Australian topographical detail to keep the reader oriented. Critics, however, were not persuaded that Kingsley's work had improved and almost unanimously doubted the accuracy of his preface that the theme of the book was love and duty.

Ignoring the criticism, Kingsley worked on and had three articles on Australian explorers accepted by *Macmillan's Magazine*. They dealt with Charles Sturt and Edward John Eyre,[36] and the article on Eyre was to involve Kingsley in public controversy before the year ended.

Domestically, Kingsley had problems. Sarah had been poorly during May but recovered sufficiently by July for Henry "to actually begin to believe in the possibility of a cherub", though as he wrote to Macmillan,[37] he saw "nothing of its appearance yet". Apart from any literary considerations, Macmillan's friendship had continued just as strongly after Henry's marriage, and he had sought to develop it by having the Kingsleys come to stay. Sarah's health, however, prevented them from accepting the invitation.[38]

About this time, after a year of marriage, a note of apprehension began to appear in Kingsley's letters about his financial position. He had been hoping that a new edition of *Austin Elliot* would have been published by June to help with the "fearful expenses of pulling a sick wife about the country, literally to save her life . . . [and the expense of] setting up a new house, [which] have superinduced an alarming financial crisis, and left me without any money at all. I suppose that one's first year is always a squeezer, but to be forced into extravagance by the Doctors is too hard. However, I can see my way quite clear if I can tide over Christmas".[39]

Macmillan in a helpful gesture sent Kingsley a story told by Mrs Carlyle, "a plain, simple story with quiet but interesting plot, [with] neither squalor nor vice nor crime". It would, said Macmillan, make a charming one-volume novel, but he advised Kingsley to "play not a bit of the fool. Quiet pathos and humour."[40] Kingsley put aside another story, "Aunt Mary",[41] and started the new novel, *Leighton Court*.[42] He agreed to Macmillan's request, but he said he would welcome any suggestions, particularly any from Dinah Maria Mulock, who on 29 April 1865 had married Macmillan's partner, G. L. Craik.[43]

With work continuing slowly on the adventure tales, Kingsley still managed by autumn 1865 to finish *Leighton Court* after, as he said, "much trouble, with no tragedy and no nonsense". Macmillan was just back from Scotland, and Kingsley, when writing to him about *Leighton Court*, expressed his own love of the Scottish countryside: "The whole of that Peebles, Selkirk, Roxburgh, and Dumfries country is sacred, every inch of it. Every name thereabouts is a dear old friend. Tweed, Yarrow, Ettrick, Teviot on one side of the hills, and Annan and Megget on the other: and up and on by the hillsides into Lanark, past Durisdeer, on to Wanlock and Cairn Table the stronghold of the Covenanters. Man! Man! every step is a verse of poetry."[44] His knowledge of the areas came from other days. In August 1862, Charles, writing to his mother from Dunkeld, had asked her to tell Henry that all that Henry had said of the grandeur of the Tay he quite agreed with: "I never saw such a river, I am sorry to say there are very few salmon up."[45] But for Henry, no trips to Scotland were in view.

Meanwhile, events were happening overseas which were to involve Kingsley. In October 1865 an angry crowd of blacks gathered outside the court-house in Morant Bay, Jamaica. Governor Edward John Eyre, well known and respected as an explorer in Australia, was accused of ruthlessness in his handling of the situation when it became known that "586 natives had been killed or executed, 600 (including women) had been flogged, and over 1000 houses had been destroyed".[46] Kingsley, because he had praised Eyre's work as protector of Aborigines on the lower Murray River, Australia, was quoted in the leading article of *The Times* on 29 November 1865, and this led to a debate between him and William Bakewell in the columns of *The Times*.[47] Kingsley's position was clear — he was not "defending Governor Eyre, he was exalting Edward Eyre, the Australian explorer".[48] In an effort to be just, he defended the "Jamaica Committee's right to bring proceedings against Eyre", although questioning their use of the term *murder*, and rejected the Eyre Defence Committee's term *disgraceful* when it was used to describe proceedings in which Thomas Hughes and J. M. Ludlow were involved.

William Bakewell (1817–70), Kingsley's opponent, was born in Staffordshire, England, and emigrated to South Australia in 1839, becoming afterwards crown solicitor of the colony.[49] His views, consequently, could be expected to carry considerable weight. On Kingsley's side the burden of his argument was simply, as he wrote in "The Two Cadets", "I greatly fear that some animals by no means dumb had been shot down in those parts." (chap. 1). For Kingsley, "those parts" meant the Glenelg River area with the adjacent portions of Victoria and South Australia. Bakewell, on the other hand, claimed in respect of the Aborigines that no war of extermination had taken place in South Australia and that Kingsley's charges were "pure and unmitigated fiction".

To some extent both Kingsley and Bakewell were right. Killings occurred on each side, and Eyre subsequently performed a magnificent job with the Aborigines between 1841 and 1844, when he won their confidence. As a result, settlement spread to the eastern areas of South Australia, and Aborigines "whose ferocity a few years before had crushed all enterprise in these regions were often employed as shepherds and storekeepers". Additionally, Eyre's influence penetrated to the Darling River, "where he was regarded as a guardian hero by the natives". At one stage, he told the imperial government that if the Aborigines of the lower Murray were deprived of "the protection and periodical presents they received" they would become exasperated and more dangerous than ever.[50] The problem of Aborigines and whites was complex and difficult, even if an Address in Reply in the House of Commons to King William IV in 1834 had prayed His Majesty "to take such steps as will secure a kindly treatment of the natives and the spread of civilisation among them".[51]

Kingsley's position on the treatment of Aborigines had been made clear two years before the debate. In June 1863 he wrote: "The old work was going on – driving sheep to new pastures, building outlying huts, butchering blacks, and all the rest of it. And, as in old times, no one to blame, my dear sir, except the blacks themselves! This, however, is an ugly subject. If people choose to reckon on the blindness of God, it is no business of a mere reviewer."[52] Earlier in 1863 he had pointed out that after Sturt's discovery of Aborigines on the River Glenelg there remained only a further fifteen years for Aboriginal occupation, after which the Aborigines' time would have come. "They are cumbering land which will, some of it, carry a sheep to four acres. They will have to be protected. Only fair play, this time, gentlemen; and let us have no arsenic dampers."[53]

Although Kingsley was a member of the Eyre Defence Committee, more was at stake for him personally than Eyre's reputation. Once Bakewell attacked him, his credibility as a reviewer of Australian affairs was threatened. Fortunately his facts were well documented and his arguments concise. With his final letter on 7 December 1865 Kingsley had the last word. Bakewell did not reply. A blow had been struck for Eyre – and Kingsley.

A letter by Eyre to Charles Kingsley on 9 June 1868 gives an idea of the intensity of the Eyre debate:

> Pray accept my best thanks for your kind, warmhearted note of the 4th June and for your congratulations upon the termination of the persistent and harping persecutions to which I have been subjected for so long a period.
>
> It is most gratifying to me to know that your good opinion and good wishes remain unchanged from what they were when I enjoyed your prompt and generous support at Southampton. No doubt the trial I have had to encounter is one which must be felt deeply by any Public man and especially so when the sudden stoppage of the career of a life time and the loss of those results which such a career entitled me to expect necessarily affect most seriously the position and prospects of those most dear to me. With you however I feel that what is ordained by the All Wise must be for the best and right and I hope and pray that I may learn from the ordeal and lessons it was intended to teach. Nor has the trial been one without much to alleviate it. But for it I should not have experienced practically how much of kindness and genuine warmhearted sympathy there is in the world for anyone who is thought to be suffering from wrong and injustice: nor should I have made the many friends, yourself amongst the most valued, if you will allow me to say so, which the circumstances I have been placed in have raised up for me, and who will I trust still be retained when these circumstances have long passed away.

Mrs. Eyre joins me in best thanks to you and in the earnest hope that we may again have the pleasure of meeting you some future day.

Stimulating as it was to be embroiled in national matters while he was holidaying at Hastings,[54] Kingsley was worried about the time involved, however, he still persisted. Writing to Macmillan generally about his clash of opinion with Bakewell, he expressed tersely his view of Australian squatters returned to settle in England: "If those short-sighted idiots, who have made fortunes on soil drenched with the blood of the natives, and have come home here and turned saint, attack me I will make hay of the whole lot. I am not going to be civil much longer. 'The Historian of Australia' as they call me in Melbourne comes of a fighting family."[55] This view of the land, the Aborigines, and the Australian squatter settled in England would also have embraced Kingsley's personal view of the events in *Geoffry Hamlyn*, in which, after emigrating to make fortunes in Australia that could not be made at home, the emigrants returned to England. Kingsley's position on this question, therefore, must modify a type of criticism seemingly applied to him personally and based solely on some of the attitudes evident in *Geoffry Hamlyn* — for example "To Kingsley the land is still waiting for history to begin, and the only history he can conceive is the history of battle. The land itself is not part of the drama, and he has no sense of the struggle which was required to make real the dreams of the settlers, nor of the change which the struggle would make to these dreams."[56] What Kingsley wrote did not represent his personal beliefs — a point he makes in *Geoffry Hamlyn* where Kingsley, rather than Hamlyn, speaks: "The narrative which I am now writing is neither more nor less than an account of what befel certain of my acquaintances" (chap. 22). Another personal statement to this effect appears in a footnote in *Ravenshoe*: "Once for all, let me call every honest reader to witness, that, unless I speak in the first person, I am not bound to the opinions of any one of the characters in this book. I have merely made people speak, I think, as they would have spoken. Even in a story, consisting so entirely of incident as this, I feel it necessary to say so much, for no kind of unfairness is so common as that of identifying the opinions of a story-teller with those of his *dramatis personae*" (chap. 44).

With the events of 1865 behind him, Kingsley started work early in 1866 on *Silcote of Silcotes,* in which he planned to embody "Aunt Mary". Following the precedent of *Leighton Court,* he intended to omit humour and fun, except for what he termed dry humour, but considered being dull an "utter mistake".[57] At this stage *Tales of Old Travel* was still in hand,[58] and *Leighton Court* was awaiting publication.[59]

Kingsley, when establishing himself at Wargrave, had hoped to let the house in summer and as a result involved himself in considerable expense. When explaining this to Macmillan, he avoided mentioning expenses incurred by Sarah's illnesses and demonstrated, rather, that his expectations were well based and his financial embarrassment temporary. He claimed his assets exceeded his liabilities by three hundred pounds, that a further twelve hundred pounds was due to him at his mother's death and five hundred pounds, similarly, from his aunt, Mrs James Wills. What he needed, therefore, was prompt payment for his writing during the year. Kingsley's appeal to Macmillan reflected a slight change in his relationship with the company. After Craik joined Macmillan's, financial dealings with Kingsley, although friendly, became more formal than they had been previously.[60]

Macmillan, much concerned at Kingsley's obvious plight, responded by trying to expedite the printing of *Leighton Court* and wanted it to go to *Fraser's Magazine,* or *Cornhill,* if earlier publication could help. As it was, Macmillan paid two hundred and seventy five pounds into Child's Bank to meet Henry's current plight, the money representing a two hundred pounds balance owing from *Leighton Court* and seventy five pounds for a small reprint of *Austin Elliot.* This payment made a total of five hundred pounds for *Leighton Court,* which Macmillan intended to recover from a two-volume edition when published and a one-volume, cheaper, edition scheduled for even later publication. One of the book's difficulties lay in its being smaller in size than that wanted for libraries, hence a first edition of only 1,250 copies was planned. But this was not the only problem affecting Kingsley's potential income. Many other writers had started since *Geoffry Hamlyn* and *Ravenshoe* had been published, and a greater volume of fiction than the reading public really demanded was now available. In fact, Macmillan at this stage had not got back his outlay on *The Hillyars and the Burtons.* The position was worrying enough for Macmillan to want a talk with Kingsley about the possibility of writing adventure books between novels to keep the "pot boiling".[61] But if this were not enough, Sarah became ill again, troubled by a cough,[62] and Henry's work was interrupted.

Leighton Court was praised by the *Saturday Review* for being free of "those senseless oddities and unmeaning freaks which in his last two novels struck everybody as being so wonderfully childish and so offensive". This "little comedy of high life in the country, though sufficiently slight", was considered by the paper to be "one of the most agreeable things that Mr. Henry Kingsley has written". On the other hand, the *Athenaeum* found the novel had a "want of harmony between the tone and position, culture and conduct of the principal actors". Small wonder that Kingsley felt, at times, beset by the demands of bills, critics, and home. For a modern reader the tale is interesting but scarcely credible. Switched identities and the reversal of a love affair are the main narrative devices used in the story, with its theme of "love will out", while the descriptions of the Devon countryside stand out as one of the book's strengths.

Shortly after this, Macmillan sent Kingsley proofs of a new work on African exploration by Samuel White Baker,[63] with whom Kingsley had at one stage discussed the "alleged bifurcation of the Zambesi and the Congo" and its relationship to the Nile.[64] As a result of Macmillan's action, Kingsley wrote three reviews, despite the trouble involved in checking the topographical detail in the Baker proofs: "I can't make out where the water-shed is. . . . Send me Speke's map and some more proofs if poss[ible]."[65] A similar feel for detail caused Kingsley to go to France with his wife in July 1866 to see "large masses of French troops manoeuvering" at Chalons.[66] From this trip came a travel article for *Macmillan's Magazine*, "A Cheap Tour near Home," as well as the information on troop movements he claimed was needed for *Silcote of Silcotes*.

Before leaving for France, Kingsley had promised to send Macmillan the completed *Tales of Old Travel*. He was troubled about his novel and, almost as if justifying his approach to writing, asserted: "I want to tell about good things and good people without being 'goody'. I want to be tragical without Braddon and Collins bigamy and poisoning. I want to write a story which shall be interesting and exciting and to make everyone the better for having read it."[67] By his direct reference to the two sensation novelists, M. E. Braddon and W. Wilkie Collins, he was trying to reassure Macmillan that his work would enlighten and better the world. He also needed money. Macmillan, aware of his personal difficulties, sent Kingsley on 13 July a cheque for forty pounds, counselling prudence in monetary affairs while assuring Henry that both he and Craik would do what they could. But, he added, they at Macmillan's also needed to be prudent.[68] Kingsley, still pressed for money, wrote to Craik after reaching France and asked him to advertise the Wargrave house for rent while he was abroad.[69]

The Kingsleys then went on with their trip. In Normandy, their route passed through Cherbourg to Saint-Lo and Caen, then westwards to Coutances,[70] from where he wrote to Craik, thence to Avranches and Saint-Malo by way of Mont-Saint-Michel.[71] He returned to England, as he told Macmillan, "full of new health, purpose and energy", but he still had to seek an extension of time for *Silcote of Silcotes*.[72] In early September Kingsley returned to Normandy after visiting his mother in Bristol,[73] undoubtedly seeking more "colour" but possibly to settle details for parts of *Austin Elliot* to be included in *Scenes de la Vie Aristocratique en Angleterre et en Russie*.[74] He completed a second article of "A Cheap Tour near Home" on his return and sent it to Macmillan in December. With this he sent the monthly instalment of *Silcote of Silcotes*, serial publication of which had begun in July, but it is evident from his letters that he was having trouble writing it. He wanted to avoid the slanginess of *Ravenshoe* and be "thoughtful", and he was troubled about the "dreary purism" of the early parts, which he thought dull.

Kingsley was frank in sharing his political sympathies with Macmillan and showed concern for the beginnings of the political change he felt inevitable. In July 1866, after disturbances in Hyde Park, he wrote:

> We want no flag and banner demonstrations in favour of reform; we *must* have it and we *will* have it: but it will not be helped by pot-

house processions. . . . I'd go for Universal Suffrage in Scotland or America but the uneducated swarming masses of England are not fit for it. . . . We have tried Aristocracy and made a mess of it. I suppose we must try Democracy now, God help us, and lose our dearly purchased freedom. To say that the Aristocracy have made a mess of it, and so that we must have Democracy, to say that the class which could have done it but wouldn't should give place to the class which would do it but can't is to say that there is no path between the Devil and the Deep Blue Sea. However it will be so. I and others are resigned.[75]

Abroad he favoured a united Germany and the possession of the Rhine frontier by France.[76] But despite his interest, forays into politics had to be limited, for writing was a constant preoccupation. He joined the London Library on 12 November to get the fifteen volumes which were allowed to borrowers[77] – his *Adventure* tales had been started almost three years earlier and were still being written.

Despite a bronchial condition which kept him at home, Kingsley worked hard revising the manuscripts he had on hand of *Silcote of Silcotes*.[78] Progress, however, was slow, largely because of the care he had to take at the same time with another work, *Mademoiselle Mathilde*, which he was writing for the *Gentleman's Magazine*. By January 1867 his financial affairs were so critical he had to sell the copyright of five books to Macmillan's. Craik told Kingsley on 14 January the copyrights concerned were valued at one hundred and twenty five pounds and the plates eighty eight pounds. He nevertheless paid Kingsley's price of three hundred and fifty pounds, from which he deducted three hundred and twenty pounds owing to Macmillan, leaving a thirty pound balance for Kingsley. Undoubtedly Macmillan and Craik were generous beyond the limits of friendship, for Craik admitted that he could not see how three hundred and fifty pounds could be made out of the books involved – *Geoffry Hamlyn, Ravenshoe, Austin Elliot, The Hillyars and the Burtons,* and *Leighton Court.* Then, as if this were not enough, Craik advanced a further two hundred and twenty pounds, which, with the thirty pounds just mentioned plus another fifty five pounds for work on hand, resulted in a cheque for three hundred and five pounds being forwarded to Kingsley.[79] As a result Kingsley felt obliged to sell the copyright of *Silcote of Silcotes* later in the year to Macmillan: "In order that if it don't go off like smoke you may recuperate out of it in a six shilling edition, without giving me anything."[80] It was the least he could do in view of the help he had received. He had had his debts remitted and was being paid in advance for his novel; in effect his publishers were accepting responsibility for the financial success or failure of his writing.

When *Silcote of Silcotes* was published, both Macmillan and Craik must have begun to doubt their judgement, much as they liked Henry personally. The faults of the work, according to both the *Saturday Review* and the *Athenaeum,* lay in the inappropriateness of the dialogue given the characters. If the *Saturday Review* detected a lack of characterization in the pursuit of sensationalism, it also found "a breach of the sensational canon" in the absence of a clearly structured plot. On the other hand, the *Athenaeum* found many of Kingsley's landscapes excellent, as was his portrayal of children; but it found a lack of consistency in characterization. What then *was* the appeal of Kingsley's work that made publishers persist with him and some critics forecast that his work would outlive that of Charles? The answer lay in an American review of 1901:

> Coincidence jostles coincidence... but you forget all this in the reading, you are led from scene to scene with no consciousness of unreality; you admire or laugh or weep under the spell of an enchanter who is never base in suggestion or mean in conception. He did not shrink from reality... but he never grovelled in the sensationalism of the stories. He was a sentimentalist, no doubt, but in the manner of Balzac and Thackeray, not of Sterne or Pierre Louys.... In some respects Henry Kingsley was one of the most faulty writers of eminence who ever lived... but even in this respect he sinned in good company, and need crave no absolution at the hands of his lovers.[81]

In short, readers felt they encountered the good and the bad in life, but enjoyed their reading while they did. As *Fraser's Magazine* had observed in 1860, Kingsley did not lack the "genial humour of bygone days" and had "power, thought and pathos. His was his own art — as in Hogarth, not Eliot, who he said was "the *model*, but we must leave her alone in her glory".

In April 1867 serialization of *Mademoiselle Mathilde* began in the *Gentleman's Magazine,* whose proprietors, Bradbury, Evans & Co., had commissioned Kingsley to write for them. The opening instalment had given Kingsley much trouble, mainly because Walford, the editor, had made clear to Kingsley that he was writing for a special class of reader who would not be interested in a colonial tale.[82] On 12 March Kingsley had written to Walford seeking more time. He was short of the required length and had to ask what constituted short copy which could be made up in April.[83] Walford apparently co-operated, for no problems with the magazine developed and the original contract was extended from nine monthly instalments to fourteen[84] at Kingsley's suggestion.[85]

In *Mademoise Mathilde* Kingsley saw one of the causes of the French Revolution as the failure of the aristocracy to recognize that the "age of swords" had passed and that the "age of gunpowder, which equalises the physical power of man" had arrived (chap. 5). Another view was repeatedly stated by Mathilde's father, D'Isigny: "The great cause which has led to these illimitable troubles, now threatening to become incalculable disasters in France, has been a want of confidence between classes" (chap. 2).

D'Isigny, a French nobleman residing in England, foreshadows the fate of his daughter, Mathilde, early in the book when he credits her with the ability to die without betraying names. This is what happens when Mathilde takes the place of her married sister in France and is executed by French revolutionaries. D'Isigny lives to see that it was his romantic concept of heroism and his wife's ill-advised entanglement in French royalist affairs that precipitated Mathilde's arrest and death.

The priest of the story, Father Martin, is drawn in such a way that his characterization offers some grounds for believing that Kingsley did not share his brother Charles's implacable opposition to Roman Catholicism. In a footnote (chap. 23), he expresses the hope that John Henry Newman would not disagree that all higher forms of religion were based on "humble inquiry of God for something more than He had revealed". Martin certainly appears humble and heroic and counterbalances the vacillating D'Isigny, who is manipulative and foolhardy.

Kingsley varies his authorial stance from omniscient to personal narrator at times, and his interpolations bring the reader back swiftly from the illusory world of adventure and romance to an England contemporaneous with the author. Despite the sustained interest, generally well-structured narrative, and acceptable characterization, the romantic values espoused of heroic self-sacrifice for family seem hardly justified. Mathilde's death seems caused mainly by her parents' folly. As in *Ravenshoe,* the question of what constituted a gentleman occurs, and Kingsley defines what he believed – irrespective of parentage. "A gentleman", he wrote, "is a man, sufficiently well educated for the duties he has to perform, and who thinks of the interests of others before he thinks of his own. And, moreover, my gentleman must not be lazy, but must try, with such powers as God has given him, to set an example, and show what a very valuable person a *gentleman* is" (chap. 55). Certainly Kingsley saw Mathilde as a gentlewoman of this type and a Christian in terms of "utter abnegation of self" (chap. 34).

Some idea of the requirements Kingsley had to meet is obtained from a letter he sent to Walford during 1867:

> Mind what you are at p24. It is rather strong meat. I have rewritten part of the paragraph on the opposite sheet, in a milder form. That is to say I have used a milder word for each expression which I have underlined. This is a case in which I must entirely trust to your older and more experienced judgement.
>
> The old fogy mind must take its gruel with a spoon. The slightest indiscretion may be disastrous: and I am a man of strong opinions. It is your place to take the flies out of the butter. They will all be replaced when the thing is published as a whole and we appeal to the general public. Meanwhile, Sylvanus Urban is my master.
>
> It is impossible that we can get into trouble by describing a Catholic priest as a perfect saint. The world is not so narrow as *that.* What I have to look to is Bradbury and Evans cash. . . . let my ignorance stand [in reference to the vestments of the priest]. It will be accounted unto us for Orthodoxy. Possibly you had *better* let it stand: or we shall both be accused of knowing more than the Philistine world consider good for us.[86]

The 1864 debate between Charles Kingsley and John Henry Newman was clearly still recent enough for elements of Roman Catholicism in the work to be considered controversial by some. The least that can be said is that Kingsley's attitude here arose from his awareness of what ought to be written to avoid giving offence and his need to give Bradbury and Evans what they wanted. Kingsley in fact showed in his letter a lively understanding of contemporaneous opinion. The year before, Lord Shaftesbury visited St Alban's Church in Holborn, well known for the ritualistic practices which had been spreading in the Church of England with an increasing use of incense, bells, and vestments; Shaftesbury was most upset at the "theatrical gymnastics". Then, while Kingsley was writing *Mademoiselle Mathilde*, a royal commission recommended that statutory action be taken to restrain the wearing of vestments.[87] Well might Kingsley wish for his ignorance of vestments to "be accounted unto him for orthodoxy". It meant being read or not read — in short, money for his work or nothing.

Despite Kingsley's preoccupation with writing and domestic troubles, Wargrave still provided some pleasant occasions. Anne Thackeray Ritchie lived for a time across the Thames at Henley after her father's death and was a neighbour of the Kingsleys. "I do not remember ever talking very much to Henry Kingsley," she wrote to Clement Shorter, "he was usually hard at work, but we used to go out in boats together, and meet at odd moments in gardens. He was perhaps more emphatic in conversation than I could comfortably respond to, but my feeling of respect and regard for him was very great, and my affectionate admiration warm and sincere." With Leslie Stephen, her brother-in-law, she remembered rowing across to the Kingsley cottage during the summer to meet, among others, another neighbour, Algernon Charles Swinburne, and remembered the Kingsley garden full of flowers and "flaming gladioli", as well as a collection of cocks, hens, rabbits, and tall dogs. Kingsley's favourite, she thought, was a collie which was never sent away when it laid its chin on Kingsley's knee at meal times. Her opinion of Kingsley as kind and chivalrous, she wrote, was not hers alone and was shared by another one of her neighbours as well.[88] Lothian Nicholson, a much younger neighbour, remembered a Kingsley who was captivating. In a letter to *The Times* in 1930, he wrote: "Somewhere about 1866–67 my father took a house on the river at Henley, and while with him in our boat at Wargrave I managed to fall in. I recollect (being about seven or eight years old) being taken to a cottage and put to dry before the kitchen fire, and that Henry Kingsley came and told me the most delightful fairy stories during the process."[89]

Charles Dodgson also visited the cottage during summer 1865, probably on 9 July, for he records in his diary: "Left for Oxley: down to Reading with a Mr. Crofts, wife and two little girls. Having incidentally found out that he was an old friend of Henry Kingsley's I soon made friends with the party."[90] On his return to London, Dodgson called at Macmillan's on 15 July 1865 to write in presentation copies of *Alice in Wonderland* and sent a copy of the book to Kingsley in appreciation of his visit. "The fancy of the whole thing is delicious" Kingsley wrote back Dodgson; "it is like gathering cowslips in springtime."[91] The link between Kingsley and Dodgson evidently continued for some time, for a diary entry made in 1872 reads: "Jan: 10 (W) . . . Called on Henry Kingsley but he was out." Then, too, on publication of *Through the Looking Glass* (1872) Kingsley wrote to Dodgson: "I can say with a clear head and conscience that your new book is the finest thing we have had since *Martin Chuzzlewit* . . . I can only say, in comparing the new *Alice* with the old, 'this is a more excellent song than the other.' It is perfectly splendid, but you have, doubtless, heard that from other quarters. I lunch with Macmillan habitually, and he was in a terrible pickle about not having printed enough copies the other day."[92] An indication of the type of friendship the two men enjoyed can be seen in the light-hearted banter which occurs at "Louis Carroll's" expense in *Valentin*: "If M. Louis Carroll would attend to his duties as a professor, instead of irritating a very high-spirited nation as the French by political poems like that of 'Humpty Dumpty' . . . " (chap. 16).

Kingsley's relationship with Swinburne by all appearances seemed friendly enough. Some of his verse Kingsley described as "simply splendid".[93] He even tried at one stage to persuade Macmillan publish him, to which Macmillan replied that he would be glad to "look at a volume of Swinburne's poems *if he wishes me to do so*. He knows my taste in these matters."[94]

Maurice Kingsley, on the other hand, in a private letter to Laurence Hutton, disclosed a somewhat different state of affairs: "While living at Wargrave, Swinbourne *[sic]* was Mrs. H. K.'s idol — whom her husband loathed; and would, on his appearance, shut himself up or run away to London."[95] One explanation for the discrepancy in the accounts could be that Henry hid any of his private resentments so as to appear a good neighbour and not give offence to an established literary figure. Some dissension between Henry and Sarah could therefore have existed while they were at Wargrave — to become apparent now, as it were, from inside the family. Kingsley's presence in London during the Wargrave years could well have been to escape dissension at home as well as from his money worries, and even, perhaps, from an unrecognized restlessness arising from his childlessness. His "strong opinions", inexpressible at Wargrave, had to find expression elsewhere.

Kingsley's indifference to criticism has already been mentioned. As time passed, however, he changed. What follows not only shows how much criticism he was now reading, but also his reactions when *Silcote of Silcotes* was published in 1867:

> Don't you think that it might be as well to put the last sentence or so of The Pall Mall review into the advertisements of Silcotes? You know best, but it seems to me that such a very pretty compliment should not be lost. If I had had to review Silcotes myself I am not sure that I should have said much else about it. With regard to Miss Jewsbury in the *Athenaeum* I honestly confess, that excepting as regards your interests, I do not care one red cent: Remember her reviews of the "Story of Elizabeth." The literary ability of The Scotsman I really *cannot* rank high with regard to works of fiction and fancy: who *could* trust to a paper which said that the letter-

press of Alices Adventures was pointless balderdash!!! From Hutton [in the *Spectator*] we of course have nothing to expect but cantankerous priggish ill-temper: what Morley [in the *Saturday Review*] will say I cannot think: the book was written to the tune of hints which I got from him myself.... I ... think him very clever.... I see that The Spectator, the week before last, congratulated you on having got rid of me, who by the by had been writing, according to The Pall Mall [Gazette] "a story without a dull page from one end to the other".[96]

In the early half of 1868 Sarah Kingsley had another miscarriage, and Kingsley's hopes of fatherhood were frustrated again. Apart from Sarah's being confined to bed, Kingsley had to suffer the chagrin of being blamed by the doctor for taking her up to London. "How was I to have him here at a guinea a mile!" he wrote.[97] He was plainly upset by Dr Massey's unconcern about the expense involved and his own inability to provide for such a contingency. Sarah had been faint and sickly and had suffered much, and it was inevitable that Kingsley's time for writing would be eroded. "What beautiful stories one could write if one was rich and had leisure," he wrote Macmillan and went on to say that he had been elected FRGS and "thought it would look well on the title page of the *Book of Adventure [Tales of Old Travel]* ".[98] Kingsley joined the Royal Geographical Society on 24 February 1868,[99] recommended by Arthur Warre, with, as supporters, J. G. Cooke and R. H. Major, keeper of the Department of Printed Maps at the British Museum.

By early summer 1868 Kingsley had written 217 pages of manuscript of *Tales of Old Travel*, enough for 140 pages of print.[100] After consulting with Charles at Eversley about the project, Kingsley sent Macmillan enough copy to make 100 printed pages. These Macmillan liked;[101] in addition he approved a short story which Kingsley had already forwarded.[102] But the writing of the *Tales*, which had been in hand since 1864, Kingsley found tiresome. To discover material strange and interesting to the public he had to read widely. Progress, necessarily slow, meant a reduced income, which in turn added to his worries.[103] In a letter of 15 September 1868 he showed his weariness: "The responsibility of having so much depending, as it will for two years longer, ages a man very fast." A longing for his old haunts was evident: "When I come to London I want to compare notes with you [Macmillan] or Malcolm as to where you have been, for I know so to speak, every stone of those mountains [Conway to Caernarvon]. I write almost in the dark."[104]

Macmillan's reply characteristically showed his solicitude, an attitude he maintained through the long years of their friendship: "I am very sorry indeed to find that the work which I thought you undertook as pleasant relaxation proves so irksome. When we agreed the matter I was to pay you two hundred pounds for a volume which should contain as much as Tom Brown's Schooldays.... I have been sorry to hear ... that which was given as pleasant and easy work turns out evidently a serious bore. Even now you have only sent enough for

200 when we ought to have about 400." Macmillan then suggested that printing go on quietly so Kingsley could see what the project would look like.[105]

To keep his output up, Kingsley began another novel and, a little later, sent Macmillan the incomplete manuscript of *Hetty*. This Macmillan passed to John Morley of the *Saturday Review* for an opinion, not revealing to Morley the identity of the author.[106] Morley must have liked what he saw, for, when sending the work and the criticism back to Kingsley, Macmillan asked to see the completed tale.[107] This Kingsley did not do, despite an offer of two hundred pounds from Macmillan,[108] and publication serially began in *Once a Week* in February 1869. That Kingsley, after getting Macmillan's help, did not publish with Macmillan underlines how strained were his resources. He could not afford to await publication, a circumstance that also resulted in Bradbury and Evans getting *Hetty*. In any case, it is more than likely Kingsley had obligated himself there, too, for a short note from Macmillan on 26 January 1869 enclosed "a cheque for the balance of Bradbury's bill".[109]

In *Hetty*, Kingsley's theme seems to have been that "all things work together for good for those who love God". The protagonist, Rebecca, is certainly an example of "the Lord chastening those whom He loves", for her progress in life is beset with problems. Hetty, the named heroine, appears late in the story and has little real contact with Rebecca, to whom Hetty sets an example of doing what is right, despite the opinion of others. Rebecca ultimately marries Hetty's father, Morley, and all three, together with Hetty's husband, set sail overseas on the missionary ship *Eirene*. Although the novel possesses interest, many of the issues that help create tension would evoke a limited response today. Kingsley's liberal Christian views, if they may be called that, are clearly present; scenes of dock life, sailors, and shipping are lively and offer some of the best prose encountered in the book.

The year had not started promisingly. As well, Sarah was sick again,[110] and a twenty-two pound bill for interest on his house mortgage had to be paid to Andrew and Atkins, Lombard Street, to "prevent foreclosure".[111] This Macmillan paid from moneys owed to Kingsley by the publishers Strahan and Co., of Ludgate Hill, and dismissed Henry's fears about asking for help: "I don't hate you very much. Do you really think I do?"[112]

But troubles had been developing for some time. From September 1868, after Kingsley and his wife had taken seriously ill at Ramsgate — presumably of food poisoning[113] — illnesses had beset both of them. Kingsley had worked on through the year, but by the end of summer 1868 he confessed himself as "sadly in want of a tonic", adding that illness and worry were "not pleasant companions for the desk".[114] After Ramsgate he wrote: "Lord if I could only get a fortnight's rest: not much chance of that."[115] And rest he did not get. By October 1868 he was seeking the address of Dr Yomano: "Here is another fellow after me, whom I must answer."[116] But misfortune did not end there.

In November he was ill,[117] and yet again in January 1869,[118] when Sarah was also sick.[119] A quick and profitable placing of *Hetty* no doubt afforded some relief from the inevitable doctors' bills, but it was insufficient to lift him beyond problems immediately at hand. Small wonder that a note of defeat appeared in a letter to Macmillan: "I lift my weary head to write to you. I am very sorry that I have miscalculated copy.... let me off as short as you can.... I am so tired, and my dear old friend, Stephen Denning, has fallen down dead at his work ... picking up a slate pencil among his boys. And like a fool I feel it. If it was not for the wife, life would be very weary to me just now. I am so tired."[120] Earlier thoughts on the illogicality of sudden death and the transience of life seem not to have been too far distant when he referred in such a way to the news about Stephen Denning. Sympathy for Kingsley, though, is qualified by the Kingsleys' life style at Wargrave, where, for instance, individually monogrammed letters suggest that the keeping up of appearances was important. The question of curtailing avoidable expenses, because of an irregular and sometimes precarious income, did not arise despite their misfortunes.

As it was finally published, *Tales of Old Travel* comprised fourteen tales of adventures drawn from many areas. The travels of Marco Polo; François Pelsaert's shipwreck on the Abrolhos Islands off the coast of Western Australia in 1629; the wanderings of a Capuchin friar, Father Denis, in the seventeenth century; the privations of seven Dutchmen on Spitzbergen Island in 1633; Alvaro Nunez's discovery of the Mississippi River in the sixteenth century; and the founding of Australia — all are among his tales of "human courage, brought to its mettle in hopeless circumstances" ("The Wanderings of a Capuchin"). The tales are in the main retold by Kingsley, who quotes freely and makes frequent observations of his own, as, for example, in "The Sufferings of Robert Everard", where he writes: "In one of the very best sailor books ever written *(Typee)* the sailor ... [despite being in a sailor's paradise] still risks his life to get back to his old hardships.... In short, your true English or American sailor always wants to be somewhere else. It has had its results: for one, among many, the language of Shakespeare bids fair to become the language of the world in time, and for a time." Kingsley's style is direct, his writing lucid, and his comments interesting. Despite his problems in finding material suitable for his purpose, he manages to sustain the interest of his tales, and the book is still acceptable as a travel and adventure book of other days.

Macmillan, with a knowledge of the book's contents and with Kingsley's interests in mind — he was inclined to think *Tales of Old Travel* would carry Kingsley's name "into new regions"[121] — had been anxious to get the book before the public in spring 1868.[122] But this was not to be. The best that Kingsley could manage for him was an edition of *Robinson Crusoe* with a biographical introduction. Still in trouble and needing more funds, Kingsley on 3 March 1869 sold the copyright of *Tales of Old Travel* to Macmillan for two hundred pounds.[123] Then, as if to make matters even more difficult for himself, he broke a leg towards the end of the month, the fracture confining him to bed and necessitating a visit by surgeons.[124] Macmillan, tactfully considerate as always, sent him three copies of *Robinson Crusoe* on 25 March "in case of accidents, say some very dear friend wants one",[125] but avoided mention of the broken leg. On 6 April Craik notified Kingsley that his mother had sent three hundred pounds to be credited to his account. Of this thirty-eight pounds was transferred to Kingsley's account at the London and County Bank, Reading, and fifty pounds was sent to him direct.[126]

Kingsley and his wife, dogged by expenses of illness, encumbered by interest on a mortgage, and handicapped by Henry's fracture, were not destined to achieve financial stability. From January to April 1869, funds known to have gone to them were considerable, totalling seven hundred pounds. By way of comparison, Edmund Gosse's income for 1875 totalled seven hundred and fifty-nine pounds, of which two hundred and six pounds came from literary efforts,[127] and Charles Kingsley's living at Eversley was worth six hundred pounds, to which was added four hundred pounds a year which his wife, Fanny, received.[128] By all accounts the Henry Kingsleys should have been able to live well and save money. That they could not was a mystery to relatives and friends alike. On 31 July 1869 Kingsley assigned to Macmillan a five hundred pounds insurance policy he had taken with the Liverpool and London and Globe Insurance Company to secure two hundred pounds plus interest which had been advanced to him.[129] Kingsley's affairs were now in such a state that Macmillan and Craik had at last acted to protect their interests. By this time his fractured leg had healed[130] – but he had been a long time incapacitated. Fate now was to take a hand, and from here on events developed quickly, which brought another radical change to Kingsley's life.

On 2 August 1869 the *Daily Review,* Edinburgh, announced the death of David Guthrie, its editor. On 27 September it announced Henry Kingsley's appointment as from 1 October, intimating that the author of *Ravenshoe,* etc, and in their opinion one of the most popular contributors to the leading magazines and journals of the metropolis, would contribute largely to its editorial and literature columns. "It is not necessary to introduce to the people of Scotland one whose reputation stands so high in our literature," the announcement went on. "Mr. Kingsley is no stranger to Scotland, nor Scotland to him, and his settlement in Edinburgh in connection with the *Review* will mark a NEW ERA IN SCOTTISH JOURNALISM" – prophetic words, which were to be fulfilled. Once again, Kingsley, putting the past behind him, looked to the future to solve the problems of the present. For the first time he was to enjoy what, for him, could only be described as the near impossible – a regular source of income.

Of *Mademoiselle Mathilde, Hetty, Tales of Old Travel,* and his edition of *Robinson Crusoe,* little more need be said. He confessed to a love of Mademoiselle Mathilde, the character, equal to that of Charles Ravenshoe. There is little doubt that he saw in their self-sacrificial roles some aspect of his own life — a manifestation of an attitude common to both characters: "Greater love hath no man than this, that a man lay down his life for his friends." In his own case there was little in the way of rewards. Belief was all that could give meaning to his life — he was enabling others to live by his efforts. *Hetty* hardly warrants such a title, for Hetty, the character, plays little part in the story. She is held out as an ideal which the other female character, Rebecca might emulate. Essentially the novel deals with religious formalism compared with good works motivated by good will, and, as well, contemporaneous expectations of women's behaviour and the conventional choices open to them. In *Tales of Old Travel* Kingsley found ample opportunity for narrator comment, and scattered in its text are fleeting references to his own experiences. Of his biographical introduction to *Robinson Crusoe,* the concluding sentence echoed what Kingsley must have been thinking about his own life: "The only rest which his fevered spirit ever had, was in writing his romances and his grave." Its relevance was to become apparent as he moved through the last two phases of his life, in Edinburgh and afterwards.

14

The Editor

The *Daily Review,* a penny journal published daily, was regarded as the Free Presbyterian Church newspaper, though the group that promoted the undertaking comprised Episcopalians and United Presbyterians as well as Free Presbyterians. They supported the journal because of press attacks on the Church and its leading ministers and also out of a desire for a newspaper that respected civil rights and religion. Started by David Guthrie of the *North British Agriculturist* on 2 April 1861, the *Review* under his guidance achieved a name for literary excellence and for its coverage of commercial and financial affairs. Despite the calibre of its management, the paper struggled throughout its life to be profitable, and was accused of sectarianism by its political opponents, who called it the *Daily Reviler.* After Kingsley left in 1871, ownership changed too, and the paper finally ceased publication in 1886. Marking its passing, the *Scotsman,* in an obituary notice, declared it had died of spleen. This, then, was the paper Kingsley came to edit — one whose proprietors hoped the Kingsley name and literary reputation would help, despite Kingsley's inexperience.[1]

In his first editorial, Kingsley stated that he hoped to keep the paper progressing as Guthrie had intended. No staff changes would be made, political and religious views would remain unaltered, contemporary affairs would be treated with liberality and without prejudice, old ideas would be developed, and new features would be introduced. Literature was to be given even more prominence than before, and books of sufficient merit would be reviewed "not with reckless, hurried sciolism but with due care and diligence". Articles of interest in quarterly and monthly periodicals would be reviewed, for "the mass of periodical writing is far too great for any ordinary reader to wade through". Public opinion abroad, in the form of extracts and translations from foreign papers, would be introduced, and a column of "Causeries" — both serious and amusing — would appear weekly. "With a programme like this, capable of great expansion," he wrote, "we hope to retain the confidence of old readers and to attract new. To sum up, all our object will be to keep our readers, with as little trouble to themselves as

High Street, Edinburgh; the *Daily Review* offices are in the buildings in the left foreground. From a photograph in the Edinburgh Room, Edinburgh Library.

possible, completely *au fait* with the latest facts and the newest ideas."[2] Relevant to his "liberality and prejudices", two letters to Edwin Arnold reveal Kingsley's personal and political views. If, as he claimed, he was a man of strong opinions, he must have found it difficult to remain non-political as an editor. The first shows a humanitarian trait:

Dear Edwin,

You don't I suppose know a *poor* literary man with an entree to the British Museum. I want him to be very poor if possible, because I should hardly like to ask a well to do man to make references for me, and what is more I most certainly could not afford to pay him. I need not tell *you* that I am a man who extends three times more courtesy to a poor man, than ever I take the trouble to do to a rich one. If you do happen to know a not very fortunate brother of the craft to whom a stray pound now and again would be of use, you would oblige me by introducing us to one another, and may possibly benefit him to the tune of a few pounds (very few I fear). I only want references made without coming to town. . . .[3]

In his second letter Kingsley not only shows where his sympathies lay but also his ability to disagree on politics while remaining friendly throughout. His style of writing was somewhat different as an editor:

My dear Eddy, [1869]

I am so sorry that I saw so little of you. We had only time for exchanging political broadsides (a most silly thing) & we had no time for a good current talk over matters, in which we should have, in the main agreed.

My dear man, you must remember that you are only 960 years old, whereas I am nearly 966. When you have lived six years more, you will begin to find out, that political and religious arguing is a weariness to the flesh, and a waste of time. If I had ever convinced anyone by argument I should despise him so heartily that I never should be civil to him any more.

That is why I hate Auberon Herbert.[4] Political faith like religious faith must be bred in the bones to come out in the flesh. You were bred tory. Stick to it old man, be earnest and true over it. It is a noble creed: I happen to think an erring one, but don't walk about this world of ours without a creed.

For me my dear Eddy I am democrat: and your tory government has turned more democrat that I am. You are Tory, well and good: but I hope to find such a dear old friend as you on the side of Peel, Salisbury and Carnarvon. *Whig* as I am I can understand *them,* and love *them.* Of Stanley I say nothing. His position is very difficult. But I love him entirely.

But do be earnest about matters. Do consider that you have no small share of ability, and *I* think of power. Stay a Tory if you choose, but stay with Salisbury and Carnarvon. Think for yourself my dearest Eddy, and don't waste a life, which may be a noble one over party formulas. That is your temptation. Be a Tory and God go with you, but follow Margaret's father and you will come to no ill.

My dear boy, I forgot to mention to you that my house is the same as if it was yours. I am always at home, and shall be delighted to see you at any time. If you meet an American or a Papist, I demand international civility. Entre nous the Americans are much nicer than the papists, and my wife takes the Americans to her bosom, while she is apt to go about with a papist. Don't *dis*believe in the Americans. Believe an old friend when he says that they are thundering fine fellows. You Tories ought to like them. I had a *Republican* here last week, and he talked such Toryism that I stopped him. His opinions about the Nigger vote were too strong. I had to point out to him that I should probably meet some of our wonderful Nigger lovers the next week, and that I wanted to keep in with them. "What are you going to do with your doctrinaire radicals," he said; "put 'em in parliament," says I. Whereupon he sniffed and said, "The best thing you can do. They will find their place."

H.K.

Kingsley's residence in Edinburgh was at Goshen Bank, Morningside. It had its own garden and grounds and an entry from Jordan Bank, and had been originally part of an estate also named Goshen Bank. In 1975 the house still stood, surrounded by high-rise residential buildings. A description given by Anne Thackeray Ritchie when writing to Clement Shorter, that it was "dark and shabby, and contrasting with sunny Wargrave",[5] tends to give a wrong impression. Together with

Canaan Lane near by, cultural associations of the district were strong. At 7 Jordan Bank, for instance, lived Samuel Bough, RSA (1822-79), a well-known landscape painter of the day, a "real Bohemian and generous to a fault",[6] and, at number 8, Thomas Brown, an artist and teacher of drawing. Sir Thomas Dick Lauder, another resident, had declined a chair of natural history in Edinburgh University in 1854, while Rev. James Hamilton later wrote that "it would be difficult to find a more charming retreat than [James Wilson's home] snugly ensconsed amidst the groves of Morningside". In short, Kingsley lived at a good address while in Edinburgh and one commensurate with his status and respectability as editor of a local newspaper.

A perusal of the *Daily Review* from 1 October 1869 until the time of Kingsley's resignation reveals many articles and critical comments. Obviously these could not have been all Kingsley's work, although overall responsibility was his. A guide to his own output may be found in Kingsley's 1875 application to the Royal Literary Fund, where he records: "[I wrote] an average of three leading articles and three columns of literature a week besides going out as war correspondent in 1870. My engagement lasted for eighteen months."[7] Given this statement, the fact that he wrote the "Causeries" column himself, and internal evidence in some of the articles, his views on a wide range of topics are evident from a reading of the *Daily Review*; they show his interest in colonial policy, education, colonies, and emigration. As an example, the problems of New Zealand colonists and Maoris were examined in the light of "a declaration of war against men [the Maoris] who were the subjects of the Queen, and which was unwise because of its placing both sides in avowedly hostile attitudes and recognising the Maoris, not as rebels, but as belligerents. Where this left the colonists and the Imperial government was a subject for debate for, in effect, the colonists had been left to complete a task begun by the Queen's officers." Lord Granville, the Colonial Minister in London, was reminded that "10,000 British troops under a British General, and colonial levies to boot did not settle the matter".[8] The authorial intrusions of Kingsley's novels were now being replaced, more satisfyingly, by comment in the *Review*'s columns.

Clement Shorter quotes a friend of that time as saying, "I remember his leaders, dictatorial, self-complacent, egotistical and ungrammatical."[9] Whether these remarks are valid or not could depend to a large extent on the viewpoint of the reader. For example, in an article entitled "The Inferior Sex" the university authorities are ridiculed for illogicality in not awarding the Hope Scholarship to a Miss Edith Pechey: "*He* means *she* when it's a question of hanging; *he* doesn't mean *she* when it is a question of voting."[10] The point was that the scholarship was given to a male student despite Miss Pechey's scholarly superiority. Judgements concerning the tone of the article could vary according to era and values, but the direct criticism makes refreshing reading.

Comments on the colony of Victoria, Australia, ten or more years after Kingsley's return were equally direct:

A very large number of people went there who were utterly unfitted for the place: not in the way of training very often, for young gentlemen, highly educated turned often into very good workmen: but utterly unfitted through want of experience, of experience which was seldom gained before the emigrant found his capital, whatever it might have been, gone, and his hands tied by poverty.... For a time the principal power of the legislative body was in the hands of the squatters — a kind of territorial aristocracy of vast wealth, who held all lands on leases from Government at peppercorn rents, and were taxed according to the number of their sheep or cattle.[11]

The article went on to state that after the 1865 Land Act in Victoria, "the system of free selection before surveying came into operation and the people came into their magnificent inheritance". With fever and ague unknown, it said, Victoria "is one of the finest heritages into which the English race have come. It offers freedom, cultivation, education, and moderate wealth to every well-conducted citizen, without any reference to birth, religion, or nation."

Other observations on Australia are worth recording. Of Queensland the *Review* stated that coolie labour was a problem for any labourer wanting to emigrate there and asserted that "in a pastoral country like Queensland the blacksmith, the wheelwright, and we are sorry to say, the publican are people of very great importance, forming with the storekeeper a small middle class between the aristocrat of the leased lands and the 'hand' or labourer.... The richest man in Australia was, we believe, a butcher." In regard to gold, the *Review*'s advice was to get rich more quickly by feeding and supplying the miners — in two words, forget it.[12] Tasmania is mentioned, but, despite the jesting tone, what was unsaid is more significant: "A melancholy example of the fate of nations... is found in... Tasmania, where, it seems, one miserable old woman... Lalla Rookh, represents what was once the race of Tasmanians — not only the 'last of a clan' but the last of a whole nation — a notable example of the tenacity of existence in women who have passed what, when we want to put it mildly, we call 'a certain age'."[13] On emigration generally the conclusion was that there was no country like the British Isles and that the key-note among thousands of emigrants was "home": "All men come back who can."

On entering Parliament in the colonies, and taking Victoria as the example, the *Review* commented: "We would only ask what the number of men is who can dare to call themselves gentlemen, either in the one legislature or the other. The Anglo-Teutonic race has desired to be ruled by the most worthless of its members and seems to have had its will. An educated migrant, if honest and decent, must give up all hopes of political life until he comes back repentant to the old country." The opinion was offered, therefore, that no *life* existed for an educated man in either America, which was discussed with reference to Iowa and Ontario, or in Australia. An emigrant had only a choice "between rowdyism and Lotos eating.... the future of Australia may be a grand one, if she keeps the scum of her large towns in order, as we do here: we can only hope that it may be something better than that of the great United States, because the position of a nation which cannot externally borrow a solitary brass farthing from any one out of Bedlam or Morningside may be grand, but is not exactly respectable."[14]

As Kingsley loved fishing, it is not surprising to find a leading article in the *Review* extolling the virtues of Rannoch, the River Tummel, Aberfeldy, and Glenlyon and remarking that "a man who puts his rod on his back will see more of the Scotch people and know more of the Scotch heart than if he took a dozen deer forests".[15] His 1863 article in *Macmillan's Magazine,* "Some Account of the Village of Inverquoich", also shows his familiarity with Scotland, a familiarity he had gained from earlier visits.

Women's rights and the education of women figured in the columns of the *Daily Review* almost from when Kingsley arrived. His wife, in letters to the editor, was the antithesis of the submissive Victorian woman. Opposing a letter whose theme for women was: "Oh! *be* thankful *that* home *is the* sphere where God has appointed *you to shine*",[16] Sarah, five days after arriving in Edinburgh, advocated more education for women, saying that women should help men by their knowledge, not retard them by their ignorance, whether they were trying to qualify as doctors or work in the sanitary cause.[17] A few days later she wrote again, arguing for the opening of universities to women, pointing out the incongruity of mothers permitting their daughters to dance with men little known to them yet being shocked at the suggestion that they should sit in a classroom with earnest students.[18] On 22 October Sarah wrote yet again to the *Daily Review,* complaining about the state of the police force when a drunk could strike a woman carrying a baby in High Street. To this Henry replied, as editor, putting the blame not on inferior police but on an inadequate number of police.[19] Two further letters written by Sarah appeared, one protesting at misleading information on programmes sold at a concert,[20] the other a long letter dealing with overcrowding, which challenged readers to act:

> It is intolerable that such a grand city as this should be defiled by the closes and wynds out of the Canongate, Cowgate, Westport, Crosscauseways, Pleasance &c. . . . We may choose to ignore but we cannot free ourselves from the responsibilities of these masses of ill housed poor close around us. It is not a time to be ignorant and idle, to be squabbling over religious details and fighting over points of doctrine. There is a great pressing work to be done; let all differences be forgot, and let Presbyterians, Episcopalians, Roman Catholics and Dissenters of all kinds work shoulder to shoulder until Edinburgh is celebrated for something nobler and greater than her public buildings and her beautiful hills.[21]

Urgent though the need may have been, the reaction of those concerned in Edinburgh may best be imagined. It was not just the publicity given to "half clothed, filthy creatures in darkness and dirt in the city", but also, in effect, the implicit condemnation of a Christianity that permitted such conditions to exist — a statement that said faith without works was dead. Leadership in social change, with gentility, was one thing; a strong-minded, outspoken woman was another — particularly when she was the wife of the *Daily Review* editor. By the end of July 1870, when Henry left for the Franco-Prussian War, the Kingsleys' arrival in Edinburgh was being looked at askance by the proprietors of the *Daily Review,* which was struggling to stay solvent.

Sarah's writings, published in her husband's paper, were not all militant. On 23 May 1870 Kingsley published a poem by his wife in which she deplored the death of a woman she had loved and reproached God for taking her life. Its content seems too personal to admit of its being a poetic exercise, while references to "fingers lingering long amidst my hair" and being "haunted by thy presence fair" were not applicable to her mother, who was still alive. Other comments, such as men "Wrangling like fools amongst their petty discontents,/ Forget that life is love: and love is service" give some indication of an emotion sublimated in terms of serving mankind. This could explain her zeal in visitation, her concern for social change and improvement, and her sense of mission. But who her inspiration was and where Henry Kingsley fitted into the picture are unanswerable questions. Of the thirty-six lines of the poem, those most of interest are:

> Memory doth bring all past hours back to me —
> I close my eyes, and feel thee near.
> When soft strong winds do stir around,
> I feel thy fingers lingering long amidst my hair;
> When night, dank, dark, and chill, does come,
> Still I am haunted by thy presence fair.
> Apart I live from hurried haunts, where men,
> Wrangling like fools amongst their petty discontents,
> Forget that life is love: and love is service —
> Apart, but not alone, for thou art with me.

Kingsley's *causeries* dealt with a variety of subjects. Of those dealing with American affairs, one on finance is typical:

> The second is from W—l s—t, — we must be very careful in these days to avoid coming under the law of libel. An English judge has laid down that it is a libel to say that a man is "no gentleman."
>
> Hush a bye baby on the tree top,
> Father's to Wall Street operations to stop.
> When the bank breaks his credit will fall,
> And down will come currency, greenbacks and all.[22]

Two other poems in the "Causeries" column have a different mood, one mourns with the widows of Leith for their men lost at sea and the prospect of a workhouse ahead,[23] the other, "Peabody's Last Voyage", is rhetorical: "Tell our brothers . . . this nation still can love, and love right well."[24]

Kingsley read widely, and many writers are treated in his columns. A brief survey shows Scott being defended against "violation of possibility for effect" on the grounds that Scott wrote a successful story; *The Times* being rebuked for saying that Tennyson was so great a poet it did not matter what he did; a memoir of Jane Austen written by her nephew being reviewed favourably; and Smollett being defended against any condemnation of "a literary man for participation in the common failings of his age . . . [as] the *ne plus ultra* of injustice". As well, the authorship of Shakespeare's plays was discussed, with reference being made at the same time to an article in a current *North British Quarterly Review (sic)*; a new edition of Chaucer was compared with earlier ones; the loss of Dickens was linked with that of Thackeray — Dickens being praised for his civilizing influence; and Nathaniel Hawthorne's notebooks were commended to "everyone interested in the critical study of English literature and English style".[25]

Three notices of his own novels appeared in the *Daily Review* — two, *Stretton*[26] and *Mademoiselle Mathilde*,[27] in the lists of new books received, and one in the book reviews:

Tales of Old Travel. Re-narrated by Henry Kingsley. Macmillan.

Of course it is impossible for us to say a word good, bad or indifferent about the letter press of this book: on the subject of the illustrations, however, we may be allowed to make a few remarks. They are probably the best that Mr. Huard has ever done, and look as well on the paper as on the wood. For grouping, the finest is probably "The Old Slave Trade," and for single figures we think that M. D'Ermenonville toiling up the fearful precipices of the Rio Grande leading his horse is even the best where all are so good. "The Desolation of Robert Everard" is also very fine. Mr. Huard now stands nearly the first among our book illustrators.[28]

One unexpected work by Kingsley was mentioned in the music reviews:

"Who will be my love." Words by Henry Kingsley. Music by W. S. Rockstro. Whether viewed from a poetical or musical point of view, this song is worthy of special approbation. Mr. Rockstro has been fortunate in securing Mr. Kingsley's elegant verse, and has succeeded in providing them with a graceful and appropriate setting. The unison of words and music is, in this instance, a happy one, and the accompaniments, while they commend themselves to the musician, present no difficulties which any player of average ability may not easily overcome. It is in the favourite key of E flat, and the compass proper embraces an octave, from E to E, so that it lies well within the reach of ordinary soprano or tenor voices.[29]

Of his other writings at this time, Kingsley's later views on the novel are important in relation to his own work. Discussing the naming of characters,[30] Kingsley maintained that very few novelists attended carefully to the invention of names, and that Dickens, Balzac and George Eliot took "their own line". Dickens had resorted to "fantacism [*sic*] as in 'Martin Chuzzlewit,' 'Nicholas Nickleby,' " and so on, "but seldom selected a 'humorous name' ". Balzac was reported to have got his names from shop doors, he claimed, "attending merely to the element of *bissarrerie*". Eliot's names were poor, Kingsley thought, and the absence of humour in her genius was strange. In fact, he maintained "half a dozen sentences in 'King Lear' or 'Twelfth Night' would exhaust all the humour in George Eliot's novels, or in any novels by any hand save those of Dickens, Thackeray or Scott". Kingsley looked for wit and aptness in the naming of characters, instancing examples from Scott such as Peter Peebles, which conveyed the idea of "loose, inconsecutive, voluble imbecility"; Drumthwackit, which suggested "a hot screed of doctrine in that parish", and finally, Jedediah Clushbotham and Habakuk Mucklewrath. For Thackeray, because the examples would be endless, he quoted as "the most splendid", Princess Potzausend Donnerwelter. His views on "word painting" are, for the purposes of trying to understand his own literary work, even more interesting.[31] They leave no doubt that Walter Scott was his model in this respect:

> Novelists of the present age have a great tendency to what is called "word painting;" in fact, among our numerous sins we have tried the thing ourselves. But let us all listen humbly to the voice of our master, Walter Scott. Ruskin has some very good passages in which he tries to bring nature before us in printer's ink, but he has, we think, no passage so splendid as the following which we quote from "The Heart of Midlothian," Chapter 40. Swinburne or Shelley have scarcely matched it anywhere, which is saying a great deal. The passage we allude to is this:— *She could see the crest of the torrent fling loose down the rock, like the mane of a wild horse!* We cannot write like that now.[32]

In his last weeks as editor, Kingsley gave an enlightened and detailed review of a new publication dealing with eighteenth century novels and manners, as portrayed in novels of that period. Whilst conceding the grossness and coarseness of the age, he maintained that there were "novels ... of a past generation with which one must have some acquaintance in order to have an intelligent apprehension of the social habits and everyday life of our grandfathers and great-grandfathers ... found in a more serviceable form in the novels of the period than in any other kind of literature. It is the business of the novelist to present pictures of social life, and there is usually not much difficulty in distinguishing between what is caricature or exaggeration and what is true portraiture".[33] The relevance of this to Kingsley's Australian novels is pertinent.

Of the many references by Kingsley to contemporary matters, two are of interest. In the first he referred to his friend C. W. Shirley Brooks and praised him for the "true wit" and the absence of "coarseness" evident in Brooks's work in *Punch*.[34] Then, when writing of the Oxford-Cambridge Boat Race, Kingsley made much of the inability of the Scots to see the value of competitive rowing. In his other remarks, he gives glimpses of himself:

> We were ourselves, while lecturing at Newcastle, in the company of the greatest oarsman whom the world has ever seen, the man Renforth. We made a pilgrimage to Renforth [James Renforth of Gateshead (1842–71)] ....
> It so happened once to an unlucky editor that he was in training with the late Robert Combes. Robert Combes' boat was ready beside

the editorial boat at Putney. We were ordered to run by the tow-path instead of rowing: we submitted to our master and ran. The tide was rushing up, and all we had to do was put our elbows up and "spin." Combes could steer himself. Combes did that course in 20 minutes 25 seconds. That is to say, that he went four miles and three quarters in that time. We were in time to help him out of his boat.[35]

While editor of the *Daily Review*, Kingsley still wrote fiction. During winter 1869, in his first months in Edinburgh, he had been ill but had on his own admission stayed up till 4 a.m. writing.[36] His letter of 9 May 1870 to John Blackwood of Edinburgh records that *Old Margaret* was nearly completed, having been written in Belgium in 1869, where he had gone for his "accessories". "Its publication has been delayed most tiresomely because I have had to put all my work into this paper," he wrote. "Would you look at it. . . . I don't think you will find much fault with it on conservative grounds."[37] The Belgium reference seems somewhat odd in view of known events of 1869 and suggests that, even if a fabrication, writing (with its income) was still a high priority.

As it happened, Blackwood was not satisfied, and Kingsley agreed on 25 July to recast the novel to meet Blackwood's views. He apologized for the delay in completing the manuscript but said that three-quarters of the story was "actually in form". At the same time he asked if he could draw on Blackwood, "for accidentally" he was "terribly poor". It was "impossible to avoid being short when one has so many dependent on one," he wrote.[38] This, then, is his admission, albeit carefully worded, that he had his mother-in-law to support, but whether Kingsley was keeping Mrs Hazelwood in his home, her home, or a nursing home is unknown. The apparent lull in his financial worries was over and, paradoxically, Kingsley already was a troubled man. Blackwood replied almost immediately (27 July) and agreed to give him forty pounds out of the one hundred and twenty pounds promised for the copyright of *Old Margaret*, but told Kingsley he was disappointed with what he had read so far.[39]

The following day Kingsley, apparently very embarrassed and reticent about making the matter known, called on Blackwood's nephew William, a former member of the Eyre Defence Committee,[40] at his office and made a rambling statement about collecting the forty pounds. Disinclined to believe Kingsley, William Blackwood acceded to Kingsley's request only when shown his uncle's letter, and when writing to his uncle later he said he thought Kingsley was "cool" in calling on him for the advance and that he was an "infernal idiot though clever enough to know money".[41] To this John Blackwood replied on 29 July 1870: "I forgot to tell you that harpy Kingsley made his appearance one day here [Blackwood's home at Strathtyrun, St Andrews] and I could not get quit of him without buying his confounded story. His novels do sell so I hope my softness will not entail loss. He has powerful interest with the vacquerie too."[42]

Two days after getting the money, Kingsley wrote to John

Blackwood again, telling of his imminent departure for the Franco-Prussian War. His reason for going was simply that "everybody funks so I have to go". Then he added that a sick wife, short money, and danger were enough to cope with and asked that their arrangements be left to stand temporarily.[43] It seems hardly possible that Kingsley did not know he was going to Europe beforehand and was, if anything, providing a slight financial reserve for Sarah before he left. But the puzzle of "short money", and why the Kingsleys, even in Edinburgh, were in financial difficulties must have been due basically to commitments from the Wargrave years and not just to "so many dependent" on him.

Blackwood may have had reservations about Kingsley's going to the war because of the loan, but others felt otherwise. His departure gave his employers an opportunity to try J. B. Gillies, another staff member, as editor, a position which he subsequently took over from Kingsley.[44] But it seems there could have been more to his going than overcoming the "funk" of others. Kingsley had criticized Church and State. On 21 May 1870 he had tilted at the Scots' professed dislike of vestments: "How curiously things dissolve when they are looked at closely. We have the very strongest objection to High Church ecclesiastical vestments: we dislike them extremely. Yet we must say, that out of Oxford we have never seen such sumptuary extravagance in the way of vestments as we saw in Mr. Moody Stuart's church on the day of Sir James Simpson's funeral." In the same column, "Causeries", he condemned the Episcopalians and the Roman Catholic clergy for not attending the funeral.[45] Then, as if to make a final impact before departure, Kingsley described Edinburgh's sanitary arrangements like reform arrangements – old mud let lie until it had got itself into a dangerous state, and "then we stir a number of venerable – smells – exactly at the wrong time," he wrote.[46] As if that were not enough, he criticized the gas company supplying South Edinburgh for having its gas lamps alight "at both ends of the night" – before sunset and after sunrise. This waste, he claimed, he saw because he went to the office early and went home in broad daylight.[47] After his departure, the proprietors of the *Daily Review* started an assessment of Kingsley's value as editor. His financial embarrassment was known to the Blackwoods, both of whom moved in the circles of Edinburgh that counted, and it seems hardly possible that others, including the owners of the *Daily Review*, were not aware of the editor's importunity.

Kingsley left Edinburgh on 5 August 1870 for Leith, intending to travel to Metz[48] through Rotterdam, Namur, and Luxembourg.[49] With Sarah recovering from sickness and finances low, the task of correspondent afforded him an opportunity for increased income and a brief respite from worries at home – precarious though the visit to the Continent might be. As the steamer approached the Dutch coast on 7 August a pilot brought news aboard of the French reverse. The Prussians had had a significant success and the French emperor had declared, "Macmahon had lost a battle, but there is no reason why matters should not rearrange themselves." Kingsley was impatient to be

The Passing Guest

ashore and suggested that the steamer ram an "abominable ferry-boat" so as to get into the canal quickly. The "ferry-boat", as he revealed three years later, turned out to be a Dutch man-of-war.[50]

Kingsley's eight weeks at the Franco-Prussian War, as recorded in his correspondence published in the *Daily Review,* falls into three phases: firstly, forays from Luxembourg into near-by hills and elsewhere to glean information, which lasted from the date of his arrival until approximately 31 August; secondly, his observation of battle areas from 1 September until approximately 15 September; and the final phase – that of accompanying medical supplies and other aid on a wagon train from Arlon to Briey.

There is little doubt that Kingsley worked hard and suffered personal privation while at the war. His time at Luxembourg, where he would have been a familiar figure with his eyeglass and glengarry, was a constant sallying forth to nearby hills, tantalized by the knowledge that Metz, his objective, was only forty kilometres away. To carry written dispatches was a breach of neutrality in Luxembourg, and the gendarmerie harassed those suspected of committing a breach. On the night of 15–16 August, Kingsley fell under suspicion and was turned out of bed and searched. Afterwards he confessed his biggest fear to have been that of imprisonment and consequent uselessness as a correspondent. Apart from this, to go into French territory was to invite being shot. "The French are greatly infuriated against everyone, and apparently desperate," he wrote from Mendorf on 11 August. As a result he decided not to attempt to cross the frontier until the battle that he predicted would happen had taken place.

Passports Kingsley found useless. He went, nevertheless, to a nearby mountain, Schomberg, from which he could observe troop movements in Sierck, then in the hands of the Prussians. "We were certainly beyond the frontier," he wrote on 11 August, "and my guilty fears transformed a herdboy into a Prussian sentinel." Of the French army he wrote on 12 August: "There has been too much fancy soldiering in the French army lately; they are splendid fellows, as everyone allows, but there has been too much pipe clay" – a reference to cleaning white gaiters, which would have been more appropriate to ceremonial than to field training. For the military efficiency of the Prussians he had the utmost respect but, despite a pro-German bias, found it difficult not to identify with the French in their humiliation.

On one occasion he set out with the *Times* correspondent and three staff officers on a night reconnaissance and became lost. Only after much trouble and some encounters with the gendarmerie did he regain his quarters. In his war correspondence he wrote on 16 August 1870:

> The night was profoundly dark, but there were innumerable stars overhead as I sat down to look over the battle-fields of that morning towards Metz. I saw nothing but a few fires, which I suppose were watch-fires, dotted about in the broad landscape. There was no movement of any kind; now and then some wandering wind, coming from the battle-field, would whisper in the ryegrass about my head, like the whispers of the dead men who lay heaped below, but that

was all I heard. Knowing what had happened below that morning, the matter became somewhat too solemn, and so I rose and left the night winds to whistle round that desolate down by themselves.

Kingsley later made fuller use of the experience in *Valentin:*

> It is not so very safe, this carrying of despatches, I can tell you. You lose your way sometimes in the dark, and, if you are close to the frontier, you may violate neutrality. Now I was close on the Dutch frontier, and I completely lost my way in the dark one night; that was before the passage of the Prince by Metz you will notice, or, to be more correct, it was the evening before the day on which Bazaine was doomed.
>
> It grew very dark, and there was no moon; my orders were for Longwy, and there were two blazing villages in a line which guided me past Metz. Then I got into a dark wood, and lost sight of them and of everything; then I got on a broad blank down, and when I got to the summit of it I found that I had entirely lost my way.
>
> There was a cluster of lights a long way off, which I made out to be Thionville. It could surely be no other place. The silence of death was all around me, and it was difficult to believe that a great battle had been fought and lost within sight of where I stood that day.*
>
> The field of battle was above twenty miles away, and yet I felt that the gentle wind which was waving the long grass on the down, was also waving the dead men's hair who lay down yonder behind the lights of Thionville.† I do not think that I ever felt so sad and lonely in my whole life.
>
> * The author is only correctly putting down personal recollections.
> † From this down you can see the cathedral at Metz, twenty miles away. I forget the name of it. [Chap. 40]

What did impress Kingsley was the co-operation and lack of distinction between all Christian denominations in the Prussian Army: "All three denominations march together... and have their place assigned to them."[51] Auberon Herbert, whom he had previously disliked, also won his admiration for helping the distressed: "As a member of Mr. Auberon Herbert's Berkshire Committee, I cannot say that gentleman turned up exactly in the place where he was wanted on the occasion of his election in '68. In fact he was rather in the way.... I can believe in him now.... many men are doing their duty here, but the leader and king of them all is Auberon Herbert, a man who might if he chose be lounging on the sofa of a club."[52] Duty, as regards service to others, Kingsley might praise; but romantic ideas about war, he was certain, were finished. "No romance or sentimentalism in the world will stand a bad stench and the stench of the battlefield is becoming intolerable."[53] He found little comfort in the sight of French women, devoid of nursing training, trying to nurse, and he had little praise for a breakdown in French supplies which left wounded men "to howl their lives out on the straw for want of proper bandaging; anyone who has broken a leg knows what that means".[54]

On 1 September Kingsley started work at 5 a.m. He was to be busy until midnight.[55] Of his journey to Esch, his encounters with streams of refugees, and the sounds of battle beyond Thionville and Longwy, he later wrote that he had witnessed and heard "the last battle *for a long time* in the open between France and Prussia. . . . I saw her [France] beaten yesterday."

It is against Kingsley's background of military training, his personal observation of war, and his concern for the wounded that his war dispatches should be read for full effect. Travelling on 1 September to Bettemberg, Esch, Audun, and Carignan, he recorded that he felt proud "to have been in sight and hearing of one of the greatest battles in the world". The historical significance of the moment was clear to him and played a large part in his feelings. Later he wrote that "no man born of woman, in the French, English and German nations, *dares* to be afraid of death in war",[56] which easily translates into "to admit the presence of fear". With Kingsley's beliefs about his lineage, being within sight and sound of battle was tantamount to proving himself and was something no other member of his immediate family had done. However else he failed, in this he had not. He had been at a war. From that knowledge came his judgements.

On 5 September he wrote from Longier, after returning from Sedan with only five hours sleep in sixty, and stated bluntly that what he had seen was not war but butchery. "If I was asked to name the punishment of the Emperor," he wrote, "I would say, let him come and look at his own work." The magnitude of the casualties appalled him, even though he wrote, "the *sight* of it is immensely beautiful: the dead men look so pretty from a little distance: they group themselves as they fall, and even when they crawl away to die they look well, for death is generally beautiful. But I should like the ex-Emperor not only to see his work at a distance, but to come near it, to touch it, and after three days to *smell* it, as I have done." A description of a French uniform by Kingsley in *Valentin* helps explain the meaning of *pretty* in the above passage: "Another three weeks and Mark came in on us, a glorious creature in scarlet breeches, blue coat, and white gaiters" (chap. 28); obviously Kingsley's *pretty* refers to the groupings of colours — not the dead. If anything, the irony in the passage wherein Kingsley wishes the emperor to see his work — not at a distance but where he could both touch and smell it — indicates Kingsley's views on the culpability of inept command and the enormity of mass killing. Similarly, "for death is generally beautiful" may be read ironically — intended for armchair readers of newspapers to whom war appeared as a news item.

What supports the presence of irony in the writing is the compassion shown by Kingsley for the first of the dead he encountered on the battlefield. Of him he wrote in prose devoid of sentimentality or romance: "Let us pass him, and feel relieved that we cannot see his face, which is deep in the mud of last night's storm. His boots are on, which is a matter of detail."[57] Then as if to dispel finally any suggestion of romanticism in his attitude to war, Kingsley's dispatch of 7 September dealt again with the picturesqueness of massed troops: "No one can say that troops in a line, under drill, are picturesque; but shatter them into heaps and they become picturesque at once. The mass of scarlet and blue clothes which lies all around you is very beautiful indeed, and the grouping (to use an artists's term) is always fine. If you go on a great field like this, however, and wish to be sentimental, you should avoid looking into dead men's faces too closely, and should hold your nose as hard as you can. The dead men are dragged away to the trench by their heels, and thrown in. . . . I had to come here to tell you what war was like, and I am telling you: the fault is not mine."

In Givonne the confusion he encountered was "an evil dream", the waste and ruin indescribable. He had to retreat from Sedan for lack of food and, by 10 September, was saturated with the horrors he had seen: "I do not care to talk about these hideous shambles — the memory of them will never be out of my mind — but some folks at home seem to think that war is all rose-water, and that men may make this ruin first and refuse to hear of it afterwards. . . . war is far more devilish than you have any conception of. . . . Allow me to speak, and to speak out: forty thousand men of the pretty French army lie out there on the hillside, a mere heap of rags, bones, entrails and brains." His realistic reporting, though, was not winning favour with his employers, who apparently shared his services with New York and London. He was on the verge of being recalled.

After joining and accompanying relief ambulance wagon trains to their destinations, Kingsley concluded his detailed descriptions of desolation and death on the battlefields with a dispatch published in the *Daily Review* on 29 September. He had, after heavy travelling, close reporting, and personal deprivaton, completed his assignment as he saw it. Back in Luxembourg he went to bed — ill with bronchitis contracted at Sedan a fortnight earlier. But he had done what he wanted — reported war as he had seen it, as it really was. In the light of later events attached to his leaving Edinburgh and the termination of his war mission, two references in his works are significant. In "The Influence of Travel", he wrote that "a man who is connected with a newspaper is not exactly free, deny it who can".[58] This is explained more fully by an excerpt from "Malmaison":

> I said to her [Marie Canzon, a nun] at once, "Come here;" and she came. I said, "Where are you going?"
> She said, "Into Metz."
> I replied, "I am a hired man and cannot go. Hired men can do nothing. Hired men have no souls. When once a man is hired and paid, he is dead for most good things: a man had better be dead and trusting to God's mercy than be hired to lie."
> "You need not lie," she said. "You never did lie in old times."
> "I never lie now," I answered, "but I am irritated, dearest Marie, by my proprietors writing and asking me to put a gloss on to matters which are perfectly obvious, to suit their politics." [Part 2]

Kingsley's experiences left him with neither romantic illusions about war nor false ideas about what was expected of him as a war correspondent, which was entertainment, not education.

In Edinburgh, by late August, Sarah Kingsley had recovered her health enough to notify in the *Daily Review* of 26 August that she was the local receiving agent for the Society for Aid to the Sick and Wounded in War. The society's headquarters were located at 2 St Martin's Place, London, but cash contributions, and cheques made payable to her, as well as any of the numerous requisites listed in the advertisement, could be left at the Kingsley residence at Goshen Bank, Morningside.

On 20 September, Dr John Brown, Scottish essayist and physician, recorded that he was glad to get "a little note from Miss Thackeray, and was very sorry to have missed her".[59] Some time after this, Anne Thackeray called on the Kingsleys at Goshen Bank. Henry, she recollected, had just returned from the Continent and "had come home for a few days only.... Mrs. Kingsley was anxious and troubled, though even then she took me in. I happened to be ill."[60] No record of Kingsley's having returned "for a few days" to Edinburgh while a war correspondent exists, though Sarah could have known he had been recalled but said that he expected to be sent back to the Continent. If this was his hope, the *Daily Review* rejected his proposals.

Ann Thackeray reported that the Kingsley's house was full of boxes and packings. However, this did not indicate, as her report could imply, that the Kingsleys were preparing to move; rather, the paraphernalia were gifts belonging to the relief society for whom Sarah had been working. Kingsley's address remained Goshen Bank, Morningside, throughout his stay in Edinburgh. That Sarah Kingsley was "anxious and troubled" could be easily understood. Her husband had employment problems and had returned ill from the war, her own work for the society awaited doing, and if that were not enough, she had been called on by an eminent but sick visitor. Sarah, nevertheless, took Anne Thackeray into her home and sent for a lady doctor, who cured her. "She also wrote to Dr. John Brown, my father's old friend, who came to see me," recalled Anne Thackeray in her account. "I left them after a couple of days and went South, grateful for their kindness, but feeling as if I ought not to have imposed upon it." No doubt she was right. But other events in the future were to trouble the Kingsleys far more than Anne Thackeray's arrival.

A contemporary report on Henry's editorship described him as "a round man in a square hole". He was regarded as knowing little or nothing about Scottish religious life and less about Edinburgh municipal matters. He could, it was granted, on occasion write a clever, sparkling article, but it was too much to expect him to master the detail of Scottish ecclesiastical controversy. Besides this, his employers could well have been troubled by the consternation with which some of his "rollicking leaders" were read in the manses of north Scotland.[61] In January 1871 Kingsley published a long poem called "Peace and War" in the *Daily Review*,[62] in the form of a dialogue between Peace and War. Peace, interceding for France, pleads for mercy and a stay of hostilities. The final stanza, a reply by War, reads:

> Are we to give up the results
>   Of St. Privat, Gravelotte, and Romain?
> Are we to go home with the insults
>   Of Gambetta and fight it again?
> They challenged: we fought and we've won.
>   They lost, but they never will say it.
> While we have a man or a gun
>   We'll not stay it; not stay it.

In April 1871 Kingsley resigned as editor of the *Daily Review*[63] after asking Macmillan and Charles Kingsley to arbitrate on what remuneration he should receive for premature dismissal. The reason given Kingsley was that the financial position of the paper required a cheaper editor.[64] In fairness to Kingsley it should be stated that the precarious financial condition of the *Daily Review* was chronic rather than acute and required more skills than his to remedy. He therefore hurried to complete *Old Margaret,* and as "family matters" kept him so poor, he asked John Blackwood for a further fifty-five pounds. He wrote three times to Blackwood[65] before getting a reply — and a decision he did not want — a rejection of the manuscript. Blackwood considered Margaret served no purpose as a character, for, he said, "her sympathies [without any reason were directed] to saving the blackguard of the piece [who had] not cast his skin by any means".[66] Blackwood felt so strongly about the matter that he told Kingsley he would rather lose the advance of forty pounds he had given and return the manuscript. Kingsley's reply was brief: "This is indeed a dreadful disappointment. I have calculated so completely on your having taken the story. Can anything be done in the way of alteration?"[67] The answer to this question was contained in a letter written on 4 May 1871 by William Blackwood to his uncle: "He [Kingsley] was in a great way about his story & after a little asked if he could get the M.S. as he had hoped he might make terms with Mr. Nimmo for its publishing and desired me to say to you that he considered you had behaved in the handsomest manner possible. . . . I am glad we are out of it."[68]

When writing to Blackwood, Kingsley mentioned that he had been ill and overworked at the *Daily Review* — "which", he said, "I now quit with thanks to heaven. What they ever had me there for will remain a mystery to the end of time. I should have conceived myself that if they had searched all Scotland or England through they could not have discovered a worse man than myself to edit a religious paper. However they would have me. I wish on the whole that they had left me alone to my old trade."[69] In another letter to Blackwood he stated that his association with the "radical Free Church paper" should have been over "six months ago". At the same time he said he would be leaving Edinburgh in three weeks — presumably towards the middle or end of May 1871.[70] It seems, then, that Kingsley encountered trouble with the paper's owners almost as soon as he returned from the Continent. J. B. Gillies, the staff member appointed to succeed Kingsley, had demonstrated during Kingsley's absence that a prominently known editor was not a necessary requirement for the continued production of the paper and that, in short, Kingsley was dispensable. By going to the war, Kingsley had prepared the ground for his return to England.

Many years later, in 1895, Blackwood's published John Skelton's reminiscences of Edinburgh, *The Table Talk of Shirley*. Writing about those who failed, Skelton discussed a Henry Westerley who came to edit the Nonconformist *Chronicle* and who was perennially impecunious to the extent even of being bankrupt. The reminiscence is obviously a portrait of Henry Kingsley, the name being taken from *Westward Ho!* and Kingsley. Other details confirm the assumption. Firstly, there was no newspaper in Scotland called the *Chronicle* owned by Nonconformist parties. Secondly, the only newspapers called "Chronicle" were the *Kelso Chronicle*, published on a Friday, and the *Rothesay Chronicle* published on a Saturday,[71] neither of which were in a position to have brought in an editor even if they had been "Nonconformist Chronicles". Finally, bankruptcy in Scotland at the time was not necessarily a public matter. There were no judicial expenses, registration, or publicity;[72] just such an arrangement with creditors as would have suited Kingsley with his desire, as expressed in his letters to Blackwood, to prevent details of his financial problems becoming known. For these reasons, then, it seems, although not beyond dispute, that Skelton was referring to Kingsley when he wrote:

> Another of the *Infanti Perduti* who from the beginning was bound to fail — failure was written upon garb and gait — was Henry Westerley. I did not know him till he was well on in life; but up to the time we met he had been failing with cheerful pertinacity. He came to edit our Nonconformist *Chronicle*; and from the day he entered the editor's sanctum, the health of the *Chronicle* declined. Though well on in life, as I have said, he always looked like a boy, somehow we treated him as such; we could not help it; he was so frank, so impulsive, so delightfully foolish and irresponsible. His Nonconformity was kept for the office; when with the Doctor, or the Principal, or myself he was a staunch Tory and Churchman. They gave him a fair salary I believe; but he was perennially impecunious. He delighted, like Fakredeen, in his debts; his creditors interested him keenly; he would entertain us with narratives and monetary adventures and moonlight flittings without the least reserve. He had a marvellous faculty of borrowing, — his success in that far from profitable calling being phenomenal; but whoever lent him a five-pound note might better have cast it into the sea. It melted like snow in summer; and on his oath he could not have told how or where it had gone. But in spite of squint and stutter, which were trying to his friends if not to himself, he was blest with the sunniest temper. Persistent ill-luck could not sour it; he took to the Court of Bankruptcy as ducks take to the water; and when he came out of the Sanctuary for his Sunday dinner with us, he was the gayest and least embarrassed of the company. Though utterly irresponsible — irresponsible as faun or satyr — he was yet — strange conjunction! — the soul of honour. He did not understand what meanness or double-dealing meant. To save his life he could not have lied. It was not in his nature. It never occurred to him. He would have been the last indeed to claim any merit for his transparent and guileless simplicity; and indeed I claim no merit for it; seeing that it

had no moral basis, nor any connection, however remote or accidental, with ethics.[73]

In May 1871, Henry and Sarah Kingsley left Edinburgh for London. Considering Kingsley's rambling statement to William Blackwood, his lack of ability to handle his monetary affairs or at least restrict his household expenses, and his failure to hold his editorial appointment, Maurice Kingsley could have been right when he wrote: "My firm conviction is that in '70 his hope was that a stray bullet on the Battlefield might end all — as, sad to say, he had become an arrant physical coward."[74]

Kingsley had written to John Blackwood that it was "all over now".[75] And indeed it was — the return to London was not a triumphant return. In 1858 there had been a future. In 1871 little could be expected but an ever-recurring shortage of money. The drama was not yet finished, though, and Kingsley, as "an observer", could only watch helplessly as it proceeded. He may have been glad to leave Edinburgh, but little in the way of gladness lay ahead.

15

The Last Years

The last years of Kingsley's life were characterized by a lack of funds and a literary output that fell steadily in quality. In consequence, income declined and three changes of residence occurred from 1871 to 1875. On arrival in London from Edinburgh, the Kingsleys lived firstly at 24 Bernard Square, then moved between March and May 1872 to 29 Fortess Terrace, Kentish Town,[1] and finally in June 1875 removed to Cuckfield, Sussex,[2] where Kingsley died of throat cancer in May 1876.

"Malmaison", written at Kingsley's Bernard Square home, shows that his war experiences were still vividly with him:

> I have only to shut my eyes now, in this quiet London street, to see the wide plains stretching far away from me, bounded by forest, brilliant near the riverside with vineyards, and overarched everywhere by a cloudless sun. I can see the spires of the village churches, some far out upon the plain among the cornfields, some nestling among the boscage of the forest, some just peeping from among the trees in a hollow by a trout-stream – nay, I can go farther than that in my imagination, for I can hear three old familiar voices calling to me, and saying, "Confess, now, that there is no place in the whole world like our Lorraine." I find myself answering, "No, and your Lorraine shall be as fair as ever again, my loved ones." And so I open my eyes again, and look on the dull London street, and the old voices are dumb for a time. [Part 1]

Unfortunately it was not as easy for Henry to shut his eyes and dismiss the worries that assailed him in his quiet London street as it was to recall the past. What remained of 1871 was to be marked by his efforts to get income. If he had received any severance payment from the *Daily Review* at all, he had still to ensure a continuity of work. Consequently, in addition to his regular writing, he sought casual work as a journalist and in December 1871 did some work for *The Times* and took a pupil.[3]

Earlier – soon after returning from Scotland – Kingsley approached Tinsley Brothers to arrange for publication of *Old Margaret* in two volumes and suggested, unsuccessfully, that Tinsley publish a small collection of poems which would be ready by October 1871.[4] Beset by money worries, he asked Tinsley in the same letter "for the balance of our acct about Margaret". But his writing activities were more extensive than this suggests. After meeting the London publisher George Bentley on 29 July 1871, Kingsley wrote to Bentley saying that his new novel, *Oakshott Castle,* part of which Bentley had perused, would run to three volumes. At this time Kingsley had approximately a volume and a half written.[5] Then, too, during the year, after Kingsley added a preface, some introductory paragraphs, and a brief closing sentence: "That is the whole story, General Halbert; and who should know it better than I, Geoffry Hamlyn?", Macmillan published chapter 30 of *The Recollections of Geoffry Hamlyn* as *The Lost Child.* Additionally, Strahan and Co. published *The Boy in Grey,* which had been serialized during 1869 and 1870 in *Good Words for the Young; Hetty,* previously serialized in 1869, was published by Bradbury and Evans; and "Jackson of Paul's" was published in *The Dark Blue* in May and June 1871 — almost as soon as he left Edinburgh. But *Old Margaret* and the short story "Malmaison" were the only two new additions — the other works had already appeared.

Old Margaret, a historical romance of the fifteenth century, received little approval. The main fault, said the critics in the *Spectator* and the *Saturday Review,* was Kingsley's not giving enough time to the "finishing" of his work and the lack of coherence in the narrative. On the other hand the *Athenaeum* disagreed with this criticism and considered there was much to redeem the book, which was marked by "plenty of action, plenty of good description, plenty of well-marked characters... and light Kingsleian touches of insight into human nature". The story, set in Ghent, appears to a present-day reader heavily laden with incident and politics and is handicapped by some improbabilities. Despite its faults, though, the novel copes tolerably well with its theme — the regenerative power of forgiveness. Martina, reputedly a "fallen" woman, is restored to society by marrying her lover, Van Dysart, a soldier of fortune. The narrative involves the House of Burgundy, Guilds, and the van Eycks; Jan van Eyck's painting "The Adoration of the Lamb" is undertaken during the period of the action. Margaret van Eyck is the "Old Margaret" of the title. On occasions the narrative provides Kingsley with the opportunity of commenting on government — for example, when he asks whether the people are fit to govern themselves or not and observes that the perfection of artillery is the death of democracy (chap. 8). As with *Hetty,* the title bears little relation to the narrative.

The other novel, *The Boy in Grey,* which Kingsley wrote in the mode of an allegory, is best understood in terms of the *Athenaeum*'s critique. It was, said the critic, an allegory for the times. The Boy in Grey represented the working classes and the poor of the world; Prince Philarete embodied the royal class; Arturio, the aristocracy; and Athanasio, the orthodox Church. The allegory represented the state of the world, with special emphasis on England, and dealt with the problems of how to reconcile democracy and royalty. The setting ranges widely and involves court scenes at Philarete's palace, India, Canada, South America, and, unexpectedly, Australia. In Australia, The Boy in Grey is kissed by Philarete and is, as a result, saved from destruction when a mob storms his palace. "I am under the impression", wrote Kingsley, "[that the Boy in Grey is] wanted not only in England, but in America" (chap. 15). Once again, despite some criticism of a superabundance of conceits, the journal praised the work. As the early critic points out, there are delightful descriptions, especially of Australian scenery, and in context the "droll conversations" between animals of various species dealing with contemporary affairs are acceptable.

Despite all this activity, Kingsley was still a troubled man. His earlier writings in *Ravenshoe,* on having a "Walpurgis night", seem strangely prophetic when read in the light of his problems:

> Oh, the weary watches! when the soul, which in sleep would leave the tortured body to rest and ramble off in dreams, holds on by a mere thread, yet a thread strong enough to keep every nerve in tense agony. When one's waking dreams of the past are as vivid as those of sleep, and there is always present, through all, the dreadful lurking thought that one is awake, and that it is all real. When, looking back, every kindly impulsive action, every heartily spoken word, makes you fancy that you have only earned contempt where you merit kindness. When the past looks like a hell of missed opportunities, and the future like another black hopeless hell of uncertainty and imminent misfortune of all kinds! Oh, weary watches! Let us be at such times on the bleakest hillside, in the coldest night that ever blew, rather than in the warmest bed that money will buy. [Chap. 41]

Well might he write, then, in the newly added opening paragraphs of *The Lost Child*: "I will tell you the real story, old as I am . . . and as I tell it I hear the familiar roar of old Snowy River in my ears, and if I shut my eyes I can see the great mountain, Lanyngerin, bending down his head like a thorough-bred horse with a curb in his mouth; I can see the long grey plains, broken with the outlines of the solitary volcanoes Widderin and Monmot. Ah! General Halbert! I will go back there next year, for I am tired of England and I will leave my bones there; I am getting old, and I want peace, as I had it in Australia."

On 13 December 1871 Kingsley accepted Macmillan's offer of £300 for publishing a thousand copies of a three-volume edition of *Oakshott Castle.* Whatever came from America or from Baron Tauchnitz was to be Kingsley's as well. Of the money offered, £200 was to be paid on publication and £100 applied against an old debt.[6] Bentley, on 24 November, had already offered £250 in cash on day of publication with a similar provision — foreign and American rights to remain with Kingsley. On 9 December Bentley withdrew his offer, as he felt that Kingsley had been unfair in not notifying his intentions by that date.[7] The charge of unfairness upset Kingsley, who replied that his plan had been to have a "certain great magazine" take the story and offer it to Bentley afterwards. Because it would not be used for some months, he had felt obliged to offer the story to the publishers of the magazine "as a whole [and] at a larger price". He denied that this was of more importance to him, though, than any of his dealings with Bentley, having tried only "to make an arrangement which would please all parties".[8]

Kingsley's financial position was obviously still acute, despite his efforts during the year, for he allowed his membership of the Garrick Club to lapse about this time[9] and during December 1871 sought the help of Lord Houghton, president of the Royal Literary Fund. According to his letter to Lord Houghton, which was addressed to him privately, he was writing at the instigation of his wife, who believed that Lord Houghton would regard him favourably because of his refusal "to relieve himself of his difficulties by law". Kingsley explained that Macmillan would not advance money against an unwritten novel *(Oakshott Castle)* despite having competed successfully for it against Bentley. His time, Kingsley explained, had been spent in writing for newspapers and consequently he had been republishing from his portfolio which was "hardly good enough". Charles, his brother, could not be approached, and indeed, must not hear of the plea for help even if it were only forty pounds that was involved. Hence the only solution was to approach another member of the literary guild.[10]

Three points in the letter raise questions. First, reference to knowledge of a way to relieve financial difficulties by law seems to be a reference to bankruptcy — which was Henry Westerley's method in Edinburgh. Would it have been too risky, for whatever reason, to be declared bankrupt in London? The second point is a reference in the letter to Kingsley's having lost everything in 1865. Did it mean that he had spent his cash reserves during his first year of marriage and had gone irretrievably into debt? Did he have to grant more than one mortgage on the Wargrave house to cope with the expense of Sarah's illnesses and the establishing of that "new house"? Any default might well have meant the loss of any equity possessed in the property. Did in fact the debts of 1865 and the recurrent interest payments constitute a handicap against which he was to struggle in vain? The questions unfortunately are unanswerable, but if repayment problems had been incurred while he was at Wargrave, much could be explained about the financial stringency he suffered when with the *Daily Review* and, previously, at Wargrave.

The third question-raising point in Kingsley's letter to Lord Houghton is the mention of an inheritance of about twelve hundred pounds expected in a few years. This probably referred to money expected from his mother's will or perhaps other expectations, including property, in which his mother-in-law had interests.[11] In a letter to George Bentley written on Christmas Day 1871 Kingsley wrote, "I am so horribly poor till February, and both my fortune and my wifes is so *wisely* tied up that neither of us can touch a penny, [and] struggle through some of the best years of our lives, I overwriting myself, she over-working herself. Hang all marriage settlements

I say."[12] This may have referred to a reversionary interest of Sarah Kingsley's and which she, at one stage, described as "the only thing we have to depend on in the future". The trustee of the interest was said to be George Kingsley, Henry's brother.[13]

In 1874 Kingsley disclosed not only the existence of "a horrible life insurance of my mother-in-law's for £34 which is murder",[14] but mentioned elsewhere that the relevant premium was for a "valuable life insurance".[15] No other details are given, but one inference which can be reasonably made is that the premiums had to be paid to secure some provision for the future, and that this was connected with Sarah's "reversionary interest". If the policy was a life policy for a major sum, Kingsley and Sarah, as beneficiaries, could be expected in return to provide for Mrs Hazelwood. The expense of Wargrave, premiums, and domestic obligations must have been onerous.

As a result of the solicitation, Lord Houghton sent Kingsley thirty pounds on 2 January 1872. Charles Kingsley heard of the matter and wrote to Lord Houghton assuming that it was Sarah who had written for help. In entreating Lord Houghton not to become involved with, or entertain any proposal from, either Sarah or Mrs Hazelwood, he said that, from his knowledge of them for twenty to thirty years, both women were quite capable of imposing on his generosity. To this Lord Houghton replied saying that he could not understand Henry's position. Charles, grieved and astonished to find Henry involved, insisted on repaying any money given so as to satisfy his own "honour and his conscience" and told Lord Houghton that the only people who knew the real mystery of what happened to Henry's earnings were "the two women who have both him and his earnings in their power".[16] That Henry misrepresented the position to Lord Houghton seems possible, for he claimed that the only new work begun in four years was *Oakshott Castle,* whereas he told Macmillan four months afterwards (April 1872) that the period was two years.[17] Kingsley added that he had evicted his tenant at Wargrave and was willing to let the premises for from two hundred pounds to two hundred and fifty pounds a year for ninety-nine years. It is clear, therefore, that he still retained some equity in the property.

The letter to Macmillan was really an overall review of Kingsley's affairs, as he wanted an advance of a hundred pounds on *Oakshott Castle*. Craik sent fifty pounds but understandably pointed out that an unwritten novel was really no security.[18] Obviously the time had arrived for Henry to produce more than intentions regarding his work, even though the sale of the completed novel was beyond doubt. Perhaps, too, there is some significance in the fact that the sum advanced equalled a legacy of fifty pounds Kingsley declared was coming to him.[19] Craik and Macmillan, however, must have considered Kingsley's plight not all due to ineptitude, for on 1 May 1872, in response to another request from Kingsley, Craik sent him twenty-five pounds, as "the doctors had ordered Mrs. K to Hastings".[20]

Despite his financial situation, Kingsley's letters to George Bentley about this time retained a light-hearted tone and were somewhat reminiscent of his early letters to Macmillan. For instance, on 12 January 1872 Kingsley observed that his conscience was kept tender by answering only one letter out of a dozen, hence he was certain no letter had come from Bentley. At the same time he mentioned that the *Daily News* considered *The Harveys,* published by Tinsley Brothers, a success: "What a pity it is that you did not have it. Tinsley is the best of men but Tinsley is not you. Men like you give a name to a book and estopp *[sic]* all the small critics."[21]

The Harveys, which Kingsley claimed in his inscription to have been written some years earlier, appears to have the merit of a better structure, and the persona of the narrator gives some unity to the book. Charles Harvey's father is an artistic clergyman who, in action, attitudes, and speech, succeeds as a character somewhat more than Kingsley usually manages. The theme of diligence leading to success is examined, while the acceptance of patronage and incursions into society are seen to be fraught with the perils that arise from double standards. The sense of the adventurous demonstrated through the narrator, rather than by authorial intrusion, also succeeds to a greater extent than usual. At times the conclusion is inescapable that the presence of the ridiculous not only serves to lighten the more serious elements of the story but also indicates what Kingsley himself saw in the world — the ridiculous and the illogical, side by side with a fate that one endured while maintaining a faith in Divine Providence.

Of *Valentin,* also published by Tinsley, little needs to be said. It is a boy's adventure story not without fault. The narrator's "heart is in France though his home is in Germany". It enables Kingsley to range freely on both sides in the Franco-Prussian war and to demonstrate in various ways aspects of national service, honourable conduct, and duty.

On the Eve of St Agnes he told Bentley that he had not been "to church today to return thanks for the P. of-Wales: you would not be less surprised however if you knew that although I am a devout churchman I only go to church about four times in the year on the average. I consider that I went to church so much too often at Chelsea and at Oxford that I am still three or four years to the good. It will be a disagreeable thing for me if I have made a miscalculation."[22] A few days later, on 25 January 1872, in yet another letter, referring to *South Sea Bubbles,* written by his brother George and Lord Pembroke, he wrote, "I never wrote a book in my life which was not actionable. 'Geoffry Hamlyn,' and the 'Hillyars and Burtons' are both gross violations of those confidences which bind man to man . . . , why the [devil (drawn on the letter)] I was not consulted (I have resorted to a rebus to avoid bad language, which I never use when not in liquor) I cannot conceive. . . . The people that Pembroke and George have attacked know perfectly well that the more they stir the mud the more it will stink."[23] A final example of his banter can be seen in his letter of 8 March, when he told Bentley: "The wife of my bosom gave me pork chops for lunch which may possible *[sic]* account for my present state of mind. The nearest bridge is I believe Waterloo."[24]

While all this was going on, Kingsley was arranging the sale of the copyright of *Hornby Mills and Other Stories* to Tinsley. This was completed on 18 March for fifty-five pounds, Kingsley reserving for himself half of whatever money Tinsley might receive from America. In his *Recollections,* William Tinsley refers to Kingsley's forgetfulness and unreliability: "He was not an earnest worker, and at times forgot that his copy was overdue to his editor or publisher, and in his later years grew quite unreliable."[25] Until now, no evidence has been available to show that Tinsley and Kingsley had at any time disagreed. As it happens, Kingsley accused Tinsley of lacking integrity when the second volume of *Hornby Mills and Other Stories* (actually printed: *Hornby Mills; And other Stories*) was being printed by Tinsley with the title simply *Hornby Mills.* Kingsley considered this would mislead the public and refused to give his name to the arrangement. He felt so strongly about the matter that he threatened to give a personal explanation in the *Athenaeum* which he considered would discomfort either Tinsley or himself.[26] Evidently he had no doubt who would win the argument, for in response to a question by Tinsley he wrote, "I merely want the title on the *boards* to be Hornby Mills and other stories the same as on the title page. That will set us both right with everyone."[27] Printing was stopped and Kingsley's demands were met.

Tinsley records a glimpse of Kingsley as he knew him at this time:

> Henry Kingsley, when not in a kind of sluggish silent mood, was a most interesting companion. But he often wanted almost dragging out of his moody manner. He was a very bad business man, and often too in want of funds — in fact I am afraid money was of very little use to him; and but for having an excellent wife, who was a good woman of business, I am afraid he would have been a very dilatory man, and stayed often very long in Bohemian haunts, or anywhere where there were boon companions and the right sort of liquor to keep good wit rolling. I published three or four novels for Henry Kingsley, but they bore no comparison in merit to "Geoffry Hamlyn," and some other fictions of his earlier years.[28]

Maurice Kingsley, of course, described Henry's marriage as "a most sad one, which drove him to drink, despair and death when a young man, and [was] a bitter, bitter source of grief to my father".[29] This was the viewpoint, no doubt, of the Charles Kingsleys, and consequently some prejudice against Sarah could be present. It seems, though, from these two reports that Henry was, to say the least, convivial. On his own evidence he lunched habitually with Macmillan, and, if Tinsley and Maurice Kingsley are correct, it seems possible that his meagre earnings did not restrict his capacity for enjoying himself.

The link with Charles Dodgson (Lewis Carroll) was kept up, as evidenced by Dodgson's diary entry of 10 January 1872 saying that he called but found Kingsley out and evidently his wife as well.[30] Sarah Kingsley at this time was secretary of a women's group called the Berners Club, in which capacity she solicited books from Richard Bentley.[31] Despite their apparently straitened circumstances, Sarah seems to have made some attempt to keep up appearances. A letter written from 24 Bernard Street records that she accompanied Henry to a special function at St Paul's, entry to which was by ticket only. This Kingsley arranged with a peer, a friend of the family, as Sarah was "exceedingly anxious to go".[32] Sarah actively helped her husband, too, for it was she who arranged to have a volume of Kingsley's works published by Tinsley, first securing Macmillan's permission to do so. This was *Hornby Mills and Other Stories,* during the publication of which, no doubt, Tinsley formed his impression of her. Additionally, she seems to have tried to conserve Kingsley's time by calling at Macmillan's to collect proofs and other material.[33]

On 1 May 1872, when Craik advanced the twenty-five pounds "on account of Oakshott", Kingsley had written, "It is like life and death to me."[34] He was again short of funds and had to move to 29 Fortess Terrace, Kentish Town, although, according to Kingsley, his own doctor wanted him to go to Clifton, Bristol.[35] By getting the advance he managed to get away, defray removal expenses, and provide for a July insurance premium of £16 7s 1d.[36] He was overtired, his health was declining, and he was approaching what he called a "death's door" illness in August 1872.[37]

From Kentish Town Kingsley often went to visit his sister-in-law Mrs George Henry Kingsley, in Southwood Lane, Highgate, and of these visits his niece Mary later wrote:

> And if in those times you could only have summoned up the courage to climb the stairs which led to the attic of that establishment, and peer through the keyhole thereof, it is probable that you would have seen Henry Kingsley in that attic writing a novel; for he had sanctuary always in that house, and fled often to that upper chamber to escape from barrel organs and watercress women and divers disagreeable things that abounded to his distraction in Kentish Town; but, if the day was sunny, it is more probable still that Henry Kingsley would have been found enveloped in a blue haze of tobacco smoke, basking on the lawn, where he would have told you such tales of corroborees, black snakes, and bushrangers as would have made sleep a curse to you for a week to come.[38]

Henry Kingsley's relations with George and his wife were evidently very close as well as cordial. In 1864, George's wife, short of funds, appealed for aid to Henry, who accepted responsibility for the two homes while George was away.[39] Then, again, it was George, aware of Henry's activities, who told Charles the news of Henry's having a pupil when they met in Denver during Charles' American tour in 1874,[40] so that George, obviously, was better informed of Henry's circumstances than Charles. Mary Kingsley's reminiscences also reveal Henry's yearning for faraway Australia in preference to the constant pressure of writing: "Henry Kingsley used to say that in England 'he could never feel the sunshine in his bones,' and often would he far, far rather have been in Australia, gazing over 'the hot, gray plains away to the white sea haze of the Southern Ocean,' or over 'the great wooded ranges, rolling away westward, tier beyond tier, till they were crowned by the gleam of the everlasting snow,' than wearily writing novels in Kentish

Town."[41] This somewhat sad impression of Henry Kingsley's private feelings in mid-1872 contrasts significantly with that of Joseph Hatton, editor of the *Gentleman's Magazine,* four years earlier, when Kingsley lived at Wargrave:

> [Henry Kingsley then] was fighting his way in literature and journalism in London; once I remember when I was editing "The Gentleman's Magazine" over the *Punch* offices in Bouverie Street. I recall his appearance as that of a bright-eyed, pleasant-looking fellow, a trifle, I should say under medium height, sensitive face and manners, with an agreeable play of features and a ready tongue that left no impression on my mind of ugliness physical or mental. He had in a comparatively small frame the carriage of an athlete, a light-weight champion, or a crack rider in an artillery regiment. ... he took no pains to let me know that he had an University education, nor did he talk about his famous brother Charles, nor in any way try to impress me with his importance socially or otherwise. He talked of his work and his hopes very modestly, and if it had fallen to my lot to meet him often, I think he was the kind of man I should have liked to be intimate with. It was a question of work which brought us together. I remember that in response to some slight bit of criticism, he remarked, "My dear Mr. Hatton, you are the editor, I am the contributor, I leave myself entirely in your hands; cut out anything you don't like, if I don't agree with you I shall restore the passages when I reprint the chapters."[42]

During 1872 Kingsley planned a series of three tales called "My Landladies.[43] Of these tales, only one appeared in *Temple Bar,* for which he received twenty guineas in August 1872.[44] That they were discontinued was no doubt due to the length of the first one: "I am so sorry to have made these stories too long because I left Oakshott for them finding it necessary to write pot boilers until my lawyers had mercy."[45] The nature of the legal problem was not disclosed.

In October 1872, ten months after acceptance, Macmillan proceeded with the printing of *Oakshott Castle* as a three-volume novel, with hopes of getting some money for Kingsley from the American market. As well, Tauchnitz offered fifty pounds for *Oakshott Castle* provided Kingsley made some corrections in *Valentin.* This Kingsley agreed to do, and the Tauchnitz edition appeared as a one-volume edition before the year ended.[46]

Any reading of *Oakshott Castle* leaves one impression – this is Kingsley at his best in banter but his worst in novels. Lord Oakshott loves Marie, wife of Arthur, his cousin, who mistreats her. For this Oakshott would kill Arthur, but a reconciliation takes place between the cousins when Arthur is shipwrecked and subsequently dies. Marie becomes a lunatic as a result of all her troubles, and Oakshott loses interest in her. His adopted daughter, Dixie, marries Arthur and Marie's son, Richard, who is also Oakshott's heir, and the novel closes with Oakshott's erection of a lighthouse at the place where Arthur was shipwrecked. If it is argued that Kingsley saw life as a farrago of incident lacking causal connections or rewards and punishments, then the novel might embody Kingsley's view. In its closing pages Charles Ravenshoe,

Austin Elliot, Lord Edward Barty, Father Tierney, and Silcote, all from earlier works, appear with the Oakshott group — as if Kingsley was making a curtain call of characters. But, in between banter and extraordinary incident, he manages to make some biting comments of his own: "Victorian Protection" was another name for prostitution, offered by highly placed personages; childlessness as a ground for separation was humbug; Americans were concerned with every detail of literary geniuses; the domestic morality of the Irish had nothing to do with creed — it was a national instinct, as evident in Londonderry as in Cork; critics were powerful enough to jest that one could be paid *not* to publish a novel; and English was the language of the future, as "French don't assimilate and French don't spread."

Oakshott Castle, because of Kingsley's obvious intelligence, involves more consideration than just its failure as a conventional novel. Its very illogicality is too obvious for even Henry Kingsley. It may well be that the novel over which he claimed to have taken so many pains is his final jest — the fine line between sense and nonsense. On 21 October Kingsley saw Macmillan and sold the copyright to him for three hundred pounds, arranging for a half share of profits after the company had recouped its outlay. This he did without telling Sarah. From this point rapid moves concerning their financial situation occurred. In January 1873 Sarah saw Craik and tried to get an advance upon the same copyright — which request Craik refused. Next day, 14 January, she wrote saying: "Henry must unfortunately negociate elsewhere through an act of carelessness on his part & the fault of a lawyer combined a sudden claim has to be met *immediately* or else everything we possess will be 'sold up' and it is little enough and then a reversionary interest of mine will be attached which is the only thing we have to *depend* on in the future. I am sorry he must involve his book."[47] Sarah was obviously unaware of what had already taken place. If this is so, Craik was indeed tactful, for the sale must have been a book entry to reduce an existing debt. What makes Sarah's action curious is that eleven days after the sale of the copyright — on 1 November 1872 — Henry had applied to the Royal Literary Fund, giving as his reason for the application "simply want of capital and ill health".[48] His supporting letter of 5 November is important, as a record of his position at this time. It was written from 29 Fortess Terrace:

My Lords and Gentlemen,
                            I am extremely sorry that I have to apply to the Literary Fund, but the reason of my doing so lies in a nutshell. I have no income except from literature and every one of my recent fictions has proved an entire failure. I do not suit the public as I did. I depended on my popularity and that has quite deserted me. The announcement of a novel by me is a sign for a perfect howl from some influential critics: this continual worry has broken me down and has seriously injured my health.

    I confess to have published three stories in one year (therefore laziness cannot be charged against me.) For "Old Margaret" (2 vols Tinsley) I received for first and second editions £70. For "The

Harveys" (2 vols Tinsley) the same sum. For 'Valentin' (2 vols Tinsley) *not one penny*. This last story has done me the most bitter harm. Next Routledge accidentally sent me £150 too much in their account about 'Stretton', I thinking this money an honorarium used it by going abroad and getting material for another novel "M. Mathilde." They pointed out their mistake to me, and I at once instead of telling them to keep their account better, said that I would "write if off." I wrote them this last year a story called "Valentin" for the young Gentlemans Magazine. This they have sold to Tinsley as a two volume novel taking from Baron Tauchnitz £40 *more than half the price of the sum I had received for my two previous novels*. I appeal to you gentlemen if a man can live decently and dress like a clerk if he is expected to write two two volume novels for £140.

I have recently been living on "Oakshott Castle" a novel which I have taken great pains about this last two years, and for which Mr. Macmillan has paid me every farthing. What I am to live on now is by no means apparent.

My middle and old age are perfectly secured, it is only the present which I care about, because I wish to work on. I have cleared off tradesmans debts so far that £150 would relieve me from trouble, the debts to those generous friends who have helped me must be cleared at my mother's death who is now 88, they are not very large but larger than I like. I cannot confess to any extravagances either on my part or my wifes, the simple thing is that it is nearly impossible to live like a gentleman by literature alone, unless you are highly popular. I am not so.

In a later letter, acknowledging receipt of a hundred pound grant, Kingsley made further reference to his popularity: "I have written so much that my later works have not sold well, ill health and domestic troubles compelled me to appeal to you." Alexander Macmillan, Edwin Arnold, and Arthur Arnold, editor of the *Echo*, all supported his application. In his letter of 5 November, Arthur Arnold mentioned that Kingsley's financial needs were apparently affecting his health and stated that there were "many circumstances, that could not be mentioned – but none discreditable". In view of Charles Kingsley's comments to Lord Houghton, Arnold's reference must have been to Sarah and her mother. While this was going on, Kingsley had the task of revising the three volumes of *Reginald Hetherege*. By 16 January 1873 the work was well in hand, although Kingsley was unhappy about any alterations to the third volume, other than expanding it. Then, because the end of the month was approaching, when a thirty-four pound premium would fall due, Kingsley asked Bentley for twenty-five pounds, being, as he said, in "Shorts Gardens a fashionable locality lying between Tiny Acre and High Holborn. Where nobody ever has any money and spends the whole of it assisting those who are worse off than themselves."[49]

The precarious financial position in which the Kingsleys found themselves caused Sarah to write to W. F. Pollock, of 59 Montague Square, on 24 January for help, without realizing his connection with the Royal Literary Fund. He in turn wrote to Octavian Blewitt, the secretary of the Royal Literary Fund: "I enclose a letter to me from

Mrs. Henry Kingsley received this morning — Before replying to it, I should like to know if you have heard of similar applications — I suppose Mrs. K. must know of the relief he had from the L.F."[50] Efforts to secure relief did not end there. Kingsley, it seems, appealed to his brother Charles, who refused. Charles's poem "The Delectable Day", written in November 1872, refers to the "fury", the "fool", and the "swindler", which Fanny Kingsley's glosses identified respectively as Sarah, Henry, and Mrs Hazelwood; his refusal can therefore be understood. In any case, Charles and Fanny were under much expense themselves, so help from them was out of the question.[51] After Charles's refusal, Henry and Sarah each wrote to Macmillan, who, when replying, explained the issues confronting the Henry Kingsleys and their relations with Charles as he saw them:

March 10 1873

My dear Henry,
    I have received your letter & your wife's. I have read through both very carefully to this result.
1. You are extremely wrong I think in your idea that there is violent hostility to you in "certain quarters." Nothing could more inaccurately describe the state of your brother's mind towards you.
2. Mrs Henry's statement of a *contingent* condition of your & her property is no statement of your affairs as they stand. These are chances of life and death, apart from the mortgages which appear to me to make this property for present practical purposes simply *nil.* Indeed Mr Andrews told me this when I saw him before you went to Edinburgh. I have no doubt that if he had altered his opinion he could now advance or get advanced money on these properties. But practically the only view a reasonable man could take of them is a possible future for making your & yr wife's later life more comfortable. The obtruding of these either for yourself or for others into a practical consideration of your affairs as they stand is I think utterly delusive.

If you were prepared to put a detailed schedule of your affairs, debts & *not including* the contingent property before your brother & myself say, or any other friends stating also what your future prospects as to *earnings* were, we *would* heartily go into it & do what we *could* fairly. But this *should* be complete & authentic.

I am sorry to say it but Mrs Henry's statement of your earnings this year is apt to mislead. I suppose it means from January. But I hope my dear Henry that during the years you have lived together she has not made a proportion of 12 to 5 of your earnings as if so, your spendings have been larger than I ever guessed. Your earnings during 1872 were surely not inconsiderable.

Mrs Henry speaks of "warning your brother through me that she means to make his conduct public." My dear Henry every step that is stirred in this direction is what used to be called worse than a crime, a blunder. I know your brother's relations to you & even from your & Mrs Henry's statements I certainly do not think it has been other than brotherly. From the first time we met in Eversley Garden, when he introduced us to each other, till last Saturday when he seemed almost broken hearted about you, no word he has uttered has ever been other than tender, even when he thought you most wrong. What are the facts. you say he refuses to advance money to you. But for the last twelve years, taking your respective claims & incomes you have been very greatly better off than him.

I really can say nothing more. Will you kindly ask Mrs Kingsley to forgive my answering her & you together. She will see from what I say that I don't agree in her view of the matter. I think that everything obtained by the processes she describes as *"begging* or *borrowing"* is a direct & fatal blow to your power of *earning* an income. That "making Charles' conduct public" is the sure way to damage you both very much indeed. I don't say that she will not cause him & your mother much pain and sorrow in the meantime, but I hardly think she will value that highly — at least in her better moods.

           Ever affectionately
           Alex Macmillan[52]

Reading between the lines of the kindly and wise counsel that Alexander Macmillan offered, it seems that Sarah *was* in a fury. Apart from Mrs Hazelwood's "murderous" insurance, Henry's spendings were greater than prudence should have allowed, and Sarah was being required to accept some of the responsibility. The property at Wargrave, with its interest on mortgages, had absorbed Kingsley's earnings to such an extent that after eight years of marriage there was little or no equity, and the final telling sentence of Macmillan's letter can only mean that Sarah was now estranged from Henry's mother as well as from Charles. Henry, consequently, financially in trouble and weary of writing, was deprived of family support and advice from two people who had been strong influences in his life. But the relations between the two Kingsley families were to undergo yet further strains. According to Maurice, Sarah Kingsley —

was taken up by a certain fashionable ladies ritualistic preacher — greatly given to confessing interesting fallen angels — who had the impertinence in 1873 to send my father and mother a moral lecture on their iniquity at dropping Mrs. H.K.

 This I had the pleasure of answering in person and he got a sound piece of my mind — I also went to see Mrs. H.K. and expostulate. Whereon she made violent love to me, clothed in a dressing gown and dishevelled hair.

 I gently called her attention to the fact that she was helping my case by making love to her nephew in her own house and fled.

 That night the story of course was rehearsed in the dear old study at Eversley, when in the midst of rage & grief my father burst into a roar of laughter with — "My dear old Joseph, I hope you didn't forget your overcoat".... shortly after I had seen his wife in '73 was the last time we met as I was going into the Euston station and he was coming out with a big book under his arm, bent for the British Museum — with a terrified start of surprise — God! how sad it was — he half turned to run — and when I called to him in the old way, seized my hand & burst out into incoherencies, which I soon got changed into chaff and we had a jolly old fashioned yarn for [an] hour or so, which, as he said when we parted again at Euston on our return from the B:M:, had done him more good than anything for years — Then, as always, he was my dear Uncle with many mutual confidences.

 Leslie Stephen might well be puzzled about her relationship with our family, as she always claimed first cousinship with her husband and signed her name after marriage Sarah Kingsley Kingsley, Sarah Hazelwood Kingsley etc. as caprice dictated.[53]

Henry Kingsley did not share his wife's enthusiasm for ritualism, having views that could only be described as broad. Earlier, in September 1864, after reading a life of Thomas Arnold, headmaster of Rugby, Kingsley commented in a letter to Macmillan that Arnold's vision of the church, consisting "not of the *clergy* but of all the faithful", was a truth "so grand and soul satisfying" that he never wearied of it.[54]

During the year Kingsley's mother died, but a codicil to her will indicates that Henry had already received his twelve hundred pounds.[55] Despite this, his position, for some reason, improved after her death, for in a letter to George Craik, he referred to his "late miserable poverty". He mentioned, too, his indifference to the criticism of his work contained in weekly journals and at the same time indicated he had taken to newspaper writing.[56] Clearly, after Charles's refusal to lend money, Henry sought outside work somewhat more determinedly than he had hitherto. Journalism was not to be the answer to his problems, however, for he wrote to his friend Ralston[57] seeking work in the British Museum. "I want to get among 'books' and away from newspapers," he said.[58] After the observations he had made in *Valentin* about hired men possessing no souls, he had realized that he had to choose — freelancing with an irregular income, or employment "among books" with financial peace of mind. Whatever his motive, he was unsuccessful.

The remaining months of 1873 were occupied in much the same way as already described — writing, revising, and seeking funds. He completed an article on Steele,[59] and wrote two columns weekly on "Sports and Pastimes" for the *Home Journal*, for which he received a hundred pounds per annum and could there, he claimed, express his own opinions.[60] In July he fell ill with whooping cough but continued to work on *Reginald Hetherege*,[61] about which in December he expressed anxiety to George Bentley, saying that it was "idle to judge me by 'young lady' standards".[62] His impatience to write as he wished, and his inability to do so, were finding utterance at last in his protest against the requirements of the drawing-room. He went on to tell Bentley that his remarks about his character, Hester Simpson, "the great novelist", should not be deleted[63] and claimed, that, in this matter, Leslie Stephen agreed with him.[64] "They can't be identified with Miss Austen in any way," he wrote, "they are more meant for Richardson."[65] On 4 May 1874, writing of the alterations made to *Reginald Hetherege* at the suggestion of Bentley's reader, Kingsley complained bitterly to Bentley: "Will you have the goodness to inform me why Charles Reade and Victor Hugo are allowed to write fiction while I am not? What in the name of confusion have I done? That I have been too virtuous I will allow, but surely under a conservative government, that should not tell against me. I will write a bawdy novel some day and make my fortune."[66]

Despite the cessation of his membership in the Royal Geographical Society on 5 May 1873,[67] any inference that his interest in overseas countries had lessened would be erroneous. The previous year he had argued in his article "The Influence of Travel" for the social and political advantages of travel, and the fact that "travelling nations are civilising, while the untravelling ones, equally able, equally brave, seem to spend the most of their time in cutting one another's throats". Travel, he felt, was a factor for peace. Men in days to come would cease to fight for a name or to maintain kingdoms, but men of different nationalities would fight for a cause. For all that, he still detested war — its only good lay in men getting to know other men.[68]

Kingsley still tried to maintain his jocularity despite his worries, and his letters to George Bentley during 1873 contain many instances of his humour. Typical is a reference to his bout of whooping cough: "Lyn Linton in the Saturday Review (anent Oakshott) said that nothing would ever prevent me from writing balderdash. That may be, but the writing of boyish balderdash does not involve infantile diseases, and I am determined to have done with them. I shall make immediate arrangements to have the chicken pox and measles. After that I may possibly write well enough to please the Saturday Review."[69]

Wry humour at his own expense appears in January 1874, when he asks Bentley to keep his confidence a *dead secret*: "If a new literary paper were started, under the editorship of a man with a beard, who gets his hair cut in Kentish Town, who wears a grey great coat, is very fond of fishing, and of looking into the shops in Regent Street, and who is a grand nephew of the Hero of Minden, General Kingsley: would you back him up by advertisements? Pray don't say a word about this. All is in nubibus."[70]

Kingsley's reference to a new literary paper may have been factual but cannot be established. Probably he was being facetious; earlier in the same letter he referred to his possessing "the Compasses, the Alembic, the Bolthead, the Menstrua, the Sublimate, the toads liver, the Athanaroth, the Poker and the Tongs all ready for making it *[Reginald Hetherege]* the finest work of fiction of the day". Bentley's advertising provoked further comment by Kingsley in a letter to Bentley dated 21 June 1874, when he wrote: "You publishers keep alive papers like The Athenaeum by your advertisements. In exchange they abuse and stop the sale of your books. Are you publishers the dirt under the feet of the Critics, 'the men who failed in Art and in Literature,' as Disraeli most truly says."[71]

Before the end of the month he almost sustained a hernia,[72] the injury from which was serious enough to worry him, as did Mrs Hazelwood's ever-recurring insurance premium which fell due for payment. The previous year importuning had caused a break with Charles. This year Henry had no alternative but to seek help elsewhere, and he turned to Bentley.[73] In his letters to Bentley's editor, the tone of his writing changed from banter to seeming irritation because he had constantly to plead for money: "An excessively truculent bootmaker (let his name go down to posterity it is Burton[)] threatens me with immediate law, and will not believe that I have not got any money, which is strictly the

The Last Years

Henry Kingsley in his later years. From an engraving in the *Illustrated London News*, 1876.

truth, as I scarcely receive enough from two sources to pay my butcher and baker. The three articles [Addison 18 pp., Steele 19 pp., Jonson 17 pp.] will cover about 58 pages of the magazine so I daresay you will let me have six pounds."[74] It is evident that Kingsley needed money and was dissatisfied with his rate of remuneration, despite Bentley's habit of paying promptly. Troubled though he was, Kingsley waited another twelve months before asking for payment to be increased: "Although you have paid me with the greatest promptitude and kindness you have never given me more than ten pounds at a time whereas some of them [articles] have gone to 14 16 and 18 pp and none under 10 pp. I know so well that you have had to keep them locked up, and I feel so thankful to you for advancing on them, but could not you let me have five pounds to save me from something very like distraction."[75]

During 1874 Kingsley completed articles dealing with Steele and Marvell and prepared a volume of "Tales and Sketches" which had mostly been, to use his word, "republished".[76] In May he told Bentley that he had done the reading necessary for a biographical and critical work: "No man living has studied British fiction more carefully than myself: in fact I attribute my present partial failure to an undue respect for authorities. You will, however, find nothing of that in Hetherege. My 'Proposal' is that we have in one volume. Steele, Addison, Ben Jonson (1). Beaumont and Fletcher (2) Marvel (3) (in hand and nearly completed) Drayton (4) (in hand) Sterne Swift and Smollet [sic] (5, 6, 7). Horace Walpole and (don't be frightened) Tennyson.... I have studied it for twenty years and I *do* know what I am talking about." *Reginald Hetherege* was at this time still unpublished, and Kingsley was amending the proofs according to the requirements of Bentley's reader.[77]

Criticism and comments, perceptive and humorous, mark his views on well-known literary and public figures: "Shakespeare may have been slightly improper at times, as in the case of Horum, Harum, Herum: but he was utterly incapable of the unutterable foulness of Beaumont and Fletcher: or the simple *coprological* dirt of Smollett. Of all this I can say nothing or next *to nothing in print.*"[78] He then goes on:

> I have come to the conclusion that Dick Steele was a tipsy humbug – I dare write no further. Addison was much worse. Smollet [sic] never made a simple joke which you dare read to Mrs. Bentley or I to Mrs. Kingsley. The only humorist of the eighteenth century who could make you laugh heartily without alluding to the coprological or priapological side of human nature was Sterne.... Sir Richard Steele is never dirty, but he is dull. *I want you very particularly my dear Mr. Bentley, to mark what I am going to say*. The value of Steele is his very dullness.... [From Steele] we get a drearily dull photograph (not picture) of the fathers of the men who conquered India and ruined France. Those dull brutes of Steele begat sons on Richardson's heroines and those sons were the greatest men the world has ever seen since the time of Leonidas. Sir Charles Grandison goes to bed with Pamela, and the result is Nelson. Let us put Gladstone in bed with Lady Herbert and watch the result with awe. We might produce something not previously contemplated.[79]

And, on Hugo, Dickens, George Eliot, and Ben Jonson he wrote:

> There is not one human being alive with one fiftieth part of the genius of Victor Hugo, now that Dickens is gone. George Elliot [sic] may end her career like the unfortunate Miss Baily of the Song, and hang herself in her garters, if she ventures to compare herself to him.... Jonson's "Bartholomew Fair" is by far the filthiest work which I have ever read. How people can quote it and not blush I do not know. The two principal ladies want to – well – I am a modest man – and there is nothing to do it in but an old broken bottle. Mrs. Ursula demands to know if she is to find a common pot for every – ... there is a great deal worse: it licks old Rabelais: but it is unlike Smollett's pure dirt in this, it is intensely witty.[80]

The Last Years

Other events in 1874 are worth noting. Charles Kingsley, on tour in America, still feared that Henry or Sarah might bother Fanny for money, and after meeting his brother George in Denver in June wrote to Fanny accordingly. What George and Charles could not know was that the addition of teaching to his other work was fatiguing Henry so much that his doctor had to order him into the country, for a day or two, to recuperate. This, for Henry, after surviving the hazards of gold-mining and the Franco-Prussian War, seems somewhat uncharacteristic. But events may have been moving beyond Henry's control. His health, delicate in youth, robust in adulthood, was now demonstrating that it had been damaged by his overseas experiences.

Reginald Hetherege was finally published by Bentley, much to Kingsley's relief. The story depends upon concealed information affecting the fortunes of an illegitimate, General Anders, who fears its revelation will bring social disgrace on him and his sister. The setting moves from London to Dorset and rests briefly in Australia. In some respects Hetherege finds, as Kingsley says in *The Hillyars and the Burtons,* "this world is no place for rewards or punishments". He reaches a stage beyond hope or sorrow, which are sentiments not unlike those Kingsley seemed to hold before his death at Cuckfield. But the novel has the inescapable coincidences and unexpected narrative developments which might contribute to its entertainment value, but find it little place today.

Despite his worries. Kingsley found time to visit Penshurst, the ancestral home of the Sidney family, before he wrote his article "Sir Philip Sidney". He was fascinated by "court after court and room after room" which displayed their treasure, but most of all by the family gallery with its Vandykes [sic] and Holbein. "The housekeeper [allowed] me to explain the portraits to *her*," he wrote, "though she was pretty well up in her work.... The Church is almost as historical as the house. The Rector made me kneel down and read a small brass. What was on it? Only 'William Sonne of Thomas Boleyn Knt. Anne Boleyn's brother.'"[81] The ancient evidence of that which no longer was still had its appeal, as it had in the old and far-off days of Chelsea.

Socially, he tried as far as he could to meet others, and when he was absent, Sarah kept up appearances. Edmund Gosse recorded in his diary on 14 October 1874: "Party at Miss Pearson's, Mrs. H. Kingsley, the MacCarthy's *[sic]*." Justin McCarthy recorded too that Henry Kingsley, Gosse, and others met in "the house of one of us, in Gower Street".[82] At one such gathering Kingsley took McCarthy's arm and, glancing towards William Black, whose book, *A Daughter of Heth,* he had just read, remarked, "There's the novelist of the year, and of many years to come. I found that out before I knew who wrote the book, and I believe I was one of the very first to find out." McCarthy thought Kingsley's accent peculiar and his manner odd. These he attributed to either the years Kingsley lived in Australia or even to Kingsley's having "some strange heroic idea that a man was 'a man for a' that' and that the ways of West End civilisation" were not an essential attribute of a gentleman. McCarthy observed also that new acquaintances were apt to be bewildered by Kingsley's bluntness and roughness of speech but that he had "the heart and spirit of a gentleman [with] a distinct touch of something like genius in him".[83]

In January 1875 Charles Kingsley died. Henry, virtually penniless, went to Eversley for the funeral. His thoughts during the journey and the ceremony can best be imagined — an era had ended and he was indeed to endure his fate alone. While he was at Eversley, Sarah was in London trying to find another thirty-five pounds. She sought it from Bentley, saying that Henry had borrowed it from her mother. The money *had* to be repaid to Mrs Hazelwood, Sarah wrote, "as she requires it to pay an insurance". January's premium henceforth would mark the anniversary of Charles's death — as well as of the break between the brothers. Whether Bentley helped is unknown, but on 2 February Kingsley appealed again to the Royal Literary Fund for help. "To conceal poverty," he wrote, "we have parted with every trinket, and have given a bill of sale on our furniture ... a month without anxiety would almost set me right." Shortly afterwards, the fund granted him fifty pounds, which he acknowledged gratefully: "I shall ... try as far as inferior powers go, not to disgrace the great name so recently lost to literature."[84] Charles was still in Henry's mind, and his death, paradoxically, reconciled Charles again to Henry in a way unpredicted by either.

Before applying to the Royal Literary Fund, Kingsley also sent a pro forma letter for Bentley to complete and forward to the fund,[85] but no record exists in the fund's file that Bentley did so; evidently he did not wish to commit himself in such terms as Henry wrote. One who did support Kingsley's request, however, was E. E. Antrobus, of 14 Kensington Palace Gardens, whose letter Henry praised highly as having "not a word too much and not a word too little".[86] Antrobus was evidently an acquaintance of long standing, and the previous year, on 1 March 1874, when telling Bentley that the American market was not worth while, Kingsley mentioned that he had accompanied Antrobus to Newgate to see the claimant in the Tichborne case.[87] Arthur Orton, an Englishman, had returned from Gippsland to claim a fortune left by Sir Roger Tichborne. He was found to be an impostor and sentenced to fourteen years imprisonment for perjury on 28 February 1874.[88] Australian aspects of the case were crucial, and Kingsley, knowing the area, was obviously more than cursorily interested.

In May 1875 Kingsley asked Bentley for the manuscript of two articles, acknowledging that, because of advances, he would have to pay Bentley for them.[89] It seems that he then sent them to Chatto and Windus, who, in good faith, published them and sent Kingsley fifty pounds. Bentley thereupon demanded twenty guineas from Chatto and Windus or the copyright of all of Kingsley's papers.[90] Chatto and Windus accordingly informed Kingsley, who became confused and upset, as he had planned to pay Bentley from other articles he had on hand — one on Canada, another on Sir Francis Drake, and one on the

Siege of Colchester — to honour his promise to pay. He wrote to Bentley: "I no more look to making another farthing out of the book than flying." However, Bentley was to publish no more of his work.

Kingsley's move to Cuckfield took place in May or June 1875. The letter written to George Bentley undertaking to pay for the released manuscripts was written in May 1875 from 29 Fortess Terrace. On 30 June Kingsley wrote again, but this time from Attrees, the sixteenth-century cottage in Cuckfield in which he was now living, apparently happy in his new circumstances: "£40 a year rent, stable let off at £4, an average of £6 worth of fruit in the garden to sell: place so healthy that the doctor (who by the way is my tenant [)] goes up and down the street swearing (at least if he doesn't he ought to)."[91] The scenery delighted him, and the rose garden, he said, was worthy of a poem. Doubtless the roses brought back memories of Eversley, where, with his mother, he had tended French roses enthusiastically; and of her meeting with Thackeray: "You know my son Charles, I should like you to know my son Henry too", and, putting a copy of *Geoffry Hamlyn* in Thackeray's hand, said, "He also can write books."[92]

Kingsley told Craik as well as Bentley that he was writing well. To help defray expenses he had been to Brighton to sell "some trinkets", but he was confident. He had much work on hand and was hoping that by November he would be better placed than he had been for some time. He had moved, he told Craik, because he and his wife could live more cheaply in Cuckfield than in Kentish Town. Whether Sarah was aware of his illness and was saying nothing is unknown. Ostensibly, economies were being practised: "I have not afforded myself any luxury except a glass of Tarragona or a glass of one and threepenny sherry at dinner for one year. Mrs. Kingsley spends what of her salary she can spare not in dressing herself but in keeping me well dressed. All this is nearly over now, so do not be angry with me if I ask your patience again, for no two people ever made a harder fight out of difficulties than my wife and I."[93] His words were prophetically ironical — over it almost was. His chest may have been giving trouble, but no sign of this is given in the letters. He was "working eight hours a day and walking six miles". On 30 June he wrote to Bentley: "God has been extremely good to us, and all the property is saved for our old age."[94] The outstanding debts on his Wargrave property may have been paid, but Kingsley's equity must have been minimal, as the whole of his estate at death was valued at only £450.[95] His comments, however, reveal an expectation of a future, not an end of life.

Much of his ready wit surfaced again in his letters and is indicative of Kingsley himself. Writing of his fellow residents, he observed that they gained an honest livelihood by standing at the corner of the street and looking at him as he passed by: "They seem to thrive at it so well that I think I shall take to standing at the corner of the street and looking at them. You have a larger experience of the world than I can pretend to: do tell me if you think it would pay. There is a middle aged man who makes a perfect fortune (from his appearance) standing in the doorway opposite my window and watching me write. If I could get him to take a turn at my desk, I could take a turn at his door. The Athenaeum would say that it was a change for the better."[96]

In later days, one of the residents from the cottages opposite Attrees — a Mrs Bates, who lived there as a child — recalled Kingsley. "[He was] a man wrapped very much in his thoughts and preoccupied," she said. Out walking, his head would be bowed and his broad shoulders very bent. Suddenly he would pull up "as if shot", stand still for a second or two staring into the distance, then, having recollected himself, he would walk on. "His small, thin figure contrasted strongly with that of 'his large masterful-looking wife'," Mrs Bates recollected. "Indeed it was commonly said among the townsfolk in Cuckfield that there was very little doubt as to which of the pair really wrote those books!" Sarah seems to have pursued her activities of former days and wrote to the Cuckfield Guardians "with some vigour — and success too" about the conditions of the old people in the Infirmary. Her eloquence at the local Penny Readings seems to have matched Henry's abruptness. On one occasion, as the family opposite was dressing for church, he rang the bell to ask brusquely of the "lady of the house" the name of a shrub. The answer was that the lady did not know. No reply or thanks from Kingsley was forthcoming. "A sort of grunted 'Oh!' and he was off. He would run in at all hours, in a rough colonial way, and borrow anything he happened to want, 'from garden tools to a corkscrew;' one day arriving in dress clothes, asking for the latter to open a bottle of wine for dinner."[97]

Henry appears to have loved the scenery of Cuckfield and its neighbourhood and admired its fine old church. To some he seemed unassuming and affable, to others extremely shy yet having the reputation of being always ready to help younger writers, his conversation marked by a breadth of information and his talk "flavoured by eccentric humour that rendered personal intercourse with him extremely pleasant".[98] From all accounts his final days were tranquil. He attended early communion and visited friends at Brighton — sisters of Percy B. Shelley, of whom they appear not to have been very proud.[99] Kingsley admired the Shelleys, and when writing to the editor of *St. James Magazine* asked that two copies of that magazine be sent to them, as members of their circle were potential buyers.[100]

The first indication that Kingsley was really ill lies in the reported presence of Barbara Allen, a cousin of Kingsley's on his mother's side,[101] who acted as his amanuensis for some time at Attrees, where *The Grange Garden, Fireside Studies, The Mystery of the Island,* and one other novel — evidently never published — *Folio and Duodecimo,*[102] were all written.

In *The Grange Garden* Kingsley deals with the securing of an inheritance despite a plot to deny the rightful beneficiaries receiving their due. The tale is more coherent and probable than some of his novels, although coincidences tend to strain credibility. *Fireside Studies,* a critical work, is interesting as a work by Kingsley but hardly rates as an enduring work of criticism. *The Mystery of the Island,* an adventure story, has brief glimpses of Australia and tells in fictional form of treasure taken by mutineers from the Dutch ship, *Batavia,* wrecked off the coastline of Western Australia in 1629. Kingsley had previously treated the affair under the heading "The Shipwreck of Pelsart" in *Tales of Old Travel,* where the account records fully the factual details on which his tale was based. The novel was published posthumously. It is not up to his usual standard; if anything, it is best adjudged a tale for children. In some respects it is a measure of Kingsley's much weakened powers as a storyteller.

In February 1876 *Grange Garden* was published.[103] The event was overshadowed by Kingsley's illness, his condition being diagnosed in April as a cancer of the throat and tongue. He was dangerously ill, and Sarah wrote to Bentley for some books to interest him. On 7 April 1876 she wrote "privately" to the Royal Literary Fund, making it clear that Henry did not know of his condition, which his physician, Dr Morell MacKenzie, considered hopeless. She also wrote, without Henry's knowledge, to Lord Derby at the Foreign Office to get support for her request, and he in turn sought information from the Royal Literary Fund. The fund's reply shows how much the Henry Kingsleys had lost credibility and reputation. Lord Derby was informed that, from what was known of them, there was little doubt Kingsley knew of the approach, "not liking to apply himself so soon after the last grant". The secretary wrote, "I may tell your Lordship that Mrs. Kingsley is one of the leaders of the party of 'strong minded women' and is not a person of much delicacy, for within a week of the grant of one hundred pounds, she wrote to one of our officers (not knowing we suppose that he was so) soliciting private relief on the plea of extreme distress and not mentioning the fact that they had received one hundred pounds from the Fund a few days before."[104] Dr Morell MacKenzie, of 19 Harley Street, Cavendish Square, physician to the Hospital for Diseases of the Throat, also wrote to the fund concerning the nature of Kingsley's illness, and this helped give substance to Sarah's claims. The fund then gave an application form to Leslie Stephen, who, with Ann Thackeray Ritchie, went to Cuckfield to see Henry. During their visit Sarah remained upstairs and Henry received them alone in the sitting-room. Ann Thackeray Ritchie's recollection of the meeting was subdued: "He was himself and yet different from himself, his eager manner was gone; he was very gentle, but he seemed collected and cheerful only. 'They tell me I am going to die.' he said, 'I can't believe it, I don't *feel* like a dying man.' He said this quite naturally, with a sort of simplicity and courage which were a part of all his life. He went on to talk of books and everyday things; he seemed pleased that we should have come to see him, and made us ashamed by making so much of it. Very soon afterwards we heard that he was gone."[105] On 30 April Sarah wrote to the Royal Literary Fund again, having "unfortunately mislaid" the application form brought by Leslie Stephen. She asked if the secretary still had the letter she had sent earlier, as she wanted it laid before the committee at their next meeting. Three days later she wrote to inform them that the illness was fatal and sent the application form with her signature scored out and Henry Kingsley's appended. His spidery writing was evidence of his weakness, and he must have signed his name with great difficulty. The fund granted sixty pounds in three instalments of twenty pounds, the first instalment being paid on 14 May.

Kingsley did not linger long and died on 24 May 1876.[106] He was buried in the local churchyard, adjacent to the church he had described as one of the most beautiful in England, "cared for like a jewel".[107] Many of the villagers as well as visitors attended, and a muffled peal rang from the church as a preliminary. His pall-bearers at the 12.30 p.m. ceremony were Robert Collinson, Edward Dicey, Lennard Lewis, and Spencer Vincent. At the gate the vicar, the Reverend T. A. Maberley, and his curates met the cortege, and the local choir, in violet robes and white surplices, brought up the rear.[108] Wreaths were placed in the grave by Sarah as well as Barbara Allen, while other mourners cast in lilies of the valley. George Kingsley was present, and others at the funeral included Dr E. W. Byass, Kingsley's doctor-tenant at Cuckfield, G. Lillie Craik from Macmillan's, Andrew Chatto, Sister Irene-Mary of East Grinstead, who nursed Kingsley in his last days, and Malcolm Lawson from the Chelsea Catholic and Apostolic Reform Church, founded by Henry Irving's father. Absent was the rector of Chelsea Church, the Reverend Gerald Blunt, who was to testify later to the Royal Literary Fund that Sarah's unthrifty extravagance was characteristic and had brought her and her husband into difficulties "even when they ought to have been comfortably off". The apologies included those of J. A. Froude, A. C. Swinburne, Miss Thackeray, Leslie Stephen, Alexander Macmillan, G. du Maurier, and the Reverend W. Harrison (Charles's son-in-law).[109]

One mourner present at the funeral but unnoted was an American journalist, Laurence Hutton, who had always admired Kingsley's works. He went, he wrote later, "from a spirit of pure affection for, and admiration of Kingsley's literary qualities". On the train to Cuckfield he met Samuel Weller, owner of "the interesting little old place in which Henry had lived, the Grange, whose garden was the scene of the novelist's own death, and of the last tale he wrote". Kingsley had apparently not lost the ability of his Oxford days to charm. His relationship with Weller was clearly such that Weller felt disposed to return to Cuckfield for the funeral and speak highly of him to Hutton.[110] Hutton had lunch with his informant and went to the funeral, where he was introduced to the family doctor and to the rector of the parish, "both of whom knew Kingsley well, and loved him". In Hutton's words: "Hetty herself it was who picked and handed me the little bunch of rosemary which I laid upon the coffin — for remembrance."[111]

In the years ahead Sarah was to survive Henry by forty-six years, dying poverty stricken in Folkestone, where she was buried. Until late in life she was burdened with the responsibility of an ailing mother, who in 1888 had a fit which affected her mentally. As a result of this, she could not recognize Sarah, could hardly see, and was therefore moved to a private asylum.[112] No further mention of Mrs Hazelwood occurs after 12 August 1889, by which time Sarah, despite a personal grant of fifty pounds from the Royal Literary Fund, had sold everything and was still seeking help to defray the expenses of her mother.[113] But all that lay in the future. For the moment Kingsley's insurance policy covered his debts to Macmillan and Co., who sent Sarah the balance of £23 19s 7d. Acknowledging receipt, she said everything was going to the creditors. Her husband's family, she went on to say, had contributed nothing to the expense of his illness, would not respond to her letters, and would not help her.[114]

Of Kingsley's death, his brother George, writing to Macmillan after the funeral, said:

> Poor Henry passed away yesterday morning without a struggle. Slept away in fact. I went down at once on getting a telegram from Sarah but it was too late.
>
> How wonderfully sudden the death of both my brothers has been. It seems as if they had lived up to the utmost tension of their power. I am very sorry for I love them both very dearly, and they were wonderful men – both of them.
>
> I have only been back from the Eastern Mediterranean about a fortnight just in time to see a little of Henry before he went – by this time he is the greatest traveller of the two.[115]

In Cuckfield churchyard Kingsley lay in a double grave over which admirers in 1931 were to erect a stone monument. His brother George, after his death, described him as the "great man – not Charles",[116] while his neice Mary was to write: "Henry Kingsley won no prizes at Oxford save silver cups, he found no fortune in Australia; all his life long he seemed to those who loved him, as all did who had even the slightest personal acquaintance with him, to squander alike brilliant talents and brilliant opportunities without attaining happiness."[117] What was to be said could not affect Henry. For him, the struggle was over; his Walpurgis nights were no more. He lay where the downs symbolically stretched towards the distant "gray plains" of that far south land where he was never more himself, where "Old Snowy" and "Father Goulburn" tumbled and growled through the long, winter nights.

Notes

CHAPTER 1

1. Owned privately in Australia, having been brought from England by Grenville Kingsley, a son of Charles and Fanny Kingsley, hereafter cited as Kingsley Bible.
2. Frances E. Kingsley, ed., *Charles Kingsley: His Letters and Memories of His Life,* 2 vols. (London: Henry S. King, 1877), 1: 5.
3. Susan Chitty, *The Beast and the Monk: A Life of Charles Kingsley* (London: Hodder and Stoughton, 1975), p. 23.
4. *The Southern Cross,* 7 August 1919.
5. F. E. Kingsley, *Charles Kingsley,* 1: 4.
6. W. D. Pink, "Kingsley of Sarratt, Canterbury, and London", *The Genealogist,* n.s.29: 214–24, and 30: 35–38, 86–94.
7. Ibid., 30: 92–93.
8. F. E. Kingsley, *Charles Kingsley,* 1: 3.
9. Archivist, Sidney Sussex College, Cambridge, to the present writer, 31 March 1976.
10. W. F. Perkins, *Boldre: The Parish, the Church and Its Inhabitants* (Lymington: King's Library, 1927), p. 52.
11. Master, Trinity Hall, to the present writer, 27 May 1976.
12. Kingsley Bible.
13. College archivist to the present writer, 31 March 1976.
14. Brenda Colloms, *Charles Kingsley* (London: Constable; New York: Barnes and Noble, 1975), p. 16.
15. Kingsley Bible.
16. F. E. Kingsley, *Charles Kingsley,* 1: 8.
17. Thomas Faulkner, *An Historical and Topographical Description of Chelsea, and its Environs* (Chelsea: Nichols and Son and Simpkin and Marshall, 1829), 1: 153, shows the dormer window clearly in an illustration of Church Place as it was in 1829, the caption giving 1641 as the year in which it was built.
18. Mary H. Kingsley, "George Henry Kingsley M.D., F.L.S., etc.", in *Notes on Sport and Travel,* by George H. Kingsley (London: Macmillan, 1900), p. 5.
19. F. E. Kingsley, *Charles Kingsley,* 1: 4–5.
20. Henry Kingsley, *Tales of Old Travel* (London: Macmillan, 1869), p. 314.
21. Robert Bernard Martin, *The Dust of Combat: A Life of Charles Kingsley* (London: Faber, 1959), p. 21.
22. F. E. Kingsley, *Charles Kingsley,* 1: 4.
23. Susan Chitty to the present writer, 15 April 1973.
24. F. E. Kingsley, *Charles Kingsley,* 1: 12.
25. Pink, "Kingsley of Sarratt", p. 37.
26. Martin, *Dust of Combat,* p. 26.
27. F. E. Kingsley, *Charles Kingsley,* 1: 17.

28. Ibid., p. 18.
29. Colloms, *Charles Kingsley*, p. 39.
30. Martin, *Dust of Combat*, p. 31.
31. F. E. Kingsley, *Charles Kingsley*, 2: 5.
32. Frances E. Kingsley, ed., *Charles Kingsley: His Letters and Memories of His Life*, abridged edition (London: Kegan Paul, 1878), vol. 2, proof copy, p. 33n, the proof copy is now in the Fryer Library, University of Queensland.
33. *Ravenshoe*, dedication.
34. F. E. Kingsley, *Charles Kingsley*, proof copy, p. 109.
35. F. E. Kingsley, *Charles Kingsley*, 1: 37.
36. Malcolm Monteith, *Chelsea's Old Rectory Garden* (1965), Chelsea Public Library.
37. F. E. Kingsley, *Charles Kingsley*, 1: 37.

CHAPTER 2

1. F. E. Kingsley, *Charles Kingsley*, 1: 36.
2. Colloms, *Charles Kingsley* p. 39.
3. M. H. Kingsley, "George Henry Kingsley", pp. 11–12.
4. J. S D. Mellick, "Henry Kingsley in Australia", *Australian Literary Studies* 6, no. 1 (May 1973): 94.
5. Sotheby sales catalogue, November 1932, lots 249–302B.
6. M. H. Kingsley, "George Henry Kingsley", p. 29.
7. F. E. Kingsley, *Charles Kingsley*, 1: 38.
8. Ibid., p. 39.
9. Chitty, *The Beast and the Monk*, p. 49.
10. Kingsley Bible records their births as 12 February 1825 (George) and 24 December 1826 (Charlotte).
11. Martin, *Dust of Combat*, p. 33.
12. Chitty, *The Beast and the Monk*, p. 14.
13. Henry Kingsley, *Fireside Studies*, 2 vols. (London: Chatto and Windus, 1876), 2: 186.
14. H. A. Harvey, King's College Archivist, interview 31 January 1975.
15. Martin, *Dust of Combat*, pp. 33–34.
16. Ibid., p. 34.
17. F. E. Kingsley, *Charles Kingsley*, 2: 131.
18. Ibid., p. 400.
19. M. H. Kingsley, "George Henry Kingsley", p. 5.
20. *Fireside Studies*, 1: 269.
21. M. H. Kingsley, "George Henry Kingsley", p. 6.
22. British Library (hereafter cited as BL), Add. MS41297, fol. 124.
23. F. E. Kingsley, *Charles Kingsley*, proof copy, p. 109.
24. Martin, *Dust of Combat*, p. 33.
25. Ibid., p. 41.
26. R. B. Martin papers, Princeton University.
27. Charles Kingsley to Mrs Knowles, National Library of Scotland (hereafter cited as NLS), Acc. no. 60, fol. 58.
28. Chitty, *The Beast and the Monk*, p. 27.
29. Martin, *Dust of Combat*, p. 52.
30. F. E. Kingsley, *Charles Kingsley*, 1: 79–90, passim.
31. *Fraser's Magazine*, n.s. 11: 401. (March 1875).
32. Maurice Kingsley, "Personal Traits of Henry Kingsley", *The Book Buyer*, 11, no. 12 (January 1895): 727.
33. Martin, *Dust of Combat*, p. 98.
34. Charles Kingsley to Ludlow, 20 October 1848, Ludlow Papers, Cambridge University Library.
35. Ludlow to Charles Mansfield, Ludlow Papers.
36. BL, Add. MS 41297.
37. Martin, *Dust of Combat* p. 98.

Notes

CHAPTER 3

1. *Tales of Old Travel*, p. 256.
2. Laurence Hutton, "The Literary Life", *The Critic* 45 (July-December 1904): 330–31.
3. Benjamin E. Martin, *Old Chelsea: A Summer-Day's Stroll,* 2nd ed. (London: T. Fisher Unwin, 1889), p. 146.
4. F. J. C. Hearnshaw, *Centenary History of King's College* (London: Harrap, 1929), p. 369.
5. *Tales of Old Travel*, p. 256.
6. Ibid.
7. Kings's College archives.
8. Kingsley Bible.
9. Colloms, *Charles Kingsley*, p. 78.
10. F. E. Kingsley, *Charles Kingsley*, 1: 134.
11. S. M. Ellis, *Henry Kingsley 1830–76: Towards a Vindication* (London: Grant Richards Pronto, 1931), p. 26, n. 1.
12. King's College archives.
13. Archivist, King's College, to the present writer, 1 April 1975.
14. King's College archives.
15. M. Kingsley, "Personal Traits", p. 730.
16. Martin, *Old Chelsea,* pp. 147–48.
17. Henry Kingsley, "Thackeray", *Macmillan's Magazine* 9: 362 (February 1864).
18. Martin, *Dust of Combat,* pp. 97–98.
19. King's College archives.
20. Martin, *Dust of Combat,* p. 97.
21. Ibid., p. 110.
22. BL, add. MS 41297, fol. 52.

CHAPTER 4

1. R. A. Sisson, *The Treasures of Time: Embroidered Kneelers in Chelsea Old Church* 2nd ed. (London: Belgrave Press, 1968), p. 1.
2. Faulkner, *Chelsea, and Its Environs,* 1: 153.
3. Martin, *Old Chelsea,* pp. 146–49.
4. Faulkner, *Chelsea, and Its Environs,* facing p. 153.
5. Alfred Beaver Elliott, *Memorials of Old Chelsea* (London: Elliott Stuck, 1892), pp. 116–17.
6. Sisson, *Treasures of Time,* pp. 6–8.
7. M. H. Kingsley, "George Henry Kingsley", p. 11.
8. "Some Account of the Village of Inverquoich", *Macmillan's Magazine* 7: 447–59 (April 1863).

CHAPTER 5

1. Joseph Foster, *Alumni Oxoniensis . . . 1715–1886* (Oxford: Parker, 1888), 2: 798.
2. F. E. Kingsley, *Charles Kingsley*, 1: 212.
3. Wellington Public Library, Turnbull Library, MS. 64, J. E. Fitzgerald, vol. 6. I am indebted to Professor P. D. Edwards, University of Queensland, for this letter. Kingsley's letters are quoted as written.
4. Kingsley to Alexander Macmillan, undated (endorsed June 1859), Berg Collection, New York Public Library.
5. Ibid.
6. John Cordy Jeaffreson, *A Book of Recollections,* 2 vols. (London: Hurst and Blackett, 1894), 1: 79–81 passim.
7. Ibid., p. 81.
8. Ibid.
9. Ibid., p. 85.

10. Ellis, *Henry Kingsley 1830–1876*, p. 38, n. 1.
11. Martin, *Dust of Combat*, p. 166.
12. Susan Chitty to the present writer, 13 June 1973 quoting unpublished letter.
13. Jeaffreson, *Book of Recollections*, p. 84.
14. Ibid., p. 100.
15. Ibid., pp. 81–84 passim.
16. Ellis, *Henry Kingsley 1830–1876*, pp. 32–33.
17. C. Kegan Paul, *Memories* (London: Routledge and Kegan Paul, 1899), pp. 142–43.
18. F. E. Kingsley, *Charles Kingsley*, 1: 292–97 passim.
19. Anne Thackeray Ritchie, "Chapters from Some Unwritten Memoirs. My Witches Caldron IV", *Macmillan's Magazine* 66: 265–70 (February 1891).
20. Martin, *Dust of Combat*, p. 131.
21. F. E. Kingsley, *Charles Kingsley*, 1: 294.
22. Martin, *Dust of Combat*, p. 136.
23. Ibid., p. 138.
24. Ludlow Papers, Cambridge University Library.
25. M. Kingsley, "Personal Traits", p. 729.
26. *The Times*, 26 June 1852, p. 8.
27. Ellis, *Henry Kingsley 1830–1876*, p. 39.

CHAPTER 6

1. Henry Pares Venables was the second son of Thomas Venables, a nephew of Captain James King, who was a companion of Captain James Cook on his last voyage to the Pacific Ocean. H. P. Venables's mother was Jane Sturt, sister of Charles Sturt. Relatives of Sturt and Venables served in the Crimean War, and R. E. C. Venables, H.P.'s grandson, believes Kingsley had access to those experiences when writing his books. Another uncle, Evelyn Sturt, owned Compton station, South Australia, which originally included the property known as Mount Gambier station when owned by Willi Mitchell before his purchase of Langi Willi, Victoria.
2. Martin, *Dust of Combat*, p. 167.
3. *Tales of Old Travel*, pp. 281–82.
4. "The Land of Gold", *Illustrated Magazine of Art*, n.s. 1, vol. 31 (1854): 42.
5. *Lloyds Register of British and Foreign Shipping 1 July 1854 to 30 June 1855* (London: Cox and Wyman, 1855).
6. Public Records Office, London, BT98/4199, document 57.
7. Ellis, *Henry Kingsley 1830–1876*, p. 41.
8. Venables MS, Baillieu Library, Melbourne University.
9. "Land of Gold", p. 43.
10. Ibid.
11. D. J. Golding, ed., *The Emigrant's Guide to Australia in the Eighteen Fifties* (Melbourne: Hawthorn Press, 1973), p. 130.
12. *Tales of Old Travel*, pp. 308–9.
13. Ibid., p. 122, in the same passage Kingsley later claimed that the *Gauntlet* "won or nearly won the race from China afterwards". The ship's papers confirm that it proceeded to Bombay and China after leaving Port Phillip. Fourteen crew members were discharged in Melbourne on 4 December 1853.
14. J.K. Loney, *Wrecks in Port Phillip Bay* (Geelong: Ken Jenkin Print, n.d.), pp. 5–6.

CHAPTER 7

1. Cuthbert Fetherstonhaugh, *After Many Days* 2nd ed. (Sydney: John Andrew, 1918), p. 23.
2. Celeste de Chabrillan, *The Gold Robbers*, trans. Lucy and Caroline Moorhead (Melbourne: Sun Books, 1970), p. 14.
3. John Sadlier, *Recollections of a Victorian Police Officer*, facsimile reprint (Ringwood, Vic.: Penguin, 1973), p. 22.
4. J. Alex. Allan, *Men and Manners in Australia* (Melbourne: Cheshire, 1945), p. 67.

Notes

5. Sadlier, *Recollections,* p. 24; see also Kingsley's "My Landladies: Chapters of a Digger's Life", *Temple Bar* 36 (October 1872): 371–90.
6. Venables MS, Baillieu Library, Melbourne.
7. Raymond Bradfield, *Castlemaine: A Golden Harvest* (Kilmore, Vic.: Lowden, 1972), pp. 10–13 passim.
8. A. W. Greig, "Letters from Australian Pioneers", *The Victorian Historical Magazine* 12, no. 46 (December 1927): 61–62. (Letter from Jas. Hodgson, 15 April 1852).
9. John Neill Macartney, *Sandhurst As It Was and As It Is* (Sandhurst: Burrows, 1882), pp. 13–14.
10. James Flett, *The Story of an Old Gold-Diggings Town: Dunolly* (Melbourne: The Poppet Head Press, 1956), p. 8.
11. L. P. G. Smith, *Centennial of The Church of St. Mary, Kingower, 1853–1971* (Ballarat: Baxter and Stubbs, n.d.), p. 6.
12. Joseph Furphy, *Such Is Life* (Sydney: Angus and Robertson, 1966), p. 205.
13. R. V. Billis and A. S. Kenyon, *Pastoral Pioneers of Port Phillip,* 2nd ed. (Melbourne: Stockland Press, 1974), p. 87.
14. G. F. James, ed., *A Homestead History, Being the Reminiscences and Letters of Alfred Joyce . . . 1843 to 1864,* 3rd ed. (Melbourne: Oxford University Press, 1969), pp. 53–54.
15. Ronald L. Carless, *Visit to "The Springs," Moliagul* (n.d.), a pamphlet prepared for the Welcome Stranger Centenary Committee, p. 2.
16. Ada Cambridge, *Thirty Years in Australia* (London: Methuen, 1903), p. 3.
17. Fetherstonhaugh, *After Many Days,* p. 42.
18. Frank Cusack, editor of *The Australian Christmas* (Melbourne: Heinemann, 1966), told this to the present writer in October 1972; he expressed a further belief that Kingsley was on the Moliagul field rather than Epsom.
19. G. H. Heaton: *The Australian Dictionary of Dates,* part 2 (Melbourne: George Robertson, 1879), p. 46.
20. *Tales of Old Travel,* p. 366.
21. Greig, "Letters from Australian Pioneers", pp. 61–62.
22. Rosilyn Baxter, "Henry Kingsley and the Australian Landscape", *Australian Literary Studies* 4, no. 4 (October 1970): 395–98.
23. La Trobe librarian, State Library of Victoria, to the present writer, 14 January 1974.
24. George H. Kingsley, *Notes on Sport and Travel* (London: Macmillan, 1900), pp. 49–50.
26. Ellis,
25. P. M. Penhallurick to the present writer, 5 March 1974.
26. Ellis, *Henry Kingsley 1830–1876,* p. 37.
27. *Tales of Old Travel,* pp. 282–83.
28. *The Ovens and Murray Advertiser* refers to this rush on several occasions between 27 January 1855 and 17 March 1855 in such terms that it is beyond doubt the hoax of *The Hillyars and the Burtons,* chap. 72. The final reference says, "Sandy Creek, Omeo and Mt. Gibbo are like dreams passed away." *The Constitution* on 12 July 1856, refers to the Omeo rush as having been "a ruinous expedition". Flett (*Dunolly,* p. 164) states "the rush to the Gibbo was a Hoax". This was September 1854.
29. Flett, *Dunolly,* p. 454.
30. The depth at which the lead was recovered and the fact that the bottom was "pink" was confirmed by H. Rodwell of Avoca, an old miner, in January 1973 when the writer interviewed him. He maintained that, as a boy in Avoca, he was befriended by the local undertaker who told him of identities who had been on the field. He was adamant that Henry Kingsley had been on Avoca, and used his old mining maps to explain where the lost lead was found.
31. *The Times Literary Supplement,* 9 January 1930, p. 28.
32. P. L. Brown, ed., *Clyde Company Papers,* vol. 6, 1854–58 (London: Oxford University Press, 1968), p. 115.
33. Billis and Kenyon, *Pastoral Pioneers of Port Phillip,* p. 172.

CHAPTER 8

1. "Charles Sturt: A Chapter from the History of Australian Exploration", *Macmillan's Magazine* 11: 204–17 (January 1865).
2. "Wild Sports of the Far South", *Fraser's Magazine* 59: 587–97 (May 1859).
3. See map of Victoria (London: John Arrowsmith, 1855).
4. "The New Church at the Mistibithiwong", *Good Words* 9 (1868): 322–28.
5. Betty Howard, *They Came to Yass Valley* (Yass, 1970), p. 18.
6. Mackenzie was the author of *The Emigrant's Guide or Ten Years' Practical Experience in Australia* (London: W. S. Orr, 1845) and *The Gold Digger* (London and Dublin: Williamson, 1852): excerpt quoted in *Friday Mount*, by Margaret Carnegie (Melbourne: Hawthorn Press, 1973), pp. 172–73.
7. Carnegie, *Friday Mount*, p. 173.
8. James S. Hassall, *In Old Australia* (Brisbane: R. W. Hews, 1902), pp. 73–78 passim.
9. The first gaol in Sydney was in Essex Street, between Harrington and George streets.
10. Geoffrey Scott, *Sydney's Highways of History* (Melbourne: Georgian House, 1958), p. 170.
11. M. Kingsley, "Personal Traits", p. 729.
12. Ellis, *Henry Kingsley 1830–1876*, p. 45.
13. Clement Shorter, memoir of Henry Kingsley, in *The Recollections of Geoffry Hamlyn* (London: Ward, Lock and Bowden, 1895), p. xvii.
14. Ibid., p. xiv.
15. F. W. Maitland, *The Life and Letters of Leslie Stephen* (London: Duckworth, 1906), p. 383.
16. Cf. Richard Mahony in Henry Handel Richardson's *The Fortunes of Richard Mahony* (London: Heinemann, 1954), p. 416: "Returning full of honours and repute, he found that the mere fact of his having lived and practised in Australia cast a slur on his good name."
17. Shorter, memoir, pp. xiv, xvii.
18. Edwin Arnold to Clement Shorter, 9 October 1894, Brotherton Library, Leeds University.
19. Henry Kingsley, review of *Reminiscences of a Thirty Years' Residence in New South Wales and Victoria*, by R. Therry, *The Reader* 1: 256 (14 March 1863).
20. *The Private Execution Act 11, Vic. No. 40. 1853* – proclaimed 10 January 1855 – required the attendance of "such constables, Military Guard, and adult spectators", as the sheriff, under-sheriff, or deputy thought necessary. Furthermore, a certificate of attendance was to be signed by the witnesses for subsequent publication in the *Government Gazette*.
21. *Rules and Regulations for the Government and Guidance of the Mounted Patrols of New South Wales* (Sydney: Government Printer, 1853), p. 7.
22. Discovered by the present writer in Archives, State Library of New South Wales, at rear of MSS 7/6291; these are the personal records concerned.
23. See note 19.
24. Frank Fowler, *Southern Lights and Shadows*, 2nd ed. (London: Sampson Low, 1859), pp. 48–49.

CHAPTER 9

1. J. V. Pendergast, *Pioneers of the Omeo District* (Melbourne, Riall Bros., 1968), p. 17.
2. See *Map of Victoria* (London: John Arrowsmith, 1855).
3. Locations of the stations are given in *Geoffry Hamlyn*, chaps. 20, 22, 23, 25, and 27.
4. W. K. Hancock, *Discovering Monaro* (Cambridge: Cambridge University Press, 1972), p. 8, favours Tubbutt for the site of Buckley's Baroona, but on inspection it is difficult to correlate its hilly, enclosed nature with the "splendidly grassed lands" of Baroona.
5. Harry C. Perry, *A Son of Australia: Memories of W. E. Parry-Okeden, I.S.O., 1840–1926* (Brisbane: Watson, Ferguson, 1928). Rosedale, Victoria, was

Notes

named after his mother, Rosalie Caroline Dutton, formerly of Chester, England. Her husband, David Parry-Okeden, served under Sir Edward Codrington at the battle of Navarino, and Sir Edward's son William was commander-in-chief at Sebastopol. He sent his own journal of the campaign to Charles Kingsley at one stage, which raises the possibility of its accessibility to Henry as a source of battle information.

6. Mary Howitt Walker, *Come Wind, Come Weather: A Biography of Alfred Howitt* (Carlton, Vic.: Melbourne University Press, 1971), p. 174.
7. Clem Ingram of Tubbutt, with whom the present writer discussed the matter in 1973, considered the route possible. Further details are given by A. M. Pearson, *Echoes from the Mountains* (Omeo, Vic.: Omeo Shire Council, 1969), p. 35.
8. Pearson, *Echoes from the Mountains*, p. 34.
9. Forests Commission, Victoria, to the present writer, 22 August 1973.
10. Ibid.
11. W. B. Clarke, *Researches in the Southern Gold Fields of New South Wales*, (Sydney: Reading and Wellbank, 1860), pp. 127, 131, 138.
12. Letter to the present writer, 20 April 1974.
13. Kingsley's original manuscript of *The Hillyars and the Burtons*, portion of which, part of chapter 49 to chapter 51, is now held in the Department of Special Collections, University of California, shows on page 448 that "Port Romilly" was substituted for "Port Bathurst". Bathurst is located on the western side of the Blue Mountains. Earlier, facing page 499, an editorial gloss "no name or imaginary" appears beside "St. George's, Hanover Square", for which was substituted "St. Nicholas Without". The Californian MS. appears to be the only surviving portion of the original and was given by Kingsley to his friend John Reid of Inverloddon, Wargrave, Berkshire about 1869.
14. *Gippsland Guardian*, 22 February 1856, p. 2.

CHAPTER 10

1. Hugh Anderson, ed., *Eureka: Victorian Parliamentary Papers Notes and Proceedings 1854–1867*, facsimile reprint, (Melbourne: Hill of Content, 1969).
2. *Tales of Old Travel*, p. 336 n.
3. "Wild Sports of the Far South".
4. Fetherstonhaugh, *After Many Days*, p. 73.
5. Perry, *Son of Australia*, p. 72; Billis and Kenyon, *Pastoral Pioneers of Port Phillip*, p. 15.
6. *Tales of Old Travel*, p. 361 n.
7. Of river characteristics, Kingsley wrote in "Charles Sturt": "Captain Sturt speaks of it [the Murray] as being perfectly clear. It doubtlessly was so in January; but later on in the summer I think he would have found it assume a brown, peaty colour. At least such is my impression. I used to notice this fact about nearly all the rivers I knew in Australia Felix. While the vegetable matter was thoroughly washed out of them and diluted by the winter floods, they were – instance the Yarra, Goulburn and Ovens – very clear. But later on in the summer, towards February, they began, as the water got lower, to get stained and brown, although not foul."
8. H. C. Gordon, *Yea: Its Discovery and Development, 1825–1920* (Melbourne: Hawthorn Press, 1954), p. 27.
9. Reference Librarian, University of Melbourne, to the present writer, 16 December 1976.
10. L. R. Cranfield, "The History of Warrandyte", *Victorian Historical Magazine* 27, no. 1 (October 1955): 19.
11. Ellis, *Henry Kingsley 1830–1876*, pp. 46–48.
12. Rolf Boldrewood, *A Sydney-Side Saxon* (London: Macmillan, 1891), p. 9.
13. Rose Browne, "Squattlesea Mere: Rolf Boldrewood's First Station", *Warrnambool Standard* 23 June 1928.
14. C. W. Darley, writing to Cuthbert Fetherstonhaugh from Longheath, Little Bookham, England, on 27 August 1919, stated that T. A. Browne stayed with Darley's father in Co. Wicklow, Ireland, and spent much time in reading

Geoffry Hamlyn. He went on to ask whether Fetherstonhaugh had ever noticed the similarity in descriptive powers of Browne and Kingsley, and attributed Browne's skills to a close study made by him of *Geoffry Hamlyn,* which Browne nearly knew off by heart. (Cuthbert Fetherstonhaugh Correspondence, Mitchell Library, no. B1504.)
15. Dunmore diary: "[16 May 1857] ... Tom and George to Post ... T.A.B. and Henry came." William Earle records Kingsley's presence at Dunmore as a guest in *Earle's Port Fairy,* ed. C. E. Sayers, 1896 (Victoria: Olinda Public Relations, 1973), p. 53. A brief discussion of Kingsley's interest in colonial problems is contained in Leonie Kramer's introduction to the facsimile edition of *The Hillyars and the Burtons* (Sydney: Sydney University Press, 1973), pp. 9–13.
16. "My Autobiography", p. 75, T. A. Browne Papers, La Trobe Library, State Library of Victoria, MSS 5767, box 145/4(a).
17. Sayers, *Earle's Port Fairy,* pp. 53–54; Capt. John Mason letter to *The Australasian,* 1 November 1890, p. 869.
18. Browne, "My Autobiography", pp. 69–72 passim.
19. William Westgarth, *Personal Recollections of Early Melbourne and Victoria* (Melbourne: George Robertson, 1888), p. 45.
20. Rolf Boldrewood, *Babes in the Bush* (London: Macmillan, 1900), pp. 230–31: the excerpt is necessarily brief.
21. Douglas Sladen, *My Long Life* (London: Hutchinson, 1939), pp. 49–58 passim.
22. Named as such in the Dunmore diary; evidence exists that Romeo was so marked, as described in "Wild Sports of the Far South" and *The Hillyars and the Burtons,* chap. 50.
23. Alexander Henderson, *Henderson's Australian Families* (Melbourne: Henderson, 1941), 1: 196–99 passim.
24. Rose Browne, "Squattesea Mere".
25. C. Stuart Ross, "The History of Settlement in the Western District", *Victorian Historical Magazine* 1, no. 2 (April 1911): 68.
26. Rolf Boldrewood, *Old Melbourne Memories,* ed. C. E. Sayers. Melbourne: Heinemann, 1969), pp. 149–50.
27. Richardson diaries; Mitchell paid a farewell visit to Gorrinn before leaving for England in 1859.
28. Departed Plymouth 15 October 1857, arrived Port Phillip 21 December 1857 (*Argus,* 23 December 1857, p. 4).
29. Shipping departures, January–April 1858, Archives, State Public Library of Victoria.
30. Fetherstonhaugh, *After Many Days,* p. 157. An oil painting of Alice Hawthorn still exists and is owned by a descendant, Robert Chirnside of Carranballac, Victoria, near Langi Willi.
31. Cusack, *The Australian Christmas,* p. 47.
32. Lorna L, Banfield, *Green Pastures and Gold* (N.p. [Vic.]: Mullaya Publications, 1974), p. 42.
33. Nathaniel Walter Swan, *A Couple of Cups Ago and Other Stories* (Melbourne: Cameron, Laing, 1885), p. xii.

CHAPTER 11

1. *Argus,* 16 January to 24 February, p. 1; 26 February, p. 4.
2. "Our Brown Passenger" was published in *Hetty and Other Stories.*
3. Ships log, Public Records Office, London, log BT98/5190 (8300–8302).
4. Public Records Office to the present writer, 9 July 1973; and ship's log.
5. *The Boy in Grey,* chap. 14.
6. "Our Brown Passenger."
7. Lat. 51°12′S. long. 161°45′E.
8. "List of Electors entitled to vote in election of members to serve in the Legislative Assembly and Council – Victoria, 21/7/1856–30/6/1857," (Melbourne: Government Printer).
9. "The Two Cadets", chap. 2.
10. *The Hillyars and the Burtons,* chap. 12.
11. Ibid., chap. 5.

12. A reference to "bush-madness" as such occurs in *The Mystery of the Island*, Chap. 11.
13. *Geoffry Hamlyn*, chap. 27.
14. "Seeking Your Fortune", published in *Hetty and Other Stories*.
15. *Ravenshoe*, chap. 57.
16. *Reginald Hetherege*, chap. 39.

CHAPTER 12

1. Ship's log.
2. Shorter, memoir, p. xvii; curiously, Tom Thurnall behaved similarly in Charles Kingsley's *Two Years Ago* (London: Macmillan, 1890, p. 465), which was first published in 1857, before Henry's return to England.
3. Later the rector, the Reverend Abel Gerald Wilson Blunt, 1860–1902; *Programme of Events... Chelsea Parish Church of Saint Luke (1824–1974)*.
4. Dedication, *Geoffry Hamlyn*.
5. Shorter, memoir, p. xvii.
6. Macmillan letters, BL, Add. MSS 55842/415 of 10 March 1873. Unless otherwise stated, correspondence referenced to the Macmillan letters is from Alexander Macmillan to Henry Kingsley.
7. Berg Collection, New York Public Library (hereafter cited as Berg Collection), letter dated 25 November 1858. Kingsley's letters in this collection are mostly undated but endorsed as belonging to a particular quarterly period, e.g., "July–Sept 1859". Undated letters are referred to hereafter by the quarter endorsed on the letter. Unless otherwise stated, correspondence referenced to the Berg Collection is from Henry Kingsley to Alexander Macmillan.
8. Berg Collection, undated (July–Sept. 1858).
9. Ibid.
10. Macmillan letters, BL, Add. MSS 55836, vol. 151, fol. 32.
11. Berg Collection, undated (July–Sept. 1858).
12. Ibid., undated (July–Sept. 1858).
13. George A. Macmillan, ed., *Letters of Alexander Macmillan* (Glasgow: Glasgow University Press, 1908), pp. 5–6. In the same letter he wrote that he had met Henry Kingsley and liked him exceedingly.
14. Berg Collection, 25 November 1858.
15. Macmillan letters, BL, Add. MSS 55836, vol. 151, fol. 86, gives the address as 121 Marina, St. Leonards.
16. Berg Collection, undated (Oct.–Dec. 1858).
17. Macmillan letters, BL, Add. MSS 55836, vol. 151, fol. 86; in this letter Macmillan queried Hamlyn's ability, as narrator, to know as much as he did about the Hawker family but allowed that Madge and Bill Lee could have told him.
18. Henry Kingsley letters, BL, Add. MSS 54916, fol. 7.
19. Berg Collection, undated (Jan.–March 1859).
20. *North British Review* 31 (1859): 400.
21. Berg Collection, 2 January 1859.
22. Ibid., undated (Jan.–March 1859).
23. Macmillan letters, BL, Add. MSS 55836, vol. 151, fol. 153.
24. Kingsley to Ticknor and Fields, 21 February 1859, Houghton Library, Harvard University; also *Harvard Library Bulletin* 12, no. 2: 216–17.
25. Berg Collection, undated (Jan.–March 1859).
26. Macmillan letters, BL, Add. MSS 55836, vol. 151, fol. 180.
27. Berg Collection, undated (Jan.–March 1859).
28. Ibid.
29. C. L. Graves, ed., *Life and Letters of Alexander Macmillan* (London: Macmillan, 1910), p. 125.
30. Macmillan letters, BL, Add. MSS 55836, vol. 151, fol. 231; on publication, Kingsley requested that copies be sent to the *Argus*, the *Age*, and the *Herald* newspapers, all in Melbourne, and also to the *Sydney Morning Herald*.
31. Macmillan letters, BL, Add. MSS 55836, vol. 151, fol. 231.
32. Berg Collection, undated (Jan.–March 1859).

33. Macmillan and Co. list dated April 1859, in Berg Collection.
34. Berg Collection, undated (April–June 1859).
35. Ibid, undated (April–June 1859).
36. *North British Review* 31 (1859): 393.
37. "Big Brothers", *The Living Age* 794 (1859): 446.
38. Berg Collection, undated (April–June 1859).
39. Ibid, undated (April–June 1859).
40. Berg Collection, 5 December 1859.
41. Ibid, undated (April–June 1859).
42. F. E. Kingsley, *Charles Kingsley,* 2: 102.
43. B.L, Add. MSS 54916, fol. 10.
44. William Tinsley, *Random Recollections of an Old Publisher,* 2 vols. (London: Simpkin, Marshall, Hamilton, Kent, 1900), 2: 284.
45. M. Kingsley, "Personal Traits".
46. Ibid., p. 730.
47. Macmillan, *Letters of Alexander Macmillan,* pp. 38, 56.
48. Ellis, *Henry Kingsley 1830–1876,* p. 62.
49. *Charles Kingsley and Eversley Church: Notes 1964* (Eversley Rectory, 1964), pp. 4–5.
50. Ellis, *Henry Kingsley 1830–1876,* p. 62.
51. Berg Collection, undated (July–Sept. 1861).
52. Ibid., 4 September 1860.
53. Ibid., undated (Jan.–March 1861).
54. T. Hughes, "The Volunteer's Catechism," *Macmillan's Magazine* 2: 191 (September 1860).
55. Department of Special Collections, University of California, Los Angeles, undated letter.
56. Ibid., undated letter.
57. Parrish Collection, Princeton University Library, undated letter.
58. Robert Lee Wolff, "Henry Kingsley", *Harvard Library Bulletin* 13, no. 2 (spring 1959): 216.
59. G. A. Macmillan, *Letters of Alexander Macmillan,* p. 181.
60. Henry Kingsley letters, BL, Add. MSS 54916, fol. 10.
61. Ellis, *Henry Kingsley 1830–1876,* p. 62.
62. Department of Special Collections, University of California, Los Angeles.
63. BL, Add. MS 41297, fol. 111.
64. Stamp Book, Inner Temple, 1862–January 1866, course data from W. W. S. Breen, Librarian, Inner Temple, London, on 29 January 1975.
65. Ellis, *Henry Kingsley 1830–1876,* pp. 62–63.
66. Data from Kingsley's marriage certificate.
67. Henry Kingsley letters, BL, Add. MSS 54916, fol. 1.
68. Berg Collection, Macmillan's presentation copies of *Austin Elliot* memorandum endorsed "Sent May 25th".
69. Henry Kingsley, letters, BL, Add. MSS 54916, fol. 1.
70. Ibid., fol. 4.
71. Ibid., fol. 21.

CHAPTER 13

1. G. A. Wilkes, "Kingsley's *Geoffry Hamlyn*: A Study in Literary Survival", *Southerly* 32 (1972), no. 4: 251.
2. *Good Words* 4 (1863): 524–26 passim.
3. M-M, "Novels of the Day: Their Writers and Readers," *Fraser's Magazine* 6: 209 (August 1860).
4. Henry Kingsley letters, BL, Add. MSS 54916, fol. 56.
5. Macmillan letters, 29 January 1866, BL, Add. MSS 55842, fol. 30.
6. Henry Kingsley letters, BL, Add. MSS 54916, fol. 22.
7. "Thackeray" *Macmillan's Magazine* 9: 356–68 (February 1864).
8. Henry Kingsley letters, BL, Add. MSS 54916, fol. 17.
9. Letters from the librarian and assistant librarian, Garrick Club, 4 April and 30 May 1973 respectively.
10. (London: George Bell and Sons, 1910), p. 491.

11. (London: Smith, Elder, 1898), p. 447.
12. Marriage certificate copy, General Register Office, London, application no. 26939, 28 January 1975.
13. Reginald Blunt, *Memoirs of Gerald Blunt of Chelsea, His Family and Forebears* (Chelsea: Truslove and Hanson 1911), p. 87.
14. Ellis, *Henry Kingsley 1830–1876,* facing page 66.
15. *Silcote of Silcotes,* chaps 41, 49.
16. *Daily Review,* Edinburgh, 9 October 1869, p. 6.
17. *Silcote of Silcotes,* chap. 49.
18. Ellis, *Henry Kingsley 1830–1876,* p. 65.
19. Michael Sadleir, "Henry Kingsley: A Portrait", *Edinburgh Review* 240 (October 1924): 332.
20. Laurence Hutton Collection, Princeton University Library.
21. Ibid.
22. Ellis, *Henry Kingsley 1830–1876,* p. 66.
23. Henry Kingsley letters, BL, Add. MSS 54916, fol. 19. In the same letter Kingsley thanked Macmillan for the gift of a butter-boat which had "so shocked and horrified" the newlyweds that they had unpacked nothing else. At this stage the Kingsleys were not in their "new house yet" but hoped "to be in about a month". Kingsley also told Macmillan that he liked *The Hillyars and the Burtons "in parts"* and went on to say, perhaps significantly, that he had heard nothing of Charles.
24. A. G. Stapleton Collection, Princeton University Library.
25. R. B. Martin papers, Princeton University Library, letter 19 January 1851.
26. F. E. Kingsley, *Charles Kingsley,* 1: 192.
27. Lewis Carroll diaries, BL, Add. MSS 54343, vol. 8.
28. Ibid., Add. MSS 54344, vol. 9.
29. R. L. Green, ed., *The Diaries of Lewis Carroll* (London: Cassell, 1953), p. 196.
30. Tinsley, *Random Recollection,* 2:284.
31. Henry Kingsley letters, BL, Add. MSS 54916, fol. 13.
32. Wolff, "Henry Kingsley", pp. 217–18.
33. Bernhard Tauchnitz, *Complete Catalogue of the Tauchnitz Edition of British and American Authors* (Leipzig, 1910), p. 75.
34. *Atlantic Monthly* 16: 121 (July 1865).
35. Henry Kingsley letters, BL, Add. MSS 54916, fol. 23.
36. "Charles Sturt: A Chapter from the History of Australian Exploration" (January 1865); "Eyre, the South Australian Explorer" (October and November 1865).
37. Henry Kingsley letters, BL, Add. MSS 54916, fol. 31.
38. Simon Nowell-Smith, ed., *Letters to Macmillan* (London: Macmillan, 1967), p. 43.
39. Henry Kingsley letters, BL, Add. MSS 54916, fol. 31.
40. Nowell-Smith, *Letters to Macmillan,* p. 43.
41. Henry Kingsley letters, BL, Add. MSS 54916, fol. 24. "Aunt Mary" never appeared as such, but found its way into *Silcote of Silcotes.*
42. Ellis, *Henry Kingsley 1830–1876,* n., p. 133.
43. In an unpublished letter to Fanny Kingsley, Mrs Craik, writing from Arran Cottage, Upper Tooting, on 11 November, said how happy she was in her marriage at the end of her days, "to a better man and a better love than any I ever drew — well that's enough — you will understand. . . . as I heard of you through Mr. Macmillan — at whose house by the bye I lately met your brother Henry and liked him very much" (letter held in Kingsley Family Album, Australia).
44. Henry Kingsley letters, BL, Add. MSS 54916, fol. 35.
45. R. B. Martin Papers, Princeton University Library, give the source as BL, Add. MSS 41297, fol. 126.
46. George H. Ford, "The Governor Eyre Case in England," *University of Toronto Quarterly* 17: 219-21 (April 1948) passim.
47. Ellis quotes most, but not all, of the article and correspondence from *The Times* in *Henry Kingsley 1830–76: Towards a Vindication.* The relevant correspondence appeared as follows in *The Times:* 30 November 1865, p. 10, (Bakewell); 2 December, p. 5, (Kingsley), 5 December, p. 7, (Bakewell), 7 December, p. 5, (Kingsley).

48. William H. Scheuerle, "Henry Kingsley and the Governor Eyre Controversy," *Victorian Newsletter*, no. 37 (spring 1970): 24–27.
49. Chas. Davies, M.D., *Biographical Cuttings*, vol. 5, p. 78 (South Australian Archives).
50. Kathleeen Hassall, *The Relations between the Settlers and Aborigines in South Australia, 1836–1860* (Adelaide: Libraries Board of South Australia, 1966), pp. 94–96, passim.
51. Alexander Sutherland et al., *Victoria and its Metropolis*, 2 vols. (Melbourne: McCarron, Bird, 1888), 1: 230.
52. "New Australian Exploration", Kingsley's review of *Tracks of McKinlay and Party across Australia,* by John Davis, *Reader,* 27 June 1863, pp. 618–19.
53. Review of *A Successful Exploration through the Interior of Australia,* from the Journals of W. J. Wills, edited by His Father, *Reader,* 21 February 1863, pp. 183–84.
54. Henry Kingsley letters, BL, Add. MSS 54916, fol. 28.
55. Ibid., fol. 30.
56. John McLaren, *"Geoffry Hamlyn* and The Australian Myth", *Segment* (journal of the School of Arts, Darling Downs Institute of Advanced Education) 2 (1973): 8.
57. Nowell-Smith, *Letters to Macmillan,* p. 44.
58. Henry Kingsley letters, BL, Add. MSS 54916, fol. 37.
59. Ibid., fol. 84.
60. Ibid.
61. Macmillan letters, 29 January 1866, BL, Add. MSS 55842, fol. 30.
62. Henry Kingsley letters, BL, Add. MSS 54916, fol. 84.
63. *The Albert N'yanza, Great Basin of the Nile Sources* (London: Macmillan, 1866).
64. Henry Kingsley letters, BL, Add. MSS 54916, fol. 56.
65. Ibid., fol. 57.
66. Ibid., fol. 42.
67. Ibid.
68. Macmillan letters, BL, Add. MSS 55842, fol. 53.
69. Henry Kingsley letters, BL, Add. MSS 54916, fol. 39.
70. "A Cheap Tour near Home", *Macmillan's Magazine* 15: 265–74 (January 1867).
71. "A Cheap Tour near Home", *Macmillan's Magazine* 16: 82–90 (May 1867).
72. Henry Kingsley letters, BL, Add. MSS 54916, fol. 40.
73. Macmillan letters, BL, Add. MSS 55253, fol. 136.
74. E. D. Forgues, trans. (Paris: Librairie de la Hachette, 1866).
75. Henry Kingsley letters, BL, Add. MSS 54916, fols. 43–46 passim.
76. Ibid., fol. 42.
77. London Library to the present writer, 26 May 1976.
78. Henry Kingsley letters, BL, Add. MSS 54916, fol. 38.
79. Macmillan letters, BL, Add. MSS 55842, fols. 64 and 66.
80. Fales Collection, New York Public Library, letter dated October 1867.
81. *Current Literature* (later *Current Opinion*) 31: 56–58 (July 1901).
82. Houghton Library, Harvard University, undated letter.
83. Parrish Collection, Princeton University Library.
84. William E. Buckler, "Henry Kingsley and *The Gentlemen's Magazine", Journal of English and Germanic Philology* 50 (1951): 90–100.
85. Houghton Library, Harvard University, letter dated 6 June.
86. Fales Collection, New York Public Library.
87. F. R. Norman, *Anti-Catholicism in Victorian England,* (London: Allen and Unwin, 1968), pp. 106–7.
88. Shorter, Memoir, p. xx-xxi.
89. *The Times,* 6 February 1930, p. 102.
90. Lewis Carroll diary, MSS 54344, fol. 8.
91. Houghton Library, Harvard University, undated letter.
92. Stuart Dodgson Collingwood, *The Life and Letters of Lewis Carroll* (London: Nelson, 1898), pp. 142–43.
93. Ellis, *Henry Kingsley 1830–1876,* p. 190.
94. Macmillan letters, 5 April 1868, BL, Add., MSS 55389, fol. 510.
95. Laurence Hutton Collection, Princeton University Library letter 14 November 1894. Maurice Kingsley continued: "A witty remark of a chum of mine

Notes

at Cambridge about that time was that Swinbourne [sic] should have entitled 'Laus Veneris,' 'Laus posteriorium' — although the greatest poet since Shelley."
96. Henry Kingsley letters, BL, Add. MSS 54916, fol. 61.
97. Ibid., fol. 77.
98. Ibid., fol. 78.
99. Kingsley's application listed his occupation as "author" and his residence as Wargrave, Berkshire, as well as the Garrick Club, London (Royal Geographical Society, London, to the present writer, 12 February 1973).
100. Macmillan letters, BL, Add. MSS 55388, fol. 331.
101. Ibid., fol. 582.
102. Henry Kingsley letters, BL, Add. MSS 54916, fol. 82.
103. Ibid., fol. 71.
104. The younger Macmillans had gone on a walking tour from Conway to Caernarvon (Macmillan letters, BL, Add. MSS 55388, fol. 582).
105. Macmillan letters, BL, Add. MSS 55388, fol. 754, letter dated 16 September 1868.
106. Ibid., fol. 939.
107. Ibid., fol. 975.
108. Macmillan letters, Add. MSS 55389, fol. 180.
109. Ibid., fol. 215.
110. Henry Kingsley letters, BL, Add. MSS 54916, fol. 84.
111. Ibid., fol. 85.
112. Macmillan letters, BL, Add. MSS 55389, fol. 376.
113. Henry Kingsley letters, BL, Add. MSS 54916, fol. 71.
114. Ibid., fol. 69.
115. Ibid., fol. 71.
116. Macmillan letters, BL, Add. MSS 55388, fol. 838.
117. Ibid., fol. 975.
118. Ibid., fol. 180.
119. Henry Kingsley letters, BL, Add. MSS 54916, fol. 84.
120. Ibid., fol. 80.
121. Macmillan letters, BL, Add. MSS 55389, fol. 355.
122. Ibid., fol. 476.
123. Henry Kingsley letters, BL, Add. MSS 54916, fol. 86.
124. Ibid., fol. 91.
125. Macmillan letters, BL, Add. MSS 55389, fol. 476.
126. Ibid., fol. 513.
127. Brotherton Collection, Gosse diaries, University of Leeds.
128. Martin, *Dust of Combat*, pp. 55–56.
129. Henry Kingsley letters, BL, Add. MSS 54916, fol. 87.
130. Ibid., fol. 89.

CHAPTER 14

1. W. J. Couper, "A Bibliography of Edinburgh Periodical Literature", *Scottish Notes and Queries,* 2nd ser. 5 (December 1903): 87-88; James Grant, *The Metropolitan: Weekly and Provincial Press* (London: George Routledge, n.d.), 3: 451–52.
2. *Daily Review,* 1 October 1869, p. 2.
3. Parrish Collection, Princeton University Library, undated letter.
4. Kingsley was on his election committee in Berkshire in 1868 (*Daily Review,* 3 September 1870, p. 6).
5. Shorter, p. xxvi.
6. William Mair, *Historic Morningside: Lands, Mansions and Celebrities* (n.p., 1947), pp. 34–36.
7. Royal Literary Fund, file no. 1899.
8. *Daily Review,* 2 October 1869, p. 2, 16 October, p. 2.
9. Shorter, memoir, p. xxii.
10. *Daily Review,* 1 April 1870, p. 2.
11. Ibid., 16 October 1869, p. 2.
12. Ibid., 26 October 1869, p. 2.

13. Ibid., 13 May 1870, p. 4.
14. Ibid., 21 May 1870, p. 2.
15. Ibid., 28 June 1870, p. 2.
16. Ibid., 4 October 1870, p. 8.
17. Ibid., 5 October 1869, p. 3.
18. Ibid., 9 October 1869, p. 6.
19. Ibid., 22 October 1869, p. 3.
20. Ibid., 2 July 1870, p. 7.
21. Ibid., 2 July 1870, p. 7.
22. Ibid., 8 January 1870, p. 2.
23. Ibid., 6 November 1869, p. 2.
24. Ibid., 11 December 1869, p. 2.
25. Ibid., 3 January 1870, p. 6; 29 January, p. 2; 7 February, p. 6; 21 February, p. 6; 9 May, p. 6; 11 June, p. 2; 31 October, p. 5.
26. Ibid., 7 March 1870, p. 2.
27. Ibid., 7 November 1870, p. 5.
28. Ibid., 18 October 1869, p. 6.
29. Ibid., 11 July 1870, p. 6.
30. Ibid., 29 January 1870, p. 2.
31. Robert Dixon writes about this in "Kingsley's *Geoffry Hamlyn* and the Art of Landscape", *Southerly* 37, no. 3 (September 1977) 274–99.
32. *Daily Review,* 19 March 1870, p. 2.
33. Ibid., 3 April 1871, p. 6.
34. Ibid., 27 December 1869, p. 2.
35. Ibid., 8 April 1870, p. 2.
36. Blackwood Collection, National Library of Scotland (NLS), MS 4262, fol. 286.
37. Ibid., fol. 218–19.
38. Ibid., fol. 220–21.
39. Ibid., MS Acc. 5643–D7 fols. 89–90.
40. Eyre Defence Committee letters, NLS, MS 4209, letter to Blackwood from Hamilton Hume, 21 September 1866.
41. Blackwood Collection, NLS, MS 4256, fols. 89–90.
42. Ibid., MS 4255, fol. 113.
43. Ibid., MS 4262, fol. 284.
44. Couper, "Bibliography of Edinburgh Periodical Literature", p. 88.
45. *Daily Review,* 21 May 1870, p. 2.
46. Ibid., 9 July 1870, p. 2.
47. Ibid., 30 July 1870, p. 2.
48. Ibid., 3 August 1870, p. 2.
49. War correspondence published in the *Daily Review* (hereafter cited as "war correspondence"), 7 August 1870.
50. "Her Majesty's Ships", *London Society* 24 (1873): 423.
51. War correspondence, 17 August 1870.
52. Ibid., 30 August 1870.
53. Ibid., 29 August 1870.
54. Ibid.
55. In his dispatch of 2 September Kingsley refers to his telegram arriving in New York and London simultaneously, so it appears that the *Daily Review* must have shared his services with an American paper.
56. "Her Majesty's Ships," p. 424.
57. War correspondence, 4 September 1870.
58. *Tinsley's Magazine* (later *Novel Review*) 10: 60 (February 1872).
59. Alexander Peddie, *Recollections of Dr. John Brown* (Edinburgh: Oliphant, Anderson and Ferrier, 1894), p. 145.
60. Shorter, Memoir, p. xxi.
61. *Scottish Notes and Queries,* 2nd ser. 5: 88, (December 1903).
62. *Daily Review,* 9 January 1871, p. 5.
63. *Scottish Notes and Queries,* 2nd ser. 5: 88 (December 1903).
64. Henry Kingsley letters, BL, Add. MSS, 54916, fol. 95.
65. Blackwood Collection, NLS, MS 4277, fols. 54, 56, 60.
66. Ibid., MS Acc. 5643–D7, letter dated 1 May 1871.
67. Ibid., MS 4277, fol. 62.
68. Ibid., MSS 4271/12, letter 7.

Notes

69. Ibid., MS 4277, fols, 56–57.
70. Ibid., fol, 54.
71. *Edinburgh & Leith Post Office Directory 1870–71*, pp. 661–62.
72. Interview, Jnuary 1975, with D. Addison, accountant of court, Edinburgh.
73. John Skelton, *The Table Talk of Shirley* (Edinburgh: Blackwood, 1895), pp. 235–37.
74. Laurence Hutton Collection, Princeton University Library, letter dated 14 November 1894.
75. Blackwood Collection, NLS, MS 4277, fol. 54.

CHAPTER 15

1. See Macmillan letters, BL, Add. MSS 55392, fol. 415, Bentley Collection, University of Illinois (hereafter cited as Bentley Collection; those letters in the Bentley Collection at the British Library are noted accordingly), fol. L4.
2. Bentley Collection, fol. L48.
3. Bentley Collection, fols. L16, L4.
4. Department of Special Collections, University of California, Los Angeles.
5. Wolff, "Henry Kingsley", p. 218.
6. Henry Kingsley letters, BL, MSS 54916, fol. 94.
7. Bentley Collection, BL, Add. MS 46643, letter dated 9 December 1871.
8. Bentley Collection, fol. L1.
9. Assistant Librarian, Garrick Club, to the present writer, 18 April 1973.
10. Una Pope-Hennessy, *Canon Charles Kingsley: A Biography* (London: Chatto and Windus, 1948), pp. 265–66.
11. Ibid., pp. 265–67.
12. Bentley Collection, fol. L3.
13. Henry Kingsley letters, BL, Add. MSS 54916, fol. 105.
14. Bentley Collection, fol. L19, undated letter, (seemingly January 1874).
15. Bentley Collection, fol. L33, letter dated 30 January 1874.
16. Pope-Hennessy, *Canon Charles Kingsley*, pp. 266–67.
17. Ellis, *Henry Kingsley 1830–1876*, p. 186.
18. Macmillan letters, BL, Add. MSS 55842, fol. 389.
19. Henry Kingsley letters, BL, Add. MSS 54916, fol. 100.
20. Ibid., fols. 96 and 102.
21. Bentley Collection, fol. L7.
22. Ibid., fol. L8.
23. Ibid., fol. L9.
24. Ibid., fol. L10.
25. Tinsley, *Random Recollections* 2: 24.
26. Mitchell Library, Sydney, undated letter.
27. Fales Collection, New York Public Library, letter dated 1872.
28. Tinsley, *Random Recollections*, p. 118.
29. Laurence Hutton Collection, Princeton University Library, letter 12 November 1894.
30. Green, *Diaries of Lewis Carroll*, p. 307.
31. S. M. Kingsley to Bentley, 19 January 1872, Bentley Collection, fol. L1.
32. Department of Special Collections, University of California, Los Angeles.
33. Macmillan letters, BL, Add. MSS 55392(1), fol. 450.
34. Henry Kingsley letters, BL, Add. MSS 54916, fol. 102.
35. Bentley Collection, fol. L11.
36. Macmillan letters, BL, Add. MSS 55392(1), fol. 618.
37. Bentley Collection, fol. L13.
38. M. H. Kingsley, "George Henry Kingsley", p. 38.
39. Henry Kingsley letters, BL, Add. MSS 54916, fol. 17.
40. R. B. Martin, ed., *Charles Kingsley's American Notes: Letters from a Lecture Tour 1874* (Princeton University Library, 1958), p. 52.
41. M. H. Kingsley, "George Henry Kingsley", p. 29.
42. Shorter, memoir, p. xix.
43. Bentley Collection, fol. L13.
44. Ibid.
45. Ibid., fol. L12.

Notes

46. Macmillan letters, BL, Add. MSS 55393(1) fol. 47.
47. Henry Kingsley letters, BL, Add. MSS 54916, fol. 105.
48. Royal Literary Fund correspondence, file no. 1899.
49. Bentley Collection, fol. L18.
50. Royal Literary Fund correspondence.
51. Chitty, *The Beast and the Monk,* pp. 279-80.
52. Macmillan letters, BL, Add. MSS 55842, fol. 415.
53. Laurence Hutton Collection, letter dated 14 November 1894.
54. Henry Kingsley letters, BL. Add. MSS 54916, fol. 13.
55. Chitty, *The Beast and the Monk,* p. 277.
56. Henry Kingsley letters, BL, Add. MSS 54916, fol. 104.
57. Probably W. R. S. Ralston (1828–89), Russian scholar and folklorist who trained for the bar and, from 1853 to 1875, worked in the British Museum Library.
58. Department of Special Collections, University of California, Los Angeles, undated letter.
59. Bentley Collection, fol. L24.
60. Ibid., fol. L25.
61. Ibid., fol. L21.
62. Ibid., fol. L25.
63. *Reginald Hetherege,* chap. 4.
64. Bentley Collection, fol. L28.
65. Ibid., fol. L31.
66. Ibid., fol. L39.
67. Royal Geographical Society to the present writer, 12 February 1973.
68. *Tinsley's Magazine* 10 (February 1872): 59–67 passim.
69. Bentley Collection, fol. L21.
70. Ibid., fol. L30.
71. Ibid., fol. L40.
72. Ibid., fol. L19.
73. Ibid., fols. L19, 20, 33.
74. Ibid., fol. L34.
75. Ibid., fol. L45.
76. Ibid., fol. L43.
77. Ibid., fol. L39.
78. Ibid.
79. Ibid., fol. L41.
80. Ibid., fol. L37.
81. Ibid., fol. L6.
82. Justin McCarthy, *Reminiscences,* 2 vols. (London: Chatto and Windus, 1899), 1: 317.
83. Ibid., 2: 272–73.
84. Royal Literary Fund correspondence, letter dated 12 February 1875.
85. Bentley Collection, fol. L44.
86. Houghton Library, Harvard University, undated letter.
87. Bentley Collection, fol. L36.
88. Heaton, *Australian Dictionary of Dates,* p. 274.
89. Bentley Collection, fol. L47.
90. Wolff, "Henry Kingsley": p. 219. While undated and with addressee unspecified, the Henry Kingsley letter held by the Houghton Library and quoted in full by Wolff seems linked with one in the Bentley Collection of May 1875; on this assumption the comments are based.
91. Bentley Collection, fol. L48.
92. Ellis, *Henry Kingsley 1830–1876,* pp. 56–60 passim.
93. Henry Kingsley letters, BL, Add. MSS 54916, fol. 107.
94. Bentley Collection, fol. L48.
95. Ellis, *Henry Kingsley, 1830–1876,* p. 110.
96. Bentley Collection, fol. L48.
97. Mary McLeod, "Stories of Henry Kingsley", *The Sussex County Magazine* 4: 488–89 (June 1930).
98. "Death of Mr. Henry Kingsley at Cuckfield," *Sussex Daily News,* 26 May 1876.
99. L. B. Walford, *Memories of Victorian London* (London: Edward Arnold, 1912), pp. 295–97.

Notes

100. William H. Scheuerle, *The Neglected Brother: A Study of Henry Kingsley* (Tallahassee: Florida State University Press, 1971), p. 159.
101. Ellis, *Henry Kingsley 1830–1876*, p. 14.
102. Henry Kingsley letters, BL, Add. MSS 54916, fol. 118.
103. Wolff, "Henry Kingsley", p. 221.
104. Royal Library Fund correspondence, letter dated 18 April 1876.
105. Shorter, memoir p. xxii.
106. According to the certificate of death, dated 27 May 1876, Kingsley died of carcinoma of the throat and tongue, the certifying doctor was E. S. Byass, the date of death 24 May 1876, and Helen C. Magrudor was present at the death.
107. *Fireside Studies*, p. 159.
108. The present Cuckfield librarian, Miss K. Mitchell, recollects that her father, present at the ceremony as a choir boy, told her that it rained and that the water from Mrs Kingsley's umbrella had trickled down his neck (Mrs Joy Carter, Cuckfield, to the present writer, 3 August 1973).
109. Bentley Collection, unidentified journal cutting "D2."
110. It seems evident that Weller knew the Kingsleys intimately, though no other references to him have so far been found.
111. Hutton, "The Literary Life", p. 331.
112. Henry Kingsley letters, BL, Add. MSS 54916, fol. 121.
113. Ibid., fol. 124.
114. Ibid., fol. 112. Kingsley's will was drawn up while he lived at 29 Fortess Terrace, Kentish Town. Witnesses were Louisa Barbara M. Allen and Lucy M. Monro. Letters of administration were granted to S. M. K. Kingsley on 4 August 1876. Seeking relief for herself from the Royal Literary Fund on 28 April 1877, she wrote: "My husband was unable to leave me any provision, in fact I was obliged to buy the furniture &c of my small house, tho' much of it had been presents to me, because *everything* had to go to the creditors. ... my mother has for some time been almost entirely dependent on my husband and myself." In a letter to the fund dated 31 October 1888, she wrote: "My husband Henry Kingsley died in 1876 leaving me nothing, the copyrights of his works all being sold. ... five years ago my mother, Mrs. Ann Hazelwood had a seizure which affected her brain, since then she has never been able to be left day or night. ... nearly all my relations are poor." Another letter, dated 7 January (1889?), refers to the mother's property: "The house in Westminster is entailed on a cousin we do not know whether he is alive or dead. I cannot raise money on it. I have to supplement my mother's small income and pay insurances on her life and interest on the money advanced on those insurances in the Eagle Insurance Office 79 Pall Mall and these with what I have to make up for her makes my real income *very* small indeed." Referring to her application, Rev. Gerald Blunt wrote: "I used to hear that there was some house property to which she was entitled on the death of her mother which would place her in independent circumstances. I do not know whether that has fallen in or not. I think it possible." Earlier in the same letter he recorded what was probably the key to Kingsley's financial difficulties: "I think however the worst that can be laid to her charge is a certain amount of unthrifty extravagance which has always characterised her and brought both her and her husband into difficulties even when they ought to have been comfortably off." Two newspaper advertisements were appended to Sarah's application to the Royal Literary Fund of 30 April 1877. One appeared in *The Times* on 7 November 1876, the other was undated. Both sought funds for Sarah. *The Times* advertisement was sponsored by Rev. G. H. Wilkinson, Chatto and Windus, and MacLaren and MacLaren. The other advertisement was inserted by the Apollo University Lodge, Oxford, of which Kingsley was a member. In a letter dated 17 April 1896, Sarah revealed that there were debts still outstanding on her mother's estate at the time of her death. Sarah, by this date, had had attacks of influenza and sustained a fall in which she struck her head against an iron gate. After the fall she suffered pain more or less intermittently.
115. Macmillan letters, BL, Add. MSS 55254, fol. 220.
116. *The Times*, 9 January 1930, p. 28, letter by G. C. Moore-Smith.
117. M. H. Kingsley, "George Henry Kingsley", pp. 5–6.

Bibliography

Diaries, letters, manuscripts, and papers held in institutions or in private collections are listed accordingly and are arranged by country and city or town where located. In section 3, articles, news items, and reviews before 1876, as distinct from books and other references of the period, are listed separately for easier critical use. After 1876, all items are listed under the name of the author, or title where authorship is unknown.

1. Works by Henry Kingsley

Details of later editions of books, of republished individual short stories, of essays and reviews, or of reprints of such, are not given. Any novel that appeared in serial form is listed in section A, any other work published before its first appearance in book form is shown in section B.

A. FIRST EDITIONS (in order of publication)

The Recollections of Geoffry Hamlyn. 3 vols. Cambridge: Macmillan, 1859. Dedication: "To my Father and Mother This Book the fruit of so many weary years of separation is dedicated with the deepest love and reverence."

Ravenshoe. 3 vols. Cambridge: Macmillan, 1862. Dedication: "To my brother, Charles Kingsley I dedicate this tale, in token of a love which only grows stronger as we both get older." Serialized: *Macmillan's Magazine,* January 1861–July 1862.

Austin Elliot. 2 vols. London: Macmillan, 1863. Dedication: "To the Reverend John Mill Chanter, and Charlotte Chanter, this book is affectionately dedicated by their brother, the Author."

The Hillyars and the Burtons: A Story of Two Families. 3 vols. London: Macmillan, 1865. Dedication: "This tale is dedicated to My Wife." Serialized: *Macmillan's Magazine,* November 1863–April 1865.

Leighton Court: A Country House Story. 2 vols. London: Macmillan, 1866. Dedication: "To my brother George this country tale is most affectionately dedicated."

Bibliography

Silcote of Silcotes. 3 vols. London: Macmillan, 1867. Serialized: *Macmillan's Magazine,* July 1866—September 1867.

Mademoiselle Mathilde. 3 vols. London: Bradbury, Evans, 1868. Dedication: "To My Wife and Miss Thackeray, in memory of the pleasant summer days during which the better parts of it were written." Serialized: *The Gentleman's Magazine,* April 1867—May 1868.

Robinson Crusoe. Edited after the original editions with a biographical introduction. London: Macmillan, 1868.

Tales of Old Travel: Re-Narrated by Henry Kingsley, London: Macmillan, 1869.

Stretton. 3 vols. London: Tinsley Brothers, 1869. Serialized: *The Broadway Annual,* September 1868—August 1869.

The Boy in Grey. London: Strahan, 1871. Serialized: *Good Words for the Young,* March—September 1869, June—July 1870.

The Lost Child. London: Macmillan, 1871.

Hetty. London: Bradbury, Evans, 1871. Serialized: *Once a Week,* February—May 1869.

Hetty and Other Stories. London: Bradbury, Evans, 1871. Contains "The Two Cadets: a Story, in two chapters, of Australian Bushrangers", "Our Brown Passenger", and "Seeking Your Fortune".

Old Margaret. 2 vols. London: Tinsley Brothers, 1871.

Hornby Mills; And other Stories. 2 vols. London: Tinsley Brothers, 1872. Dedication: "Dedicated by Henry to Barbara" [Louisa Barbara M. Allen]

Valentin: A French Boy's Story of Sedan. 2 vols. London: Tinsley Brothers, 1872.

The Harveys. 2 vols. London: Tinsley Brothers, 1872.

Oakshott Castle: Being the Memoirs of an Eccentric Nobleman. 3 vols. London: Macmillan, 1873.

Reginald Hetherege. 3 vols. London: Richard Bentley, 1874.

Number Seventeen. 2 vols. London: Chatto and Windus, 1875.

The Grange Garden: A Romance. 3 vols. London: Chatto and Windus, 1867. Serialized: *St. James Magazine,* April 1875—August 1876.

Fireside Studies. 2 vols. London: Chatto and Windus, 1876. Dedication: "To the Earl of Pembroke and Montgomery. My Lord, — To use the words of another, 'I bring you here a nosegay of a few culled flowers, with nothing of my own but the string which binds them.' Henry Kingsley."

The Mystery of the Island. London: William Mullan, 1877.

B. SHORT STORIES, ESSAYS, REVIEWS, POEMS, PAINTINGS
    (in alphabetical order)

"About Salmon". *Macmillan's Magazine* 12: 127—36 (June 1865).

"Addison". *Temple Bar* 41: 319-37 (June 1874). In *Fireside Studies* 1 as "The Fathers of 'The Spectator' ".

"An American Guide". Review of *Harper's Handbook for Travellers in Europe and the East,* by W. Pembroke Fetridge. *The Times,* 18 November 1871, p. 4.

"Baker's Exploration of the Nile Sources". *Macmillan's Magazine* 14: 205—18 (May—October 1866).

Bibliography

"Baker's Explorations in Central Africa". Review of *The Albert N'yanza, Great Basin of the Nile, and Explorations of the Nile Sources,* by Samuel White Baker. *North British Review* 44: 363–88 (June 1866).

"Ben Jonson". *Temple Bar* 42: 35–40 (August 1874). In *Fireside Studies* 1 as "The Master of the Mermaid".

"Berjeau's Varieties of Dogs". Review of *The Varieties of Dogs, as They Are Found in Old Sculptures, Pictures Engravings, and Books...,* by Ph. Charles Berjeau. *The Reader,* 6 June 1863, pp. 547–48.

"Cain's Brand". *Good Words* 2 (1861): 376–84, 422–31.

"Charles Sturt: A Chapter from the History of Australian Exploration". *Macmillan's Magazine* 11: 204–17 (January 1865). In *Hornby Mills and Other Stories* as "The March of Charles Sturt".

"A Cheap Tour near Home". *Macmillan's Magazine* 15: 265–74 (January 1867), 16: 82–90 (May 1867).

"Christmas Books". Review of *The Albert N'yanza,* by Sir Samuel Baker. *The Times,* 20 December 1871, p. 4.

"The Discovery of the Albert N'yanza". Review of *The Albert N'yanza...,* by Samuel White Baker. *Fortnightly Review* 5: 654–69 (August 1866).

"An Episode in the Life of Charles Mordaunt". *London Society* 21 (1872): 1–18. In *Hornby Mills; And other Stories.*

"Eyre, the South Australian Explorer". *Macmillan's Magazine* 12: 501–10 (October 1865), 13: 55–63 (November 1865). In *Hornby Mills and Other Stories* as "Eyre's March".

"Fletcher and Beaumont". *Temple Bar* 42: 460–71 (November 1874). In *Fireside Studies* 2.

"Gossip about the Paris Exhibition". *Macmillan's Magazine* 15: 91–96 (May 1867). Authorship likely, but not conclusively established.

"Her Majesty's Ships". *London Society* 24 (1873): 417–25.

"Hornby Mills Garden". *Argosy* 1: 394–407 (April 1866). In *Hornby Mills and Other Stories.*

"The Influence of Travel". *Tinsley's Magazine* 10: 59–67 (February 1872).

"Jackson of Paul's". *The Dark Blue* 1: 302–13 (May 1871); 1: 456–65 (June 1871). In *Hornby Mills; And other Stories.*

"The Last Two Abyssinian Books". Review of *The Nile Tributaries of Abyssinia,* by Sir Samuel White Baker, and *Narrative of a Journey through Abyssinia in 1862-3,* by Henry Dufton. *Fortnightly Review* 8: 547–58 (November 1867).

"Malmaison". *Tinsley's Magazine* 9: 560–67 (December 1871), 9: 672–91 (January 1872). In *Hornby Mills; And other Stories.*

"Meerschaum". *London Society* 26 (1874): 21–34.

"Miss Milton". *Argosy* 18: 352–60 (November 1874).

"My Landladies: Chapters of a Digger's Life". *Temple Bar* 36: 371–90 (October 1872).

"The Mystery of St. Remi". *Belgravia,* no. 33, pp. 1–21 (holiday number 1877, bound in some libraries at the back of no. 34).

"The Navies of France and England". With Augustus G. Stapleton. *Macmillan's Magazine* 2: 249–58 (August 1860).

"New Australian Exploration". Review of *Tracks of McKinlay and Party across Australia,* by John Davis. *The Reader,* 27 June 1863, pp. 618–19.

Bibliography

"New Books of Sport and Natural History: A Gossip for September". *Macmillan's Magazine* 2: 385–93 (September 1860).

"The New Church at Mistibithiwong". *Good Words* 9 (1868): 322–28.

"New Year's Day at Windsor, 1327: Sir Henry Mullory's Story". *Argosy* 1: 173–85 (January 1866). In *Hornby Mills; And other Stories*.

"Olaf the Sinner and Olaf the Saint". *Good Words* 3 (1862): 23–25.

"Oliver Shand's Partner". *Good Words* 4 (1863): 768–74.

"Our Suspicious Neighbours". *Belgravia*, no. 29 (1876), pp. 217–37.

"Our Widow". *Argosy* 20: 111–25 (August 1875).

"Peabody's Last Voyage: 'Quis desideris sit pudor aut modus/Tam chari capitus?' ". Poem. *Daily Review*, 11 December 1869, p. 2.

"Peace and War". Poem. *Daily Review*, 9 January 1871, p. 5.

Review of *Reminiscences of a Thirty Years' Residence in New South Wales and Victoria*, by R. Therry. *The Reader*, 14 March 1863, pp. 256–57.

Review of *South Sea Bubbles*, by the Earl of Pembroke and G. H. Kingsley. *The Times*, 5 February 1872, p. 4.

Review of *A Successful Exploration through the Interior of Australia*, from the Journals of W. J. Wills, Edited by His Father. *The Reader*, 21 February 1863, pp. 183–84.

"Richard Steele". *Temple Bar* 40: 103–21 (March 1874). In *Fireside Studies* 1 as "The Fathers of 'The Spectator' ".

"Sir Henry Mullory's Story". *Every Saturday* (Boston), 17 February 1866, pp. 182–88.

"Sir Philip Sidney". *New Quarterly Magazine* 3: 416–42 (January 1875). In *Fireside Studies* 2.

"Some Account of the Village of Inverquoich". *Macmillan's Magazine* 7: 447–59 (April 1863). In *Hornby Mills; And other Stories*.

"Thackeray". *Macmillan's Magazine* 9: 356–68 (February 1864).

The Times. Correspondence, 2 December 1865, p. 5; 7 December 1865, p. 5.

"Travelling in Victoria". *Macmillan's Magazine* 3: 140–50 (January 1861).

"The Two Cadets". *Once a Week*, 23 February 1867, pp. 214–20, 2 March 1867, pp. 246–53.

"Views in Victoria". Nine watercolours with annotations. Mitchell Library, Sydney, MS A2071.

"Who Will Be My Love". Words by Henry Kingsley and music by W. S. Rockstro. London: Chappell, n.d.

"Why Lady Hornbury's Ball Was Postponed". *Argosy* 12: 200–19 (September 1871). In *Hornby Mills and Other Stories*.

"The Widows of Leith". Poem. *Daily Review*, 6 November 1869, p. 2.

"Wild Sports of the Far South". *Fraser's Magazine* 59: 587–97 (May 1859).

"William Blake". *Macmillan's Magazine* 11: 26–33 (November 1864).

"The Wooden Soldier". *London Society* 24 (1873): 27–38.

"A Word of Remonstrance with Some Novelists". *Good Words* 4 (1863): 524–26.

C. UNLOCATED WRITINGS

"Andrew Marvell". [See letter, n.d., fol. L4, Bentley Collection, University of Illinois.]

"The Arctic Expedition". [See letter (1873-74?), Parrish Collection, Princeton University Library.]

"Bees". [See letter (1873-74?), Parrish Collection, Princeton University Library.]

"Billiard Markers". [See letter, circa 30 August 1872, fol. L13, Bentley Collection, University of Illinois.]

"The Boy Who Ran Away". [See letter (1873-74?), Parrish Collection, Princeton University Library.]

"A Child's Garden". [See letter (1873-74?), Parrish Collection, Princeton University Library.]

"Debra Mavsne [?]". [See letter, 8 March 1872, fol. L10, Bentley Collection, University of Illinois.]

"Marlowe". [See letter, n.d., fol. L4, Bentley Collection, University of Illinois; also, "The Father of Irregular Drama" in *Fireside Studies* 2.]

"Siege of Colchester". [See Robert Lee Wolff, "Henry Kingsley", p. 219.]

"Sir Frances [sic] Drake". [See Robert Lee Wolff, "Henry Kingsley," p. 219.]

"Sports and Pastimes". *Home Journal,* circa 1873. [See letter, 6 December 1873, fol. L25, Bentley Collection, University of Illinois.]

"Xmas Day at Windsor". [See letter, 8 March 1872, fol. L10, Bentley Collection, University of Illinois.]

2. Diaries, Letters, Manuscripts, Papers

AUSTRALIA

Private Collection

Hall, Rev. William, Diaries. Mr J. Gillespie, Kingower.
Jamieson Papers. Robert Jamieson, Stony Point, Darlington.
Jauncey, J. "Travels in the Monaro", 1833-42. A. B. Jauncey, Bega.
Kingsley Family Album and Bible. Location withheld at owner's request.
MSS and papers. Brian Elliott, Adelaide.
Richardson diaries, circa 1850. Mrs E. Richardson, Ararat.
Scott diaries, circa 1850. Mr and Mrs R. J. Scott, Scotsburn.
Whittakers, C. M., ed. "The Whittakers Story". Vol. 1. C. J. Ingram, Tubbut.

ADELAIDE

South Australian Archives

Davies, Chas., M.D., "Biographical Cuttings" 5: 78.
Spence, Catherine Helen, "Description of a Visit to England, 1865-66". MS. A434/A3, 273.

Bibliography

BRISBANE

Fryer Library, University of Queensland
Kingsley, Henry. ALS to unknown addressee, n.d.

MELBOURNE

Baillieu Library, University of Melbourne
Venables, H. P. Three watercolours.
Venables, R. E. C. MS.

Department of Crown Lands and Survey
Mercer, W. D., and G. D. Lockart. Application to the superintendent, Port Phillip, for a lease of Plains Station [Baroona], 14 June 1851.
Mitchell, Willi. Application to chief secretary for transfer of lease, 15 July 1859.

La Trobe Library, State Library of Victoria
Browne, T. A. (Rolf Boldrewood). ALS to James H. Irvine. H16684, box 32/9. MS 7849, box 260/5(a)
T. A. Browne Papers. MSS 5767, box 145/4(a); 6107, box 41/1(2).

Victorian State Archives
Shipping Arrivals, September–December 1853.
Shipping Departures, January–April 1858.

SYDNEY

Mitchell Library, Library of New South Wales
Browne, T. A. (Rolf Boldrewood). ALS to James H. Irvine. H16684,
Darley, C. W. ALS to Cuthbert Fetherstonhaugh (1919). Rose Browne Correspondence, no. B1504.
Fetherstonhaugh Correspondence, 1915–19, no. B1504.
Kingsley, Henry. ALS to William Tinsley, n.d. MS A1, p. 7.

New South Wales Police Department
Financial Pay Records for Foot and Mounted Patrols, 1854–56.
Register of Enlistments for Foot and Mounted Police, 1851–62.

State Archives
Mounted Patrol and Gold Escort Police Register, 1853–66. MS 7/6291.

WARRNAMBOOL

Warrnambool Public Library
Macknight, C. H. Dunmore diaries. With comment by Conway Macknight.

ENGLAND

CAMBRIDGE

Cambridge University Library
Ludlow Papers: 122 ALSs from Charles Kingsley to J. M. Ludlow, Add. 7348/5, 62 ALSs from J. M. Ludlow to Charles Kingsley, Add. 7348/16.

LEEDS

Brotherton Library, University of Leeds
Brotherton Collection: ALS from Edwin Arnold to Clement Shorter, 9 October 1894, ALS from Walter Besant to Clement Shorter, Shorter Correspondence; Gosse Correspondence and Diaries.

LONDON

British Library
Bentley Collection: Register of agreements with authors and others, with dates and details of publication, Add. MS 46629; *Reginald Hetherege,* agreement for publication, 23 December 1873, Add. MS 46618, fol. 312; 2 ALSs from George Bentley to Henry Kingsley, 9 December 1871, 24 November 1872, Add. MS 46643, Address book of Richard Bentley, Add. MS 46680.
Carroll, Lewis. Diaries for 1860–76. Add. MSS 54343–45.
Kingsley, Charles. ALS to Maurice Kingsley, Add. MS 41297, fol. 124, ALS to John Skelton, 26 February 1862, Add. MS 41299, fol. 237(a).
Kingsley, Henry. Letters and documents. Add. MSS 54916, fols. 1–108.
Macmillan Letters. Private letter books. Add. MSS 55253–54, 55388–93, 55836, 55842.
Macmillan's Magazine Index. Add. MS 55998.
Skelton, John. ALS to Mrs F. E. Kingsley, 13 February 1876. Add. MS 41299, fol. 237(b).

Family Division of the High Court of Justice
Letters of Administration, Henry Kingsley, 4 August 1876.
Will, Henry Kingsley, 16 April 1873.

General Register Office
Death Certificate (copy), Henry Kingsley, 27 May 1876. Marriage Certificate (copy), Henry Kingsley and Sarah Maria Kingsley Hazelwood, 19 July 1864.

Inner Temple Library
Stamp Book 1862–January 1866, Warrants for admission. . . .

King's College, Archives
Kingsley, Charles. 2 ALSs to Principal, King's College, 5 July, 18 September 1848.
Kingsley, Henry. School Report.
"Information from Student Nomination or Admission Form".

Public Records Office
Certificate of British Registry No. 315. PRO BT 107/347/315. Document 57 BT 98/4199.
Log of *Swiftsure.* BT98/5190 (8300–8302).
Ships Logs, Adm. 53, 1799–1920.
Ships Logs, Supplementary Series I, Masters Logs (Adm. 54).

Royal Literary Fund
Correspondence file no. 1899, including, from Henry Kingsley, 5 ALSs and 3 applications for funds and 3 receipts (1872, 1875, 1876).

Bibliography

NEW ZEALAND

WELLINGTON

Turnbull Library, Wellington Public Library
Kingsley, Henry. ALS to J.E. Fitzgerald, March (?) 1850. MS 64, vol. 6.

SCOTLAND

EDINBURGH

National Library of Scotland
Blackwood Collection: 2 ALSs from John Blackwood to Henry Kingsley, 27 July 1870, 1 May 1871, MS Acc. 5643-D7, ALS from John Blackwood to William Blackwood, MSS 4255; 2 ALSs from William Blackwood to John Blackwood, 28 July 1870, 4 May 1871, MSS 4256, 4271; 9 ALSs from Henry Kingsley to John Blackwood, 1870-71; MSS 4262, 4277, receipt for *[Old] Margaret*, 28 July 1870, MS 4262.
Eyre Defence Committee letters. ALS from Hamilton Hume to William Blackwood, 21 September 1866. MS 4209, fol. 64.
Kingsley, Charles. Acc. no. 60, fol. 58.

University of Edinburgh Library
Brown, John. MS E70/49.

UNITED STATES

CAMBRIDGE, MASS.

Houghton Library, Harvard University
Kingsley, Henry. ALS to Ticknor and Fields, Boston, 21 February 1859; 4 ALSs to various addressees (1867–78?).
Ticknor and Fields. Cost Book of Publication, III, January 1857–April 1863.

LOS ANGELES

Library of the University of California at Los Angeles
Kingsley, Henry. *The Hillyars and the Burtons* MS. (part chap. 49 to chap. 51). Given to John Reid, Inverlodden, Wargrave, Berks., circa 1869; 8 ALSs to various addressees (1860–74?).

NEW YORK

New York Public Library, Astor, Lenox and Tilden Foundation
Henry W. and Albert A. Berg Collection: 25 ALSs from Henry Kingsley to Alexander Macmillan, 1858–61; 4 documents, 1859–63.
De Coursey Fales Collection: 7 ALSs from Henry Kingsley to various addressees, 1861–72.

PRINCETON

Princeton University Library, Manuscript Division
Laurence Hutton Collection: esp. "The Literary Life" MS. and 4 ALSs

from Maurice Kingsley to Laurence Hutton, 1, 12, 14, November 1894, 8 January 1895.
R.B. Martin Papers and Correspondence: esp. ALS from Elizabeth B. Mueller to Robert B. Martin, 25 May 1949.
Morris L. Parrish Collection: 8 ALSs from Henry Kingsley to various addressees (1860–74?).
A. G. Stapleton Collection, Kingsley letters.

URBANA-CHAMPAIGN

University of Illinois
Bentley Collection: 48 ALSs from Henry Kingsley to George Bentley, 1871-75, and 2 documents; 8 ALSs from S.M.K. Kingsley to George Bentley, 1872–78.

3.   **Other Works**

A.   *ARTICLES, NEWS ITEMS, AND REVIEWS*

Academy
Review of *Grange Garden.* 9 (January–June 1876): 554.

Argus
"Victorian Jockey Club – October Meeting". 3 October 1857, p. 4.
"The Great Match". Editorial. 5 October 1857, p. 5.
"Non Mi Recordo". Correspondence. 8 October 1857, p. 6.
Shipping Intelligence. 23 December 1857, p. 4, 26 February 1858, p. 4.
" 'Swiftsure' Sailing". Advertisement. 11, 16 January, 12, 19, 23, 24 February 1858, p. 1.
"Ararat Bushfire". 3 February 1858, p. 4.

Athenaeum
Review of *The Recollections of Geoffry Hamlyn.* 7 May 1859, pp. 610–11.
Review of *The Hillyars and the Burtons.* 27 May 1865, pp. 716–17.
Review of *Leighton Court.* 24 February 1866, p. 266.
Review of *Silcote of Silcotes.* 16 November 1867, pp. 643–44.
Review of *Stretton.* 5 June 1869, pp. 759–60.
Review of *Tales of Old Travel.* 16 October 1869, p. 497.
Review of *The Boy in Grey.* 8 April 1871, p. 431.
Review of *Old Margaret.* 22 July 1871, p. 109.
Review of *Hetty.* 19 August 1871, pp. 232–33.
Review of *The Harveys.* 16 December 1871, p. 790.
Review of *Hornby Mills and Other Stories.* 1 June 1872, pp. 686–87.
Review of *Valentin.* 21 September 1872, p. 357; 28 September 1872, p. 403.
Review of *Oakshott Castle.* 22 March 1873, p. 375.
Review of *Reginald Hetherege.* 20 June 1874, p. 825.
Review of *Number Seventeen.* 12 June 1875, p. 779.
Review of *Fireside Studies.* 25 March 1876, p. 424.
Obituary. 27 May 1876, p. 731.

Bibliography

Atlantic Monthly
Review of *The Hillyars and the Burtons.* 16: 121 (July 1865).
Review of *Stretton.* 37: 239–40 (February 1876).

Evening Post
"Death of Henry Kingsley". 25 May 1876, p. 2.

Fraser's Magazine
M-M. "Novels of the Day: Their Writers and Readers". 61: 205–17 (August 1860).
"Jamaica and the Recent Insurrection There". 73: 161–79 (February 1866).
King, R. J. "Charles Kingsley". N.s. 11, no. 63 (March 1875): 397–406.

Gippsland Guardian
" 'Storm Bird' Sailing". Advertisement. 22 February 1856, p. 3.

Illustrated London News (Supplement)
"The Late Mr. Henry Kingsley". 3 June 1876, p. 545.

Illustrated Magazine of Art
"The Land of Gold". N.s. 1, vol. 31: 43–45.

Living Age
"Big Brothers". 794 (1859): 446–48.

Macmillan's Magazine
Hughes, T. "The Volunteer's Catechism". 2: 191–99 (September 1860).
Martineau, John. "Volunteering, Past and Present". 2: 394–403 (September 1860).
T.A. "Recent Novel Writing". 13, no. 75 (January 1866): 202–9.

New York Times
"Henry Kingsley the Novelist". 2 July 1876, p. 4.

North American Review
Review of *The Reminiscences* [sic] *of Geoffry Hamlyn.* 88 (October 1859): 547.
Review of *The Hillyars and the Burtons.* 101 (July 1865): 293–99.

North British Review
Review of *The Recollections of Geoffry Hamlyn.* 31 (1859): 384–403.

Reviews and Literary Notices
Review of *The Hillyars and the Burtons.* July 1865, p. 121.

Saturday Review
Review of *Austin Elliot.* 6 June 1863, pp. 731–32.
Review of *The Hillyars and the Burtons.* 13 May 1865, pp. 576–77.
Review of *Leighton Court.* 10 March 1866, pp. 299–300.
Review of *Silcote of Silcotes.* 4 January 1868, pp. 25–26.
Review of *Mademoiselle Mathilde.* 23 May 1868, pp. 693–94.
Review of *Stretton.* 19 June 1869, pp. 814–16.
Review of *Old Margaret.* 8 July 1871, pp. 56–57.
Review of *Hetty.* 2 December 1871, pp. 728–29.
Review of *Valentin.* 28 September 1872, pp. 412–13.
Review of *Oakshott Castle.* 26 April 1873, pp. 563–64.

Review of *Reginald Hetherege*. 18 July 1874, pp. 92–93.
Review of *Number Seventeen*. 3 July 1875, pp. 29–30.

Spectator
Review of *Ravenshoe*. 7 June 1862, pp. 637–38.
Review of *The Hillyars and the Burtons*. 6 May 1865, pp. 501–2.
Review of *Old Margaret*. 19 August 1871, pp. 1014–15.
Review of *Hornby Mills and Other Stories*. 18 May 1872, pp. 632–33.
Review of *Valentin*. 2 November 1872, pp. 1401–2.
"Henry Kingsley the Novelist". 3 June 1876, pp. 706–7.
Review of *Fireside Studies*. 24 June 1876, pp. 803–4.

Southern Cross (Sydney)
Review of *The Recollections of Geoffry Hamlyn*. 19 November 1859, p. 5.

Sussex Daily News
"Death of Mr. Henry Kingsley at Cuckfield". 26 May 1876.

The Times
"Oxford Boat Race". 1 April 1852, p. 8; 5 April 1852, p. 5.
"Henley Royal Regatta". 26 June 1852, p. 8.
"Henley Regatta". 13 June 1853, p. 8.
Editorial (Eyre). 29 November 1865, p. 8.
Bakewell, W. Correspondence. 30 November 1865, p. 10; 5 December 1865, p. 7.
Review of *Hetty*. 16 September 1871, p. 4.
Review of *The Lost Child*. 25 December 1871, p. 4.
Review of *Oakshott Castle*. 18 April 1873, p. 4.
Review of *Fireside Studies*. 24 April 1876, p. 4.
Obituary. 25 May 1876, p. 5.
Funeral Notice. 27 May 1876, p. 12.
Advertisement for Funds. 7 November 1876, p. 6.
"Funds for Henry Kingsley". 9 November 1876, p. 8.

Town and Country Journal (Sydney)
"Mr. Henry Kingsley". Obituary. 12 August 1876, p. 253.

"Funeral of Henry Kingsley." Unidentified newspaper cutting. Univ. of Illinois, Urbana-Champaign.

B.   BOOKS AND OTHER REFERENCES BEFORE 1876

Clarke, W. B. *Researches in the Southern Gold Fields of New South Wales*. Sydney: Reading and Wellbank, 1860.
Edinburgh and Leith Post Office Directory. 1870–71.
Faulkner, Thomas. *An Historical and Topographical Description of Chelsea, and its Environs*. Vol. 1. Chelsea: Nichols and Son and Simpkin and Marshall, 1829.
Forgues, E. D., trans. *La Revue des Deux Mondes (Austin Elliot)*. Paris: Librairie de la Hachette, 1864.
———. *Scènes de la Vie Aristocratique en Angleterre et en Russie*. Paris: Librairie de la Hachette, 1866. Scenes from H. Kingsley, *Austin Elliot*; N. Tolstoy, *Nickolinka*, H. Shakespeare, *Chasses dans l'Inde*.

Fowler, Frank. *Southern Lights and Shadows: Brief Notes of Three Years' Experience of Social, Literary and Political Life in Australia.* 2nd ed. London: Sampson Low, 1859.

Grant, James. *The Metropolitan: Weekly and Provincial Press.* Vol. 3. London: George Routhledge, n.d.

―――. *The Newspaper Press.* 2 vols. London: Tinsley Bros, 1871.

King's College Calendar for 1848.

Kingsley, Charles. *Two Years Age.* Cambridge: Macmillan, 1857.

Levey, William, ed. *Victorian Stud Book.* Vols. 1 and 2. Melbourne: Bell's Life Office, 1859.

Lloyds Register of British and Foreign Shipping 1 July 1854 to 30 June 1855. London: Cox and Wyman, 1855.

New South Wales Government Gazette, 1854–57.

Philips' Emigrant's Guide to Australia. London: George Philip, 1852.

The Private Execution Act II, Vic. No. 40, 1853. Sydney, n.d.

Rules and Regulations for the Government and Guidance of the Mounted Patrols of New South Wales. Sydney: Government Printer, 1853.

Sherer, John. *The Gold-Finder of Australia.* London: Clarke, Beeton, 1853.

Victorian Electoral Roll, 21 July 1856 to 30 June 1857.

C. BOOKS AND ARTICLES SINCE 1876

Adcock, A. St. J. "The Kingsleys" *The Bookman,* 25: 167–73 (January 1904).

Allan, J. Alex. *Men and Manners in Australia.* Melbourne: Cheshire, 1945.

Anderson, Hugh. "The Composition of *Geoffry Hamlyn*: A Comment." *Australian Literary Studies* 4, no. 1 (May 1969): 79–80.

―――, ed. *Eureka: Victorian Parliamentary Papers Notes and Proceedings 1854–1867.* Facsimile reprint. Melbourne: Hill of Content, 1969.

Argyle, Barry. *An Introduction to the Australian Novel 1830–1930.* London: Oxford University Press, 1972.

Austin, K. A. *The Lights of Cobb and Co.: The Story of the Frontier Coaches, 1854–1924.* Adelaide: Rigby, 1967.

Back to Beaufort. Beaufort: Centenary Celebrations Committee, 1936.

Banfield, Lorna L. "Ararat from Mining Camp to City." *Victorian Historical Magazine* 33, no. 131 (February 1963): 358–79.

―――. *Green Pastures and Gold: A History of Ararat.* N.p. [Vic.]: Mullaya Publications, 1974.

Barnes, John. *Henry Kingsley and Colonial Fiction.* Melbourne: Oxford University Press, 1971.

―――. "A Young Man Called Kingsley." *Meanjin Quarterly* 30, no. 1 (March 1971): 72–84.

Baxter, Rosilyn. "Henry Kingsley and the Australian Landscape." *Australian Literary Studies* 4, no. 4 (October 1970): 395–98.

Beer, N. H. "The Presentation of War in English Prose Fiction, with special reference to the work of Captain F. Marryat, Henry Kingsley, H. Rider Haggard, H. G. Wells, R. H. Moltram and Evelyn Waugh." Diss., University of London, 1970.

Bibliography

Benalla Past and Present: Illustrated History of the Town and District 1838 to 1920. Benalla: Back to Benalla Carnival Committee, 1920.

Beston, John. "Land of Hope for Britain's Lower Classes." Review of *The Hillyars and the Burtons,* with introduction by Leonie Kramer. *Sydney Morning Herald,* 29 September 1973, p. 27.

Billis, R. V., and Kenyon, A. S. *Pastoral Pioneers of Port Phillip.* 2nd ed. Melbourne: Stockland Press, 1974.

————. *Pastures New: An Account of the Pastoral Occupation of Port Phillip* (1930). Melbourne: Stockland Press, 1974.

Blackie, J. S. *Notes of a Life.* Edited by A. Stodart-Walker. Edinburgh: Blackwood, 1910.

Blunt, Reginald. *Memoirs of Gerald Blunt of Chelsea, His Family and Forebears.* Chelsea: Truslove and Hanson, 1911.

Boas, Guy. *The Garrick Club 1831–1964* (1948). London: Garrick Club, 1964.

Boldrewood, Rolf. *Babes in the Bush.* London: Macmillan, 1900.

————. *Old Melbourne Memories.* Edited by C. E. Sayers. Melbourne: Heinemann, 1969.

————. *A Sydney-Side Saxon.* London: Macmillan, 1891.

"The Bookman". "Henry Kingsley". *South Australian Institutes Journal,* 29 February 1932, pp. 12–13.

"Books and Bookmen". *Sussex County Magazine,* February 1930, p. 156.

Bradfield, Raymond. *Castlemaine: A Golden Harvest.* Historical Briefs Series, no. 3. Kilmore, Vic.: Lowden, 1972.

Bride, Thomas Francis. *Letters from Victorian Pioneers.* Melbourne: Heinemann, 1969.

Brown, P. L., ed. *Clyde Company Papers.* Vol. 6, 1854–58. London: Oxford University Press, 1968.

Brown and Forrest, D. W., ed. *Letters of Dr. John Brown.* London: Adam and Charles Black, 1907.

Browne, Rose. "Squattlesea Mere: Rolf Boldrewood's First Station." *Warrnambool Standard,* 23 June 1928. Reprinted from *The Sydney Morning Herald.*

Buckler, William E. "Henry Kingsley and *The Gentleman's Magazine.*" *Journal of English and Germanic Philology* 50 (1951): 90–100.

Burke, Keast. "Henry Kingsley in Australia". *Etruscan* 23, no. 3 (September 1974): 29–32.

Byrom, Thomas, Introduction to *Ravenshoe* (1862). Reprinted London: Dent, 1970.

Byrne, Desmond. *Australian Writers.* London: Richard Bentley, 1896.

Cambridge, Ada. *Thirty Years in Australia.* London: Methuen, 1903.

Carless, Ronald L. *Visit to "The Springs," Moliagul.* Welcome Stranger Centenary Committee, n.d.

Carnegie, Margaret. *Friday Mount: First Settlement at Holbrook and the South-Western Slopes of New South Wales.* Melbourne: Hawthorn Press, 1973.

"Charles Kingsley". *Southern Cross,* 7 August 1919.

Charles Kingsley and Eversley Church: Notes 1964. Eversley Rectory, 1964.

Chitty, Susan. *The Beast and the Monk: A Life of Charles Kingsley.* London: Hodder and Stoughton 1975.

Churchill, D. M., and A. de Corona. *The Distribution of Victorian Plants.* Melbourne: Royal Botanic Gardens and National Herbarium and Botany Department, Monash University, 1972.

Collingwood, Stuart Dodgson. *The Life and Letters of Lewis Carroll.* London: Nelson, 1898.

Colloms, Brenda. *Charles Kingsley.* London: Constable; New York: Barnes and Noble, 1975.

Couper, W. J. "A Bibliography of Edinburgh Periodical Literature". *Scottish Notes and Queries,* 2nd ser. 5 (December 1903): 87–88.

Cowan, Peter M. "Venables, Henry Pares (1830-1890)". *Australian Dictionary of Biography,* 6: 1851-1890. Carlton, Vic.: Melbourne University Press, 1976.

Cowan, R.M.W. *The Newspaper in Scotland.* Glasgow: George Outram, 1946.

Cranfield, L. R. "The History of Warrandyte". *Victorian Historical Magazine* 27, no. 1 (October 1955): 1–26.

Critchley, L. G. "The Explorations of Von Mueller". *Walkabout,* 1 September 1953, p. 19.

Croft, Julian. "Is *Geoffry Hamlyn* a Creole Novel?" *Australian Literary Studies* 6, no. 3 (May 1974): 269–76.

Cusack, Frank, ed. *The Australian Christmas.* Melbourne: Heinemann, 1966.

"Death of Mrs. Henry Kingsley: Temperance and Social Worker". *Folkestone Herald,* 19 August 1922.

De Castella, Francois. "Early Victorian Wine Growing". *Victorian Historical Magazine* 19, no. 76 (December 1942): 140–67.

De Castella, Hubert. *John Bull's Vineyard.* Melbourne: Sands and McDougall, 1886.

Dixon, Robert. "Kingsley's *Geoffry Hamlyn* and the Art of Landscape". *Southerly* 37, no. 3 (September 1977): 274–99.

["Douglas Sladen–Langi Willi"]. *The Book Buyer* 11 (1894): 244.

Dutton, Geoffrey. *The Hero as Murderer: The Life of Edward John Eyre, Australian Explorer and Governor of Jamaica, 1815–1901.* Sydney: Collins, 1967.

Earle, William. *Earle's Port Fairy* (1896). Edited by C. E. Sayers. Olinda, Vic.: Olinda Public Relations, 1973.

"Early Port Fairy". *Gazette* (Port Fairy), 4 December 1973, p. 2.

Elliott, Alfred Beaver. *Memorials of Old Chelsea.* London: Elliott Stuck, 1892.

Elliott, Brian. "Antipodes: An Essay in Attitudes". *Australian Letters* 7, no. 3 (August 1966): 66.

—————. "The Composition of *Geoffry Hamlyn*: The Legend and the Facts". *Australian Literary Studies* 3, no. 4 (October 1968): 271–89.

Ellis, S. M. *Henry Kingsley 1830–1876: Towards a Vindication.* London: Grant Richards Pronto, 1931.

Fetherstonhaugh, Cuthbert. *After Many Days.* 2nd ed. Sydney: John Andrew, 1918.

Finnin, Mary. "The Mahogany Ship Mystery". *Bulletin,* 14 March 1956, p. 27.

Flett, James. *The History of Gold Discovery in Victoria.* Melbourne, 1970.

———. *The Story of an Old Gold-Diggings Town: Dunolly.* Melbourne: Poppet Head Press, 1956.
Ford, George H. "The Governor Eyre Case in England." *University of Toronto Quarterly* 17: 219–33 (April 1948).
Foster, Joseph. *Alumni Oxonienses: The Members of the University of Oxford, 1715–1886.* Oxford: Parker, 1888.
Fuller, Hester Thackeray, and Violet Hammersley, eds. *Thackeray's Daughter: Some Recollections of Anne Thackeray Ritchie.* Dublin: Euphorion, 1952.
Furphy, Joseph. *Such is Life* (1903). Sydney: Angus and Robertson, 1966.
"*Geoffry Hamlyn*: An Australian Classic?" *Bulletin,* 22 October 1952, p. 2.
Gettman, Royal A. *A Victorian Publisher: A Study of The Bentley Papers.* Cambridge: Cambridge University Press, 1960.
Golding, D. J., ed. *The Emigrant's Guide to Australia in the Eighteen Fifties.* Melbourne: Hawthorn Press, 1973.
Gordon, George, et al. Correspondence. *Times Literary Supplement,* 10 April 1930, p. 318.
Gordon, H. C. *Yea: Its Discovery and Development, 1825–1920.* Melbourne: Hawthorn Press, 1954.
Graves, Charles L. *Life and Letters of Alexander Macmillan.* London: Macmillan, 1910.
Green, R. L., ed. *The Diaries of Lewis Carroll.* London: Cassell, 1953.
Greig, A. W. "Letters from Australian Pioneers". *Victorian Historical Magazine* 12, no. 46 (December 1927): 21–108.
Groome, Francis H. "Henry Kingsley". *Bookman,* 8 June 1895, pp. 74–75.
Hainsworth, Roger. "Facsimiles and Reprints". Review of *The Hillyars and the Burtons,* with introduction by Leonie Kramer. *Australian Book Review* 2: 91-92 (July 1973).
Hamer, Clive. "Henry Kingsley's Australian Novels". *Southerly* 26 (1966): 40–57.
———. "The Surrender to Truth in the Early Australian Novel". *Australian Literary Studies* 2, no. 2 (December 1965): 103–16.
Hamilton, J. C. *Pioneering Days in Western Victoria: A Narrative of Early Station Life.* Melbourne: Exchange Press, n.d.
Hancock, W. K. *Discovering Monaro: A Study of Man's Impact on his Environment.* Cambridge: Cambridge University Press, 1972.
Harding, Eric. *Bogong Jack: The Gentleman Bushranger.* Melbourne: Yandoo, 1967.
Hassall, James S. *In Old Australia.* Brisbane: R. S. Hews, 1902.
Hassall, Kathleen. *The Relations Between the Settlers and Aborigines in South Australia, 1836–1860.* Adelaide: Libraries Board of South Australia, 1966.
Hearnshaw, F. J. C. *Centenary History of King's College.* London: Harrap, 1929.
Heaton, G. H. *The Australian Dictionary of Dates.* Melbourne: George Robertson, 1879.
Henderson, Alexander, ed. *Early Pioneer Families of Victoria and Riverina.* Melbourne: McCarron, Bird, 1936.
———. *Henderson's Australian Families.* Vol. 1. Melbourne: Henderson, 1941.

"Henry Kingsley". *Current Literary Thought and Opinion* 31 (July 1901): 56–58.
"Henry Kingsley". *Times Literary Supplement,* 17 March 1930, p. 85.
"Henry Kingsley's Grave". *Times Literary Supplement,* 15 June 1931, p. 135.
[Henry Kingsley: Identity] *Notes and Queries* 7S, III, pp. 160, 194.
Hergenhan, L. T. *"Geoffry Hamlyn* Through Contemporary Eyes". *Australian Literary Studies* 2, no. 4 (December 1966): 289–95.
Hetherington, John. "Bindi's Weathered Walls Have Seen Omeo's History Made". *Age,* 28 September 1963, p. 12.
Hodgson, James. *Historic Port Fairy.* Port Fairy Historical Society, n.d. *The Victorian Historical Magazine* 12, no. 46 (December 1927): 61–62.
Hone, J. Ann. "Macknight, Charles Hamilton (1819–1873)." *Australian Dictionary of Biography.* Vol. 5: 1851–1890. Carlton, Vic.: Melbourne University Press, 1974.
Horner, J. C. *"Geoffry Hamlyn* and its Australian Setting". *Australian Literary Studies* 1, no. 1 (June 1963): 3–15.
Hoskins, W. G., ed. *Dartmoor.* National Park Guide, no. 1. London, 1957.
Howard, Betty. *They Came to Yass Valley.* Yass, 1970.
Hutton, Laurence. "Henry Kingsley". *Book Buyer* 11, no. 12 (January 1895): 723–25.
——. "The Literary Life". *Critic* 45: 321–33 (July–December 1904).
Huxley, Elspeth, ed. *The Kingsleys: A Biographical Anthology.* London: Allen and Unwin, 1973.
James, G. F. *A Homestead History, Being the Reminiscences and Letters of Alfred Joyce of Plaistow and Norwood, Port Phillip, 1843 to 1864.* 3rd ed. Melbourne: Oxford University Press, 1969.
Jeaffreson, John Cordy. *A Book of Recollections.* 2 vols. London: Hurst and Blackett, 1894.
Jenkins, J. E. "Early Ararat." *Victorian Historical Magazine* 8, no. 1 (November 1920): 137–43.
Jennings, G. H. "The Forgotten Brother". *Sussex Life,* May 1976, pp. 33–35.
Kiddle, Margaret. *Men of Yesterday: A Social History of the Western District of Victoria, 1834–1890* (1961). Carlton, Vic.: Melbourne University Press, 1967.
Kingsley, Frances E., ed. *Charles Kingsley: His Letters and Memories of His Life.* 2 vols. London: Henry S. King, 1877. Abridged edition, London: Kegan Paul, 1878.
Kingsley, George H. *Notes on Sport and Travel.* With a Memoir by Mary H. Kingsley. London: Macmillan, 1900.
Kingsley, Mary H. "George Henry Kingsley M.D., F.L.S., etc.". In *Notes on Sport and Travel,* by George H. Kingsley.
Kingsley, Maurice. "Personal Traits of Henry Kingsley". *Book Buyer* 11, no. 12 (January 1895): 727–31.
"The Kingsley Pedigree". *Notes and Queries* 11S. V, pp. 41–42, 158, 217, 373; 12S. II, pp. 70, 136, 253; 12S. VII, p. 174.
"Kingsley's Stand at Minden". *Notes and Queries* 10S. VII, pp. 109, 158, 294–95, 378.

Kramer, Leonie J. *Henry Kingsley: Some Novels of Australian Life.* The Commonwealth Literary Fund Lectures, 1954.

———. Introduction to *The Hillyars and the Burtons.* Facsimile reprint. Sydney: Sydney University Press, 1973.

Kunitz, S. J., and H. Haycraft, eds. *British Authors of the Nineteenth Century.* London: H. W. Wilson, 1936.

Lansbury, Coral. *Arcady in Australia: The Evocation of Australia in Nineteenth-Century English Literature.* Carlton, Vic.: Melbourne University Press, 1970.

Leslie, John W., and Helen C. Cowie, eds. *The Wind Still Blows... Early Gippsland Diaries.* Victoria: H. C. Cowie and J. W. Leslie, 1973.

Levitki, Leon, trans. *Van Eyck.* Edited by George Szekeley. London: Abbey Library, n.d.

Loney, J. K. *Wrecks in Port Phillip Bay.* Geelong: Ken Jenkin Print, n.d.

———. *Wrecks on the Gippsland Coast.* 3rd ed. N.p., 1971.

Lord, Walter Frewen. "The Kingsley Novels". *Nineteenth Century* 60: 996–1004 (June 1904).

———. "The Kingsleys". In *Mirror of the Century.* London: John Lane, 1906.

Macartney, John Neill. *Sandhurst As It Was and As It Is.* Sandhurst: Burrows, 1882.

McCarthy, Justin. *Reminiscences.* 2 vols. London: Chatto and Windus, 1899.

MacInnes, J. D. "Some Western District Pioneers". *Victorian Historical Magazine* 11, no. 44 (June 1927): 259–70.

McLaren, John. *"Geoffry Hamlyn* and the Australian Myth". *Segment* 2 (1973): 6–12.

McLeod, Mary. "Henry Kingsley at Cuckfield". *Sussex County Magazine* 4: 251–53 (March 1930). Also letters and replies, April 1930, p. 340; May 1930, p. 428–29.

———. "Stories of Henry Kingsley". *Sussex County Magazine* 4: 488–89 (June 1930).

Macmillan, George A. *Letters of Alexander Macmillan.* Glasgow: Glasgow University Press, 1908.

Mair, William. *Historic Morningside: Lands, Mansions and Celebrities with "Annals of the Parish" and Some Account of Ecclesiastical Morningside.* N.p., 1947.

Maitland, F. W. *The Life and Letters of Leslie Stephen.* London: Duckworth, 1906.

"Marat in his *Mademoiselle Mathilde*". *Notes and Queries* 12S. II, pp. 409, 475; 12S. III, p. 14.

Martin, Benjamin E. "Old Chelsea". *Century Magazine* 33 (1886): 225–36.

———. *Old Chelsea: A Summer-Day's Stroll.* 2nd ed. London: T. Fisher Unwin, 1889.

Martin, Robert Bernard, ed. *Charles Kingsley's American Notes: Letters from a Lecture Tour 1874.* Princeton: Princeton University Press, 1958.

———. *The Dust of Combat: A Life of Charles Kingsley.* London: Faber, 1959.

Mason, John. Correspondence. *Australasian,* 1 November 1890, p. 869.
Matthews, Leslie, and Moberly Bell. *Chelsea Old Church: Bombing and Rebuilding 1941–1950.* First published 1958. Chelsea: Chelsea Vicarage, 1973.
"Meerschaum". *Notes and Queries* 11S. VIII, p. 247.
Mellick, J. S. D. "Henry Kingsley in Australia". *Australian Literary Studies* 6, no. 1 (May 1973): 91–94.
———. "Henry Kingsley – Mounted Policeman?" *Australian Literary Studies* 7, no. 4 (October 1976): 416–20.
———. "Henry Kingsley: A Biography", Ph.D. University of Queensland, 1978.
Melville, Lewis. *Victorian Novelists.* London: Archibald Constable, 1906.
Monteith, Malcolm. *Chelsea's Old Rectory Garden.* N.p., 1965.
Moorhead, Lucy and Caroline, trans. *The Gold Robbers,* by Céleste de Chabrillan. Melbourne: Sun Books, 1970.
Moore Smith, G. C. Correspondence. *Times Literary Supplement,* 9 January 1930, p. 28.
Murray, James. Introduction to *The New South Wales Illustrated: The Sketches of F. C. Terry* (1855). Melbourne: Lansdowne, 1973.
Murray's Handbook for Travellers in Devon and Cornwall (4th ed. 1859). London: David and Charles, 1971.
Newnham, W. H. Introduction to *Victorian Illustrated 1857 and 1862: Engravings from the Original Edition by S. T. Gill and N. Chevalier* (1859). Melbourne: Lansdowne, 1971.
Nicholson, Lothian. Correspondence. *Times Literary Supplement,* 6 February 1930, p. 102.
Norman, E. R. *Anti-Catholicism in Victorian England.* London: Allen and Unwin, 1968.
Nowell-Smith, Simon, ed. *Letters to Macmillan.* London: Macmillan, 1967.
O'Dwyer, Joseph, ed. *Bard in Bondage: Essays of P. I. O'Leary.* Melbourne: Hawthorn Press, 1954.
Oldham, J. E., and A. T. Sterling. *Victorian: A Visitor's Book.* Melbourne: Brown, Prior, 1934.
Paul, C. Kegan. *Memories.* London: Routledge and Kegan Paul, 1899, reprinted 1971.
Pearson, A. M. *Echoes from the Mountains.* Omeo, Vic.: Omeo Shire Council, 1969.
Peck, Harry H. *Memoirs of a Stockman* (1942). Melbourne: Stock and Land, 1972.
Peddie, Alexander. *Recollections of Dr. John Brown.* Edinburgh: Oliphant, Anderson and Ferrier, 1894.
Pendergast, Jane Vince. *Pioneers of the Omeo District.* Melbourne: Riall Bros, 1968.
Perkins, W. F. *Boldre: The Parish, the Church, and Its Inhabitants.* Lymington: King's Library, 1927.
Perry, Harry C. *A Son of Australia: Memories of W. E. Parry-Okeden I.S.O., 1840–1926.* Brisbane: Watson, Ferguson, 1928.
———. *Pioneering: The Life of the Hon. R. M. Collins, M.L.C.* Brisbane: Watson, Ferguson, 1923.
Pink, W. D. "Kingsley of Sarratt, Canterbury, and London". *Genealogist,* n.s. 29 (1913): 212-24; 30 (1914): 35-38, 86-94.

"The Point of View". *Scribner's Magazine* 19: 23–24 (January 1896).
Pope-Hennessy, Una. *Canon Charles Kingsley: A Biography*. London: Chatto and Windus, 1948.
"Portrait of Henry Kingsley". *Critic* 45: 331 (October 1904).
Programme of Events Being Held to Commemorate the One Hundred and Fiftieth Anniversary of Chelsea Parish Church of Saint Luke, 1824–1974. [Chelsea], n.d.
"Punch Derby's Prophecy". *Punch,* 27 May 1871, 217–18.
Quiller-Couch, Sir Arthur. *Adventures in Criticism*. Cambridge: Cambridge University Press, 1924.
"The Rambler". "Miscellaneous Jottings". *Book Buyer* 11 (1894): 244.
Review of *The Hillyars and the Burtons. Critic,* 15 February 1896, p. 108.
Review of *Ravenshoe, Austin Elliot, Geoffry Hamlyn. Critic,* 9 March 1895, p. 176.
Review of *The Recollections of Geoffry Hamlyn. Bulletin,* 28 September 1895, p. 1.
Ritchie, Anne Thackeray. *Chapters from Some Memoirs*. London: Macmillan, 1894.
―――. "Chapters from Some Unwritten Memoirs. My Witches Cauldron". *Macmillans Magazine* 66: 265–70 (February 1891).
Ross, C. Stuart. "The History of Settlement in the Western District". *Victorian Historical Magazine* 1, no. 2 (April 1911): 51–72.
[Russell, G. W. E.]. "One Who Has Kept a Diary". *Collections and Recollections*. London: Smith, Elder, 1898.
Russell, G. W. E. *Sketches and Snapshots*. London: George Bull, 1910.
―――. *Selected Essays on Literary Subjects*. London: Dent, 1914?].
Ryan, J. S. "The Prose Style of Henry Kingsley". *Armidale and District Historical Society Journal and Proceedings,* no. 19 (April 1976), pp. 63–72.
Sadleir, Michael. "Henry Kingsley: A Portrait", *Edinburgh Review* 240 (October 1924): 330-48. Revised as "Henry Kingsley", *Times Literary Supplement,* 2 January 1930, pp. 1–2.
―――. *Things Past*. London: Constable, 1944.
Sadlier, John. *Recollections of a Victorian Police Officer* (1913). Facsimile reprint. Ringwood, Vic.: Penguin, 1973.
Saintsbury, George *Collected Essays and Papers of George Saintsbury, 1875–1920.* 4 vols. London: Dent, 1923.
Scheuerle, William H. "Henry Kingsley and the Governor Eyre Controversy". *Victorian Newsletter,* no. 37 (spring 1970): 24–27.
―――. "Magdalen at Michael's Gate: A Neglected Lyric". *Victorian Poetry* 5 (Summer 1967): 144–46.
―――. *The Neglected Brother: A Study of Henry Kingsley*. Tallahassee: Florida State University Press, 1971.
―――. "Periodicals in the Novels of Henry Kingsley". *Victorian Periodicals Newsletter,* no. 12 (June 1971): 11–14.
―――. Introduction to *Ravenshoe*. Lincoln: Nebraska University Press, 1967.
―――. "Romantic Attitudes in *Geoffry Hamlyn*". *Australian Literary Studies* 2, no. 2 (December 1965): 79–91.
Scott, Geoffrey. *Sydney's Highways of History*. Melbourne: Georgian House, 1958.

Bibliography

Shorter, Clement. *The Recollections of Geoffry Hamlyn.* New edition. With a memoir of Henry Kingsley. London: Ward, Lock and Bowden, 1895.

———. *Victorian Literature: Sixty Years of Books and Bookmen.* London: James Bowden, 1897.

Simpson, Charles. Correspondence. *Times Literary Supplement,* 10 April 1930, p. 318.

Sisson, R. A. *The Treasures of Time: Embroidered Kneelers in Chelsea Old Church.* 2nd ed. London: Belgrave Press, 1968.

Skelton, John. *The Table Talk of Shirley: Reminiscences of and Letters from Froude, Thackeray, Disraeli, Browning, Rossetti, Kingsley, Baynes, Huxley, Tyndall and Others.* Edinburgh: William Blackwood, 1895.

Sladen, Douglas. *My Long Life.* London: Hutchinson, 1939.

Smith, L. P. G. *Centennial of The Church of St. John The Baptist, Rheola, 1870–1970.* Ballarat: Baxter and Stubbs, 1970.

———. *Centennial of the Church of St. Mary, Kingower, 1853–1971.* Ballarat: Baxter and Stubbs, n.d.

Sotheby and Co. Sales Catalogue, 14 December 1925. Lots 106–18. Property of Mrs. St. Leger Harrison ("Lucas Malet").

———. Sales Catalogues, 14–15 November 1932. Lots 188–238, 248–302. Kingsley Library and Papers.

Spence, C. H. *Catherine Helen Spence: An Autobiography* (1910). Facsimile reprint, Adelaide: Libraries Board of South Australia, 1975.

Sutherland, Alexander, et al. *Victoria and Its Metropolis.* 2 vols. Melbourne: McCarron, Bird, 1888.

Sutherland, Bruce. "Henry Kingsley and Australia". *Australian Quarterly* 17, no. 2 (June 1945): 98–105.

Swan, Nathaniel Walter. *A Couple of Cups Ago and Other Stories.* Melbourne: Cameron, Laing, 1885.

Tauchnitz, Bernard. *Complete Catalogue of The Tauchnitz Edition of British and American Authors.* Leipzig: Tauchnitz, 1910.

Temple, E. *The Kiewa Valley and its Pioneers.* Maryborough, Vic.: Hedges and Bell, n.d.

Thirkell, Angela. "Henry Kingsley". *Nineteenth-Century Fiction* 5: 175–87 (December 1950).

———. "The Works of Henry Kingsley". *Nineteenth Century Fiction* 5: 273–93 (March 1951).

Tinsley, William. *Random Recollections of an Old Publisher.* 2 vols. London: Simpkin, Marshell, Hamilton, Kent, 1900.

Toynbee, Paget. Correspondence. *Times Literary Supplement,* 9 January 1930, p. 28.

Trevelyan, Sir George Otto. Correspondence. *Times Literary Supplement,* 21 June 1923, p. 422.

Walford, L. B. *Memories of Victorian London.* London: Edward Arnold, 1912.

Walker, Mary Howitt. *Come Wind, Come Weather: A Biography of Alfred Howitt.* Carlton, Vic.: Melbourne University Press, 1971.

Westgarth, William. *Personal Recollections of Early Melbourne and Victoria.* Melbourne: George Robertson, 1888.

Wilkes, G. A. *"Geoffry Hamlyn*: A Study in Literary Survival". In *The Australian Experience,* ed. W. S. Ramson. Canberra: Australian National University Press, 1974.
———. "Kingsley's *Geoffry Hamlyn*: A Study in Literary Survival." *Southerly* 32 (1972), no. 4: 243–54.
Wolff, Robert Lee. "Henry Kingsley". *Harvard Library Bulletin* 13, no. 2 (spring 1959): 195–226.

Index

Aborigines, 110-12
Alexander, Mount, 43, 47, 49, 52, 54
Allen, Barbara, 164, 166
America, 129-31, 146, 151, 161, 162
Anderson's Creek, 70
Annesleys, 96, 107
Antrobus, E.E., 162
Ararat, 52, 70, 74
Argus (Melbourne), 74, 77, 90
Arnold, Arthur, 154
Arnold, Edwin, 30, 33, 34, 57, 97, 126-27, 154
Arnold, Thomas, 157
Athenaeum, 113, 115, 116, 119, 145, 150, 158, 164
Austen, Jane, 132, 157
Austin Elliott, 27, 43, 78, 96, 98, 100, 108, 109, 113-15
Australia, 8, 17, 25, 32, 38, 40, 44, 45, 78, 80, 83, 84, 85, 86, 89-92, 108-112, 129, 151, 152, 165, 167
Avoca, 49, 52, 53
Avoca River, 53

Baker, Samuel White, 113
Bakewell, William, 110-112
Ballarat, 43
Balzac, H. de, 116, 132
Barnack, 1, 2
Baroona, 72
Beechworth, 49, 52, 55, 67, 69
Belloury River, 62
Bendigo, 43, 47, 48, 52, 76
Bendigo Advertiser, 48
Ben Nevis (Australia), 49, 72
Bentley, George, 145-49, 154, 157-63 *passim*, 165
Bentley, Richard, 150
Bideford, 4
Blackie, John Stuart, 96
Black, William, 161
Blackwood, John, 134, 135, 141, 143
Blackwood, William, 134, 141, 143
Blewitt, Octavian. *See* Royal Literary Fund

Blunt, Gerald, 6, 104, 166
Boldrewood, Rolf. *See* Browne T.A.
Bournemouth, 13, 20
Boy in Grey, The 55, 145-46
Brackenbury, Mrs 49-50
Bradbury, Evans Co., 116-19, 121, 145
Braddon, M.E., 114
Brooks, C.W. Shirley, 104, 133
Brown, Dr John, 140
Browne, T.A., 70-73, 91
Buckley, Patrick Cody, 64
Buckley's Crossing, 63, 64
Buninyong, 49, 73, 74
Bushrangers, 82

Cabbage Tree Creek, 64, 65, 67
Caledonia Diggins, 69
Cambridge, 2, 13, 20, 87-89, 98
Cambridge, Ada, 49
Cambridge University, 19, 37, 133
Campbell, Henry, 49, 69, 96, 103
Canada, 37, 38, 129, 162
Cann River, 61, 63, 65, 67
Carlyle, Mrs Thomas, 109
Chabrillan, Céleste de, 45
"Charles Sturt: A Chapter from the History of Australian Exploration", 54, 69
Chatto and Windus, 162
"Cheap Tour near Home, A", 114
Chelsea, 5-7, 17, 23, 25, 27, 21-28 *passim*, 40, 65, 86, 105, 161
Chelsea Old Church, 24, 28
Chelsea Public Library, 17-18
Chirnside Bros, 74
Chronicle (Kelso), 142
Clarke, Marcus, 48
Clovelly, 3-5, 7, 27, 29
Cockney, 25, 26, 82
Cole, Mount, 49, 73
Colebrook, 20, 29, 40
Collins, W. Wilkie, 114
Combes, Robert, 133-34
Comet, 74
Constitution, 52

Index

Convicts, 80, 81, 82
Cornhill, 113
Cornwall, 59, 60
Craik, G.L., 113-15, 123, 148, 151, 153, 157, 163, 166
Cranfield, L.R., 69
Crediton, 29
Crimean War, 46
Critic, 92
Cuckfield, 144, 161, 163-67

Daily News, 92, 149
Daily Review (Edinburgh), 123, 124, 128-32, 134-36, 139, 140, 141, 144
Daisy Hill, 52, 70
Dandenong Ranges, 70
Dark Blue, The 145
Dartmoor, 29
Delamere Forest, 1
Derby, Lord, 165
Devon, 3, 29, 89, 90, 93, 98, 113
Dicey, Edward, 18, 166
Dickens, Charles, 132, 133, 160
Dodgson, Charles, 107, 108, 118-19, 150
Donkeywoman's Flat, 53
Dressors, 86
Drosier, Thomas, 20, 29, 30
Duckworth, R.J., 108
du Maurier, Gerald, 166
Dunmore, 70, 72
Dunmore Cottage, 70, 71
Dunolly, 48

Echo, 154
Edinburgh, 96, 123, 124, 127-28, 130, 133, 135, 139, 140, 141, 143, 144, 145, 147
Electra, 68
Eliot, George, 116, 132, 133, 160
Ellis, S.M., 32, 51, 57, 96, 104
Emu Creek, 73
Emu, Mount, 73
"Episode in the Life of Charles Mordaunt, An", 29
Erskine, Thomas, 97
Essex House, 3, 6, 21, 22
Eureka, 68
Eversley, 13, 27, 86, 88, 90, 93, 96, 155, 156, 162, 163
Exeter, 29
Expedition Pass, 49, 54
Eyre, Edward John, 54, 68, 71, 72, 109-110

Faithful's Station, 55
Faulkner, Thomas, 21-23
Feathertop, Mount, 65
Ferntree Gully, 70
Fetherstonhaugh, Cuthbert, 45, 49, 72
Field Lane Home for Boys, 96
Fiery Creek, 73

Fireside Studies, 9, 11, 164
Fitzgerald, J.E., 29
Folio and Duodecimo, 164
Folkestone, 166
Forest Creek, 43
Fortess Terrace, 144, 151-53, 158, 163
"Foundation of an Empire, The", 44
Fowler, Frank, 59
France, 114-16, 140
Franco-Prussian War, 135-38, 149, 161
Fraser, Malcolm, 48
Fraser's Magazine, 103, 113, 116
Froude, J.A., 32, 107, 166
Furphy, Joseph, 48

Garrick Club, 104, 147
Gauntlet, 41-44, 46
Geelong, 74
Gentleman's Magazine, 115, 116, 154
George, Lake, 54, 56
Germany, 35, 36, 115
Gippsland, 45, 63, 64, 66, 67
Glenalbyn Grange, 48
Glengower, 48
Good Words for the Young, 145
Gordon, Adam Lindsay, 48
Gosse, Edmund, 123, 161
Goulburn River, 54, 68, 69, 167
Grange Garden, 164, 165

Hall, William, 48
Hamlyn. *See* Williams, James Hamlyn
Harrison, W., 166
Harveys, The, 8, 9, 12, 15, 16, 19-20, 31, 41, 56, 149
Hawthorne, Nathaniel, 132
Hazelwood, Mrs, 106, 107, 134, 147, 148, 155, 156, 158, 162, 167
Hazelwood, Sarah Maria Kingsley. *See* Kingsley, Sarah Maria
Henley, 32, 34, 36, 118
Herbert, Auberon, 127, 137
Hetty, 121-24, 145
Hillyars and the Burtons, The, 2, 4, 6, 9, 21-27 *passim,* 38, 43-46, 51-54, 62, 65-66, 69, 73, 79-80, 84, 88, 95-99, 108, 113, 115, 161
Hogarth, William, 102, 116
Holne, 2
Home Journal, 157
Hornby Mills and Other Stories, 150, 151
Horn, Cape, 77-79
Houghton, Lord, 147, 148, 154
Howitt, A.W., 63
Hughes, Thomas, 106, 110
Hugo, Victor, 157, 160
Hume and Hovell, 48, 54
Hunt, Holman, 96
Hutton, Laurence, 15, 105, 119, 166

Index

Ilfracombe, 3
Indi River. *See* Murray River
"Influence of Travel, The" 139, 158
Inner Temple, 99
Inverary, 98
Irvine, James, 70
Irving, Martin, 18, 34, 69, 90, 91

Jeaffreson, John Cordy, 30-33
Jonson, Ben, 160

Kentish Town. *See* Fortess Terrace
Ker, W.L. (Dr), 69
Kiewa River, 55
King Island, 77, 78
Kingower, 48
King River, 53, 55
King, R.J., 13
King's College, 8, 9, 14, 15-18, 20, 29
King's College School, 15, 16
Kingsley, Charles (father), 1, 3, 5, 7, 9, 10, 12, 13, 17, 30, 89, 93
Kingsley, Charles (grandfather), 2
Kingsley, Charles (brother), 1-14 *passim*, 17, 19, 20, 24, 27, 29, 32, 35-36, 60, 72, 86-100 *passim*, 104, 108, 110, 112, 116, 117, 120, 123, 141, 147-51 *passim*, 154-58 *passim*, 161-63
Kingsley, Mrs Charles, 32
Kingsley, Charlotte, 3, 11
Kingsley, F.E. (Fanny), 1, 2, 3, 4, 7, 11, 13, 14, 17, 40, 91, 94, 95, 100, 106, 123, 155, 161
Kingsley, George Henry (brother), 7, 8, 11, 13, 49, 90, 93, 95, 104, 148, 151, 161, 166, 167
Kingsley, Mrs George Henry, 151
Kingsley, Gerald, 9, 13, 17, 19
Kingsley, Grenville, 3, 7, 94
Kingsley, Herbert, 4
Kingsley, Mary (mother), 1, 3, 5, 10, 12, 14, 30, 89, 91, 114, 123, 154, 156, 157
Kingsley, Mary (niece), 3, 7, 8, 11, 12, 27, 151, 167
Kingsley, Maurice, 12, 13, 19, 93, 105, 119, 143, 150, 156
Kingsley, Rannulph de, 1
Kingsley, Sarah Maria, 57, 95, 104-113 *passim*, 119-22, 130, 131, 139, 140, 143, 147-56 *passim*, 161-67 *passim*
King's Row, 25
Korong, Mount, 49
Kosciusko, Mount, 64, 65

Laidlaw, Mrs, 71, 72
Lanarkshire, 98
Langi Willi. *See* Willi Mitchell
Langworthy, Willie, 33
Lander, Sir Thomas Dick, 128
Lawrence, Thomas, 24

Lawson, Henry, 50, 51, 83
Leighton Court, 3, 29, 109, 112-15
Liddell, Dean, 108
Linton, Lyn, 158
Llangeryn, Mount, 73, 146
Lost Child, The, 89, 145, 146
Lucas, Nathan, 3, 7, 8
Ludlow, J.M., 10, 14, 20, 36, 110
Luxembourg, 136, 139

Maberley, T.A., 166
McCarthy, Justin, 161, 162
Macartney, John Neill, 47
MacKnight, Charles Hamilton, 70-74 *passim*, 91
MacLehose, James, 87
Macmillan, Alexander, 86-100 *passim*, 103, 106-109, 112-15, 119-23 *passim*, 146-57 *passim*, 166, 167
Macmillan, Daniel, 86
Macmillan's Magazine, 93, 97-99, 103, 109, 114, 130
Mademoiselle Mathilde, 115, 116, 118, 123, 132
"Malmaison", 12, 37, 139, 144, 145
Martin, B.E., 19, 21, 23
Martin Chuzzlewit, 119
Martineua, John, 3
Mary, 44
Maryburnong River, 62
Masson, David, 103, 108
Maurice, F.D., 107
"Meerschaum", 96
Melbourne, 45-47, 54, 66-68, 74, 76, 77, 84
Melville (bushranger), 49
Menzies, R.G., 48
Merimbula, 61, 63
Miller, Maxwell, 30
Mistibithiwong. *See* Mount Murramurrangbong
Mitchell, Willi, 53, 54, 72-74, 76, 91
Mitta Mitta River, 53, 55
Moliagul, Mount, 48, 49, 52
Monaro, 48, 56, 61-64
Morley, John, 121
Mounted Police, 56-59
Mount William Station. *See* Chirnside Bros
Mudie's Circulating Library, 90
Mueller, Baron von, 64
Munro, Alexander, 96
Murramurrangbong, Mount, 55
Murray Gates, 64, 65
Murray River, 61, 65, 67
"My Landladies: Chapters of a Digger's Life", 53, 56, 57
Mystery of the Island, The, 50-51, 164, 165

Nerrin Nerrin, 72
"Navies of France and England, The" 13

Index

Newman, John Henry, 117
"New Church at the Mistibithiwong, The", 55, 60
New Quarterly, 92
New South Wales, 45, 48, 57-59
New Zealand, 78, 128
Norfolk Island, 68

Oakshott Castle, 3, 4, 145-48, 151, 153, 154, 158
Old Margaret, 134, 141, 144, 145, 153
Omeo, 52, 57, 61, 63, 65, 67
Once a Week, 121
"Our Brown Passenger", 17
Ovens and Murray Advertiser, 52
Ovens River, 49, 53
Oxford, 2, 12, 20, 25, 29-39 *passim*, 40, 91, 107, 133, 135, 167

Pall Mall Gazette, 119, 120
Parry-Okeden, David, 63, 64, 68
Paul, C. Kegan, 34
"Peace and War", 140
Phillips' Emigrant Guide to Australia, 43
Port Albert, 66, 67
Port Fairy, 70, 91
Port Phillip, 44, 45, 54, 68, 74, 78
Pryce, W.B., 77, 79, 84
Punch, 133

Queensland, 129

Ravenshoe, 3, 9, 11, 29-42 *passim*, 44, 48-52 *passim*, 60, 62, 71, 82, 91, 93, 96-103 *passim*, 108, 112-17 *passim*, 123, 146
Reade, Charles, 157
Reading, 97
Recollections of Geoffry Hamlyn, The, 3, 8, 11, 12, 16, 21, 29, 41, 43, 48, 49, 52, 55, 56, 60-65 *passim*, 70-76 *passim*, 79-84 *passim*, 87-95 *passim*, 98, 99, 101, 103, 108, 112, 113, 115, 145, 163
Reginald Hetherege, 4, 10, 17, 56, 62, 63, 154, 157-61 *passim*
Renforth, James, 133
Richardson, Samuel, 157, 160
Richardsons (Gorrinn Station), 73
Ritchie, Anne Thackeray, 35, 118, 127, 140, 165, 166
Robertson, George, 87, 90
Ross, C. Stuart, 72
Rothesay Chronicle, 142
Routledge, George, 154
Royal Geographical Society, 120, 157
Royal Literary Fund, 128, 147, 153, 154-55, 162, 165-67
Ruskin, John, 133
Russell, George, 104
Russell, Philip, 53, 71

Sadlier, John, 45
Sandhurst. *See* Bendigo
Saturday Review, 92, 100, 113, 115, 120, 121, 145, 158
Scotland, 100, 109, 123, 130, 140, 141, 144
Scotsman, 119, 125
Scott, Sir Walter, 102, 131, 133
Shaftesbury, Lord, 118
Shelley, Percy Bysshe, 133, 164
Shorter, Clement, 57, 118, 127, 128
"Siege of Colchester", 163
Silcote of Silcotes, 20, 98, 104, 107, 112, 114, 115, 119
"Sir Francis Drake", 162
"Sir Phillip Sidney", 161
Skipton, 73-76
Sladen, Douglas, 71, 75
Smollett, Tobias George, 132, 160
Snowy River, 61-66 *passim*, 146, 167
"Some Account of the Village of Inverquoich", 27, 130
Sophia, 77
Southern Cross (Australia), 92
Spanish Galleon, 70
Spectator, 99, 120, 145
"Sports and Pastimes", 157
Squattlesea Mere, 70, 71, 93
Steele, Richard, 160
Stephen, Leslie, 57, 118, 157, 165, 166
St George's Workhouse, 96
St James Magazine, 164
St Leonard's, 88, 91
St Luke's Church, 5, 23
Strahan and Co., 121, 145
Stretton, 30, 32, 37, 44, 132, 154
Sturt, Charles, 40, 54, 109
Sturt, E.P.S., 68
Swan, Nathaniel Walter, 76
Swiftsure, 43, 74, 77-79, 84, 86
Swinburne, Charles, 118, 119, 133, 166
Sydney, 54, 55, 61

"Tales and Sketches", 160
Tales of Old Travel, 15, 16, 40, 51, 68, 77-78, 79, 103, 112-15, 120-24 *passim*, 132, 165
Tasmania, 48, 74, 80, 129
Tauchnitz, Bernard, 99, 107, 108, 146, 154
Taylor, Tom, 92, 107
Tennyson, Alfred, 91, 96, 131
Thackeray, Anne. *See* Ritchie
Thackeray, William Makepeace, 19, 35, 102, 103, 132, 133, 163
Thames, river, 26, 118
The Springs, 48
Tichborne case, 162
Ticknor and Fields, 89, 100, 108
Times, The (London), 32, 36, 88, 110, 118, 131, 144
Tinsley Brothers, 144, 149, 151

Tinsley, William, 93, 108, 150, 154
"Travelling in Victoria", 68, 74, 75, 76
Treasure, S.J., 65
Tubbutt, 61, 63, 67
"Two Cadets, The", 48, 49, 82, 83
Two Years Ago, 87

Union Hotel, 76

Valentin, 12, 16, 119, 137, 138, 149, 154, 157
Vancouver Island, 29, 37
Van Diemen's Land. *See* Tasmania
Venables, Henry Pares, 31, 40-47 *passim*, 52, 68, 80, 91
Venables, Roger, 31
Victoria, 45, 128-29

Wales, 100, 120
Walford, Edward, 116, 117
Walker, Mary Howitt, 63

Wargrave, 97, 104, 108, 112, 118, 119, 127, 135, 147, 148, 156, 163
Warrandyte, 69
Western District of Victoria, 48, 69, 73
Westward Ho!, 86, 89, 142
"Who will be my love", 132
Widderin, Mount, 72
"Wild Sports of the Far South", 68, 76, 84-85
William, Mount, 74
Will O' The Wisp, 44
Wills, Mrs James, 113
Wilson, Daniel, 95-96
Wilson, George, 92, 93
Worcester College, 29, 30, 33, 34, 37, 91
"Word of Remonstrance with Some Novelists, A", 102

Yarra River, 68, 69
Yering, 68

LIBRARY OF DAVIDSON COLLEGE